Voices of the Civil War

Voices of the Civil War · Shiloh

By the Editors of Time-Life Books, Alexandria, Virginia

Contents

THE FIELD AT SHILOH

The Battle of Shiloh raged for two days in the woodlands and clearings west of the Tennessee River, beyond the bluffs of Pittsburg Landing. An artist's rendering depicts the terrain of the battlefield.

Corinth–Pittsburg Road

Shiloh Church

Hamburg–Purdy Road

Hornet's Nest

Locust Grove Creek

Peach Orchard

Hamburg–Savannah Road

Tennessee River

Lick Creek

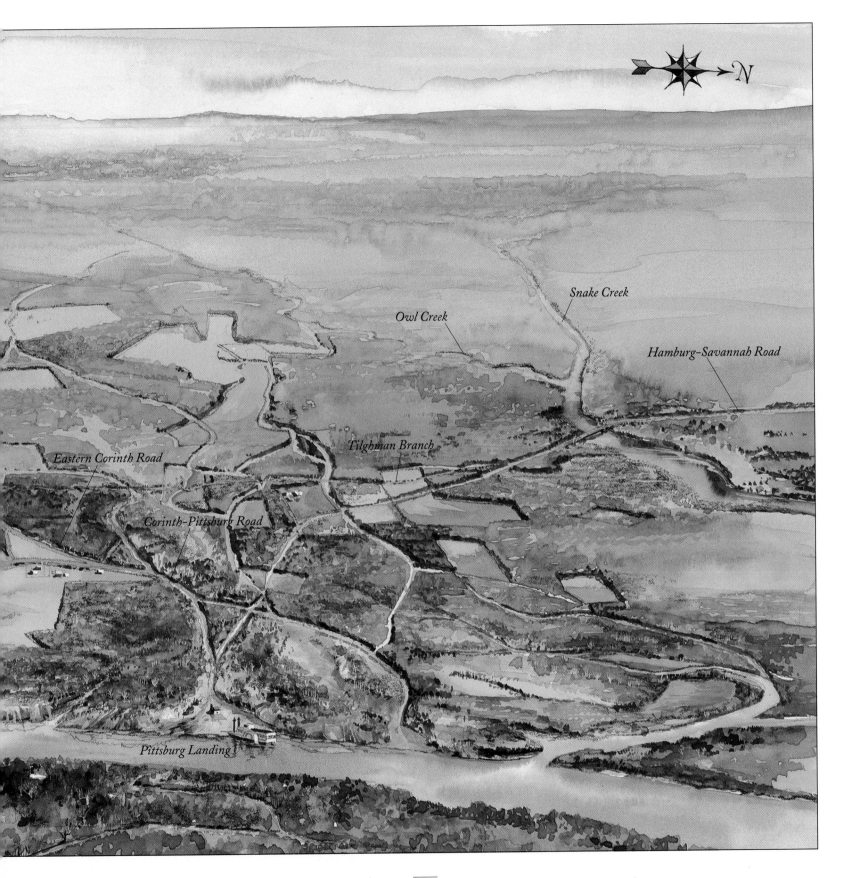

Snake Creek

Owl Creek

Hamburg–Savannah Road

Tilghman Branch

Eastern Corinth Road

Corinth–Pittsburg Road

Pittsburg Landing

Yankees on the Move in the West

It took only two days after arriving at his new headquarters in Nashville, Tennessee, in September 1861 for General Albert Sidney Johnston to conclude that the situation for the Confederacy in the western theater of war was desperate. He fired off a telegram to his friend Jefferson Davis, president of the Confederacy, pleading for help. "We have not over half the *armed* forces that are now likely to be required," Johnston lamented. What was worse, there were no rifles or muskets to give to the recruits who were straggling in, no uniforms or other equipment of any sort.

Gloomy as it was, Johnston's telegram was an understatement. He had been given the most daunting task assigned to any general in this first year of the Civil War—to take command of the entire western two-thirds of the

Confederacy and protect it from Union invasion. This meant trying to defend a line more than 300 miles long from the Cumberland Mountains in the east all the way to the Mississippi River. In addition, Johnston was to make sure the Federals did not control the Mississippi itself or play havoc beyond the river in Missouri and Arkansas.

To guard the huge area, Johnston found that he had fewer than 20,000 men, most of them untrained and untested and armed with old shotguns and flintlocks brought from home, if anything. As one of Johnston's aides bluntly put it, "He had no army."

Johnston had been assigned the job because it was agreed throughout the South— this before Robert E. Lee had fought a battle—that he was by all odds the best officer in the Confederate army. A handsome, courtly 58-year-old West Point graduate, Johnston had had a somewhat checkered career that included resigning from the U.S. Army twice to become a farmer and then a cotton planter. But by the time the Civil War began he had been promoted to brigadier general and named the army's top commander on the West Coast. He then had led a company of fellow Southern sympathizers, bent on join-

Typical of the Confederates called upon to defend Tennessee, members of the Clinch Rifles, Company A, 5th Georgia Volunteers, lounge before a wall tent with their black servant. In April 1862 they helped guard the Cumberland Gap and then marched west to participate in the siege of Corinth.

ing the Confederate army, on a hair-raising trek across 800 miles of mountains and desert from San Francisco to Texas.

Finally reaching the Confederate capital of Richmond by railroad, Johnston had been given a hero's welcome—and almost immediately was sent to Nashville to save the western Confederacy from the Union threat. "I hoped and expected that I had others who would prove generals," President Davis said, "but I knew I had one, and that was Sidney Johnston."

The threats were not as menacing as the Confederate leaders in Richmond thought, at least for the moment. In the fall of 1861 the Federal forces scattered about Kentucky, Illinois, and Missouri numbered about twice as many men as Johnston had, but they, too, were mostly raw recruits lacking arms and other gear. And the western forces on both sides would remain ill equipped for some time, getting leftovers and hand-me-downs after the armies in the East were supplied.

But the perils Johnston faced in the long run were very real, in large measure because of geography. The western Confederacy was divided by long, wide rivers navigable for hundreds of miles by gunboats and transports. Unlike the smaller streams in the East, which generally flowed west to east across the paths of the marching armies, the western rivers flowed north to south for much of their length—huge daggers pointing deep into the Southern heartland.

Greatest of the rivers, of course, was the Mississippi, which figured prominently in the Union's overall strategy, the so-called Anaconda Plan devised by the U.S. Army's savvy commanding general, Winfield Scott. According to Scott's master plan, Federal forces would conquer the length of the Mis-

sissippi and, combining this with a naval blockade of the South's seaports, slowly squeeze the Confederacy to death as if in the coils of a giant snake.

Nearly as critical for Johnston were two other big rivers, the Tennessee and the Cumberland, which, flowing out of the southern highlands, emptied into the Ohio before that river met the Mississippi. The Cumberland, hooking through the Confederate state of Tennessee, flowed right through Nashville, an exceedingly important city that was busily manufacturing guns, ammunition, and other war matériel for the Confederate armies.

Just as crucial was the northward-flowing Tennessee, a ready-made 200-mile-long invasion route stretching all the way into Alabama. In a few months, in the spring of 1862, a Federal army would plunge south on the Tennessee almost to the Alabama border. There, in a forlorn backwoods region marked only by a tiny Methodist meeting house called Shiloh Church, the invading Federals and Johnston's army would hammer each other in the first huge and crucially important battle of the Civil War, a ferocious and bloody two-day clash in which more men would be killed and wounded than in all the battles of all the nation's previous wars, and one that would have lasting effects on the course of the entire conflict.

For the time being, though, Johnston tried mightily to stretch his tiny force in a defensive line clear across southern Kentucky. His first aim was to hang on to at least parts of the key border state, hoping—though Kentucky had declared itself officially neutral—that the Southern partisans there might still swing the state over to the Confederate side. He also desperately needed to shield Nash-

ville and prevent the Federals from rampaging south on the rivers.

Anchoring the line's western end were about 11,000 men under Major General Leonidas Polk at the Mississippi River town of Columbus, Kentucky. The 55-year-old Polk, a dignified, silver-haired West Pointer, had early abandoned a military career to take religious orders, eventually becoming the Episcopal bishop of Louisiana. He had been persuaded by President Davis, however, to put on a uniform again and help organize Confederate forces in Tennessee.

Not known as an aggressive officer, Polk had nonetheless moved quickly to seize the strategic high bluffs at Columbus in early September 1861, before Johnston arrived. Placing scores of guns on the heights overlooking the river, Polk was ready to blast anything afloat and block any Federal thrust down the Mississippi.

To protect Nashville, Johnston sent Brigadier General Simon Bolivar Buckner, a capable West Pointer from Kentucky, along with a column of troops, to the town of Bowling Green, 60 miles north of Nashville. There two rivers, the Green and the Barren, formed a barrier against any southward Federal attack. As the winter of 1861-1862 progressed, Johnston added troops to this main force until it numbered about 22,000 men, and he put Major General William J. Hardee, the old army's expert on drill and tactics, in overall command.

Having covered what he thought were the likeliest points of attack, General Johnston sent a Nashville politician and newspaper editor by the name of Felix Zollicoffer far to the east to command a tiny army of 4,000 men guarding the Cumberland Gap. Finally Johnston dispatched a few troops and some military engineers to hurry the construction of two heavily armed bastions already being built on bends in the Tennessee and Cumberland Rivers just south of the Tennessee line. If made as formidable as Johnston fervently hoped, Fort Henry and Fort Donelson would block any Federal attempts to steam up the rivers with gunboats and smash the center of his line.

Facing the Confederates were two Federal armies totaling more than 37,000 men when Johnston arrived and growing rapidly as new regiments flowed in from the various midwestern states. Union forces in the West were split between two commands, the Department of the Ohio, with a forward headquarters in Louisville, Kentucky, and the Department of the Missouri, headquartered in St. Louis.

The officer in charge in St. Louis during the summer and early fall of 1861 was the dashing, handsome Major General John Charles Frémont. Known as the Pathfinder, Frémont had gained fame before the Civil War by exploring and mapping—sometimes incorrectly it turned out—several of the passes through the Rocky Mountains.

Frémont made his share of mistakes in St. Louis as well. He occasioned much ridicule by strutting about with a sort of personal royal guard, a company of Unionist Kentuckians all six feet or so tall. He also cluttered his staff with European fortune hunters—footloose officers from a half-dozen European armies eager to associate with the famous Frémont, who wore flashy uniforms draped with gold and silver bangles that contemptuous Missourians called "chicken guts."

In the fall of 1861 Frémont did something far more foolish, and dangerous. Alarmed by the number of Confederate guerrilla bands spreading havoc in Missouri—like Kentucky it was a border state with many Southern sympathizers—Frémont issued a proclamation declaring martial law and decreed that any citizen caught with a gun in Federally controlled areas would be court-martialed and shot. In doing so, General Frémont invited the wholesale killing of Unionists in reprisal by the Confederates and a wild escalation of internecine bloodshed in Missouri and elsewhere. In addition, Frémont's proclamation declared that the slaves of Southern sympathizers would be set free, a move that would have alienated millions in Missouri, Kentucky, and parts of the North who favored the Union cause but still opposed any idea of emancipation.

The inflammatory proclamation alarmed President Abraham Lincoln, who quickly annulled it and two months later relieved Frémont of his job. But while still in St. Louis Frémont unwittingly performed an invaluable service for the Union. Needing a commander for the Federal force forming at Cairo, Illinois—the strategic spot where the Ohio River met the Mississippi—he chose a seemingly unlikely candidate, a rather scruffy-looking brigadier general named Ulysses S. Grant. He had been strongly impressed, Frémont said, by Grant's "dogged persistence" and "iron will."

The Ohio-born Grant was a man under a cloud, as he remained for some time. A West Point graduate, he had fought with bravery and dash in the Mexican War of 1846-1848, escaping his dull behind-the-lines job as a regimental quartermaster to take part in two of the war's bloodier battles.

After the war, however, Grant was assigned to a remote, forlorn post in California. Separated from his wife and family, whom he could not afford to bring along, serving under a martinet, and feeling a failure, he took to the bottle—or so the story went. Whether Grant drank enough to interfere with his duties is not known, but he got the reputation in the old tight-knit officer corps of being a drunk. In 1854 he was in effect forced to resign from the Regular Army.

In the following years Grant tried farming and failed at it, then drifted from one ill-paying job to another, ending up at age 39 as a lowly clerk in a Galena, Illinois, leather goods store run by his brother. But with the coming of war Grant saw his opportunity. Pulling a few strings, he gained command of a new regiment, the 21st Illinois Infantry, which had mutinied against its incompetent colonel. "In a very few days," one soldier wrote, Grant quietly "reduced matters in camp to perfect order."

His efficiency noticed, Grant was promoted to brigadier general in July 1861, taking over in Cairo in early September. There he again got things running smoothly by imposing organization and discipline on the Federal troops massing there, despite the fact that the old, low-lying river town was a nightmarish spot. Cold and damp, Cairo was infested with gambling halls, bordellos, and bars that kept drunken soldiers circulating through the guardhouse.

Grant was a born general with a genius for military organization—and a taste for fighting. The purpose of war, he said simply, was to "find out where your enemy is, get at him as soon as you can and strike him as hard as you can, and keep moving on." Grant's troops, who dubbed him "the quiet man," trusted him because, without any of the posturing common among generals of the time, he looked out for their welfare and got things done fast and against all odds. "He habitually wears an expression," one soldier said, "as if he had determined to drive his head through a brick wall and was about to do it."

Once in command at Cairo, Grant showed his penchant for fast action by immediately moving 50 miles up the Ohio with part of his force to occupy Paducah, Kentucky, which controlled access to the mouths of the Cumberland and Tennessee Rivers. General Polk had intended to capture the strategically vital town, but Grant forestalled him, sending in infantry and artillery before Polk's troops arrived. It was not the last time Grant would get to a place faster than Bishop Polk.

Grant also proved his willingness to fight by loading about 3,000 men on river transports to assault Belmont, Missouri, a one-horse hamlet on the west bank of the Mississippi across from General Polk's main position at Columbus. The attack failed when Polk sent reinforcements across the river and then blasted the Federals with his artillery. But Grant extricated his men with aplomb, showing a coolness in crisis that would become his hallmark.

By no means as prone to action was Grant's new superior in St. Louis, Major General Henry W. Halleck, who succeeded Frémont in November 1861. The ultimate desk general, the 47-year-old Halleck had spent most of his time in the army doing staff work—and carefully cultivating his own career. He was by universal agreement a master at covering his own flanks through caution and never doing anything rash.

But Halleck also had a reputation for being highly intelligent—his army nickname was Old Brains—and with having an acute sense of strategy. Ultimately Halleck would give Grant the green light to smash at A. S.

Johnston's line in the campaign that would culminate at the Battle of Shiloh—but not without imposing delays that caused Grant fits of frustration.

The other Federal force facing Johnston, the army of the Department of the Ohio, was commanded through the late fall and early winter of 1861-1862 by a fellow Ohioan and near classmate of Grant's at West Point, Brigadier General William Tecumseh Sherman. Red-headed, rail thin, intense, and as voluble as Grant was silent, Sherman talked so incessantly when ideas flashed through his mind that his aides complained the chatter made them dizzy. But Sherman became, like Grant, a past master at military movement, a daring tactician, and—as he would prove at Shiloh—an imperturbable leader in battle.

Sherman's high-strung nature caused him a reversal, however. While Sherman was in charge at Louisville, Johnston proceeded to do what any smart general would when facing a larger enemy—stage an elaborate bluff to trick the enemy into inaction while building up one's own force. Urged on by Johnston, General Buckner sent his infantry regiments marching and countermarching around Bowling Green making shows of force. At the same time Confederate cavalry patrols—some led by a future terror to the Federals named Nathan Bedford Forrest—ranged through central and southern Kentucky, smashing a small, isolated Union camp at Barboursville and occupying briefly the towns of Albany and Hopkinsville.

Mistaking bluff for reality, Sherman became highly alarmed, sending messages to Washington demanding to be reinforced with a fantastic number—200,000 men—to meet an imagined Confederate offensive all across Kentucky. Soon he was in the throes

of something like a nervous breakdown and was briefly relieved of duty. By early 1862, however, he was commanding a new division at Paducah and would shortly find himself in the vanguard of Grant's army.

Taking Sherman's place in Louisville was Brigadier General Don Carlos Buell, an exceedingly methodical 44-year-old West Pointer who believed he must have his troops thoroughly equipped and trained before doing anything whatever. Buell was not much concerned by Buckner's saber rattling—but he made no move to attack the Confederates at Bowling Green either, even when his army had grown to an impressive 45,000 men. In fact, when Halleck unleashed Grant to attack, he was forced to threaten and cajole Buell before the latter agreed to join the Federal move southward.

While Buckner's troops at Bowling Green were making feints toward Louisville, Felix Zollicoffer, the politician-general guarding eastern Kentucky, actually advanced toward the enemy, moving his 4,000 men to the northwest from near the Cumberland Gap to Mill Springs, Kentucky. Sadly for Zollicoffer, he maneuvered himself into an untenable position on the north bank of the rain-swollen Cumberland River—and then found that a Federal force commanded by a capable West Pointer, Brigadier General George H. Thomas, was bearing down on him.

The Confederates' only option was to attack first and hope for the best. This they did on the morning of January 19, 1862, with a couple of regiments, bone-weary from slogging through winter mud, lunging at the Federal line. General Thomas struck back hard, crushing in the rebel flanks. Zollicoffer himself was shot dead when he nearsightedly blundered into a Federal unit, and the demoralized remnants of his force only escaped across the Cumberland River by scrambling aboard some barges and an old river steamer.

With the disastrous little Battle of Mill Springs, Johnston's right flank was destroyed, but the terrain in eastern Kentucky was so rough that Thomas could not press his pursuit. Still, the war was closing in on Johnston's main forces. Spring was coming and with it, surely, a Federal attack. To his despair, Johnston found that Forts Henry and Donelson, guarding the Cumberland and the Tennessee, were by no means as strong as he had hoped.

Fort Henry had been poorly sited to begin with, standing on such low ground that its lower works flooded whenever the Tennessee River rose. While loudly bemoaning "its wretched military position," the post commander, a Kentucky-born West Pointer and brigadier general named Lloyd Tilghman, had inexplicably delayed construction of works on the strategic heights directly across the river from Fort Henry. Nor had he done much to bolster the far better situated Fort Donelson, 12 miles away across a stretch of rugged, hilly land separating the Tennessee from the Cumberland.

General Johnston tried to spur Tilghman to action, but it was essentially too late. Federal scouts had reported that Fort Henry was vulnerable, and Grant was chafing to attack—as was an equally feisty U.S. Navy man, Flag Officer Andrew Hull Foote, recently sent west to command a freshwater fleet of gunboats that had grown steadily in the past few months. A passionate evangelical Christian, Foote preached hellfire sermons to his crews—and cut their grog ration—but like Grant he thought the way to

wage war was to hit the enemy with implacable fury and get it over with.

The builder of Foote's strange fleet was a single-minded civilian named James B. Eads, a St. Louis riverman and expert at salvaging hulks wrecked on Mississippi sand bars. The first gunboats were three ordinary river steamers, their sides armored with thick oak beams. They immediately proved useful on reconnaissance runs, their wooden sides easily deflecting small arms fire. But everyone knew they would be shot to splinters by heavy guns like the ones Leonidas Polk had at Columbus, or the ones that poked through embrasures at Forts Henry and Donelson.

So Eads developed on the spot an entirely new sort of vessel armored with heavy iron plating, each boat 175 feet long and carrying 13 heavy cannon. Eads' gunboats were appallingly ugly and scowlike—they resembled enormous turtles, one observer said— but they had powerful steam engines and shallow draft and were ideal for river warfare.

Eads' shipyards, working with furious haste, produced seven of these gunboats, all named for western river ports: *Cairo, Louisville, Pittsburgh, Carondelet, Mound City, Cincinnati,* and *St. Louis.* To them Eads added a pair of older boats he had fitted with iron sides, the *Essex* and the *Benton.*

With these fearsome vessels wharved at Cairo, Grant and Foote impatiently wired General Halleck, pleading for permission to steam up the Tennessee and smash Fort Henry. The arrogant Halleck abruptly put them off. But soon he felt heavy pressure from President Lincoln and others in Washington to do something to hit the Confederates. Mindful of his reputation as always, Halleck grudgingly gave the go-ahead,

wiring Grant to "make your preparations to take and hold" the fort.

Grant immediately got the vanguard of a 17,000-man force aboard a fleet of transports. On February 2, 1862, the entire flotilla, Foote's gunboats in the lead, churned up the Ohio giving off dense clouds of Stygian smoke and then turned to the right, splashing their way southward into the mouth of the Tennessee toward Fort Henry. It was the first leg of an offensive that would take them up the Tennessee to Pittsburg Landing and the fateful collision with the Confederate army at Shiloh Church.

CHRONOLOGY

January 10, 1862	*Battle of Mill Springs*
February 6	*Capture of Fort Henry*
February 12-16	*Siege of Fort Donelson*
February 26	*Occupation of Nashville*
April 6-7	*Battle of Shiloh*
May 29-30	*Evacuation of Corinth*

The war in the West—that vast region between the Appalachian Mountains and the Mississippi River—began with small-scale clashes between local forces in Missouri. But by November of 1861, the lines were drawn for a greater war between major armies, with Kentucky and Tennessee as the battle ground. Most of the battles would be fought for Confederate-held rail-hub towns and forts on the Mississippi, Cumberland, and Tennessee Rivers, which served as avenues of invasion for Federal forces spearheaded by flotillas of gunboats. In the first year of the war, the Federal campaign to take the strategic town of Corinth, Mississippi, would bring Yankee and Rebel armies to battle at Shiloh on the banks of the Tennessee.

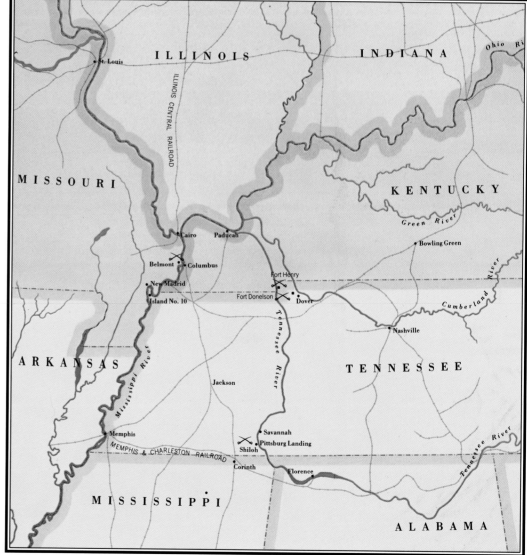

ORDER OF BATTLE   (Battle of Shiloh)

ARMY OF THE MISSISSIPPI   (Confederate)

Johnston/Beauregard   47,000 men

1st Corps Polk		2d Corps Bragg		3d Corps Hardee	Reserve Corps Breckinridge
Clark's Division	Cheatham's Division	Ruggles' Division	Withers' Division	*Hindman's Brigade*	*Trabue's Brigade*
Russell's Brigade	*Johnson's Brigade*	*Gibson's Brigade*	*Gladden's Brigade*	*Cleburne's Brigade*	*Bowen's Brigade*
A. P. Stewart's Brigade	*Stephens' Brigade*	*Anderson's Brigade*	*Chalmers' Brigade*	*Wood's Brigade*	*Statham's Brigade*
		Pond's Brigade	*J. K. Jackson's Brigade*		

ARMY OF THE TENNESSEE   (Federal)

Grant   48,000 men

1st Division McClernand	2d Division W. H. L. Wallace	3d Division L. Wallace	4th Division Hurlbut	5th Division Sherman	6th Division Prentiss
Hare's Brigade	*Tuttle's Brigade*	*Smith's Brigade*	*Williams' Brigade*	*McDowell's Brigade*	*Peabody's Brigade*
Marsh's Brigade	*McArthur's Brigade*	*Thayer's Brigade*	*Veatch's Brigade*	*Stuart's Brigade*	*Miller's Brigade*
Raith's Brigade	*Sweeny's Brigade*	*Whittlesey's Brigade*	*Lauman's Brigade*	*Hildebrand's Brigade*	
				Buckland's Brigade	

ARMY OF THE OHIO   (Federal)

Buell   17,900 men

2d Division McCook	4th Division Nelson	5th Division Crittenden	6th Division Wood
Rousseau's Brigade	*Ammen's Brigade*	*Boyle's Brigade*	*Garfield's Brigade*
Kirk's Brigade	*Hazen's Brigade*	*Smith's Brigade*	*Wagner's Brigade*
Gibson's Brigade	*Bruce's Brigade*		

JEFFERSON DAVIS
PRESIDENT, CONFEDERATE STATES OF AMERICA

By September 1861, when General A. S. Johnston arrived in Nashville to take charge of the Confederate forces, a line running from Forts Henry and Donelson to the Cumberland Gap marked the Confederacy's thin defenses in the West. In his 1881 memoirs, The Rise and Fall of the Confederate Government, Davis summarized the precarious situation.

General Johnston, on his arrival at Nashville, found that he lacked not only men, but the munitions of war and the means of obtaining them. Men were ready to be enlisted, but the arms and equipment had nearly all been required to fit out the first levies. Immediately on his survey of the situation, he determined to occupy Bowling Green in Kentucky, and ordered Brigadier General S. B. Buckner, with five thousand men, to take possession of the position. This invasion of Kentucky was an act of self-defense, rendered necessary by the action of the government of Kentucky and by the evidence of intended movements of the forces of the United States. It was not possible to withdraw the troops from Columbus in the west, nor from Cumberland Ford in the east, to which General Felix K. Zollicoffer had advanced with four thousand men. . . . East of Columbus, Fort Henry, Fort Donelson and Hopkinsville were garrisoned with small bodies of troops; and the territory between Columbus and Bowling Green was occupied by moving detachments which caused the supposition that a large military force was present and contemplated an advance. A fortified camp was established at Cumberland Gap as the right of General Johnston's line, and an important point for the protection of East Tennessee against invasion. Thus General Johnston located his line of defense, from Columbus on the west to the Cumberland Mountains on the east, with his center at Bowling Green, which was occupied and intrenched.

COMMANDER HENRY WALKE
U.S.S. CARONDELET

A veteran of the Mexican War with 30 years of naval service, Henry Walke took command of the powerful ironclad Carondelet in January 1862. Walke and his vessel were to be assigned to the formidable fleet of river gunboats then being constructed at Carondelet, Missouri, and Mound City, Illinois, under the direction of riverman and shipbuilder James Eads.

While Foote was improvising a flotilla for the Western rivers he was making urgent appeals to the Government for seamen. Finally some one at the Navy Department thought of the five hundred tars stranded on Shuter's Hill, and obtained an order for their transfer to Cairo, where they were placed on the receiving ship *Maria Denning*. There they met fresh-water sailors from our great lakes, and steamboat hands from the Western rivers. Of the seamen from the East, there were Maine lumbermen, New Bedford whalers, New York liners, and Philadelphia sea-lawyers. The foreigners enlisted were mostly Irish, with a few English and Scotch, French, Germans, Swedes, Norwegians, and Danes. The Northmen, considered the hardiest race in the world, melted away in the Southern sun with surprising rapidity.

On my gun-boat, the *Carondelet,* were more young men perhaps than on any other vessel in the fleet. Philadelphians were in the majority; Bostonians came next, with a sprinkling from other cities, and just enough men-o'-war's men to leaven the lump with naval discipline. The *De Kalb* had more than its share of men-o'-war's men, Lieutenant-Commander Leonard Paulding having had the first choice of a full crew, and having secured all the frigate *Sabine*'s reënlisted men who had been sent West.

During the spring and summer of 1861, Commander John Rodgers purchased, and he, with Commander Roger N. Stembel, Lieutenant S. L. Phelps, and Mr. Eads, altered, equipped, and manned, for immediate service on the Ohio and Mississippi rivers, 3 wooden gun-boats—

the *Tyler,* of 6 8-inch shell-guns and 2 32-pounders; the *Lexington,* of 4 8-inch shell-guns and 2 32-pounders, and the *Conestoga,* of 4 32-pounder guns. This nucleus of the Mississippi flotilla (like the fleets of Perry, Macdonough, and Chauncey in the war of 1812) was completed with great skill and dispatch; they soon had full possession of the Western rivers above Columbus, Kentucky, and rendered more important service than as many regiments could have done. On October 12th, 1861, the *St. Louis,* afterward known as the *De Kalb,* the first of the seven iron-clad gun-boats ordered of Mr. Eads by the Government, was launched at Carondelet, near St. Louis. The other iron-clads, the *Cincinnati, Carondelet, Louisville, Mound City, Cairo,* and *Pittsburgh,* were launched soon after the *St. Louis,* Mr. Eads having pushed forward the work with most commendable zeal and energy. Three of these were built at Mound City, Ill. To the fleet of iron-clads above named were added the *Benton* (the largest and best vessel of the Western flotilla), the *Essex,* and a few smaller and partly armored gun-boats.

Workmen at the Carondelet shipyards near St. Louis stand on the unfinished gun decks of two Eads ironclads. Dubbed Pook's Turtles for their designer, naval architect Samuel Pook, the powerful ironclads with their low, armored superstructures were intended to challenge the Rebel shore batteries along the rivers.

"It is officially reported that certain women are in the habit of approaching the vicinity of the military prison, and waving hostile flags for the purpose of insulting our troops."

MAJOR GENERAL GEORGE B. CRITTENDEN
COMMANDER, DISTRICT OF EASTERN TENNESSEE

Kentuckian and West Point graduate George Crittenden commanded Kentucky volunteers in the Mexican War and rose to the rank of lieutenant colonel with the Regular Army. He resigned his commission in 1861 to side with the Confederacy. In an address to the citizens of eastern Kentucky, Crittenden gave his reasons for the Confederate occupation of portions of their state.

Division Headquarters, Mill Springs, Ky.,
January 6th, 1862
To the People of Kentucky

When the present war between the Confederate States and the United States commenced, the State of Kentucky determined to remain neutral. She regarded this as her highest interest, and balancing between hope for the restoration of the Union and love for her Southern sisters, she declared and attempted to maintain a firm neutrality.

The conduct of the United States Government toward her has been marked with duplicity, falsehood and wrong. From the very beginning, the President of the United States, in his messages, spoke of the chosen attitude of Kentucky with open denunciation, and on the one hand treated it with contempt and derision, while, on the other hand, he privately promised the people of Kentucky that it should be respected. In violation of this pledge, but in keeping with his first and true intention, he introduced into the State arms which were placed in the hands of persons known or believed to be in favor of coercion, thus designing to threaten the Confederate States. Then the government of the Confederate States in self-defense, advanced its arms into your midst, and offered you their assistance to protect you from the calamity of Northern military occupation.

The Louisville Citizen Guards, photographed in their bivouac at the Louisville Fair Grounds in August 1860, were part of the 5,000-man Kentucky State Guard, commanded by General Simon Bolivar Buckner. When Kentucky proclaimed neutrality, the governor ordered the state guard to repel incursions from either side.

MAJOR GENERAL HENRY W. HALLECK
COMMANDER, DEPARTMENT OF THE MISSOURI

Cautious and methodical, and an excellent administrator, General Halleck was the architect of the Federal plan to advance along the line of the Tennessee River. As department commander he was also responsible for the suppression of pro-Rebel sentiment in the southern cities occupied by his troops.

BRIGADIER GENERAL DON CARLOS BUELL
COMMANDER, DEPARTMENT OF THE OHIO

In a congratulatory general order, Buell praised Brigadier General George Thomas for his victory over Brigadier General Felix Zollicoffer's 4,000-man Confederate force at Mill Springs, Kentucky, on January 19, 1862. The Federal success wrecked the eastern end of the Confederate defensive line in the western theater.

The President, Secretary, Librarian, Directors, and other officers of the Mercantile Library Association, the President, Secretary, Directors, and other officers of the Chamber or Chambers of Commerce of this city [St. Louis] are required to take the oath of allegiance prescribed by article 6 of the State ordinance of October 16, 1861.

Any of the above officers who shall neglect to file in the office of the Provost Marshal General, within ten days of the date of this order of the oath so superscribed, will be deemed to have resigned, and any who, after neglecting to file his oath of allegiance within the time prescribed, shall attempt to exercise the functions of such office will be arrested for contempt of this order and punished according to the laws of war.

2d. It is officially reported that carriages bearing the enemy's flag are in the habit of driving to the vicinity of the military prison in McDowell's College. The commanding officer of the prison will seize and take possession of any carriage bearing the enemy's flag, and the horses, carriage, and harness be confiscated.

3d. It is officially reported that certain women are in the habit of approaching the vicinity of the military prison, and waving hostile flags for the purpose of insulting our troops and carrying on communications with the prisoners of war. The commanding officer of the prison guard will arrest and place in confinement all women so offending.

4th. Any carriage or other vehicle bearing a hostile flag in the city will be seized and confiscated. The city police and patrol guards are directed to arrest persons in vehicles under such flags; also, persons wearing or displaying a hostile flag in the city.

Headquarters Department of the Ohio
Louisville, Ky., Jan. 23, 1862.
General Order, No. 40.
The General commanding has the gratification of announcing the achievement of an important victory, on the nineteenth inst., at Mill Springs, by the troops under Gen. Thomas, over the rebel forces, some twelve thousand strong, under Gen. George B. Crittenden and Gen. Zollicoffer.

The defeat of the enemy was thorough and complete, and the loss in killed and wounded was great. Night alone, under cover of which his troops crossed the river from his entrenched camp and dispersed, prevented the capture of his entire force. Fourteen or more pieces of artillery, some fifteen hundred horses or mules, his entire camp equipage, together with wagons, arms, ammunition, and other stores to a large amount, fell into our hands.

The General has been charged by the General-in-Chief to convey his thanks to Gen. Thomas and his troops for their brilliant victory. No task could be more grateful to him, seconded as it is by his own cordial approbation of their conduct.

By command of Brig.-Gen. Buell
James B. Fry,
A.A.G., Chief of Staff.

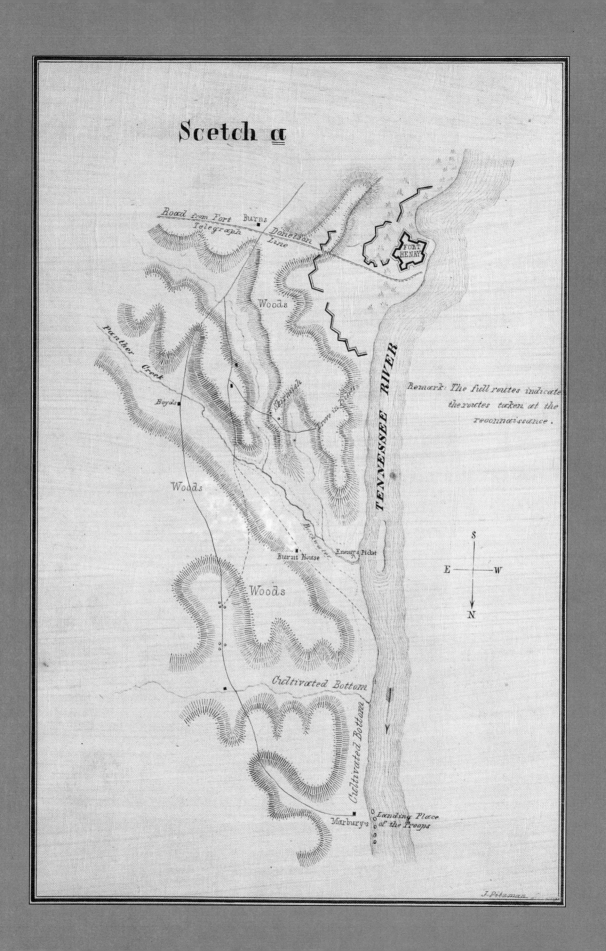

Struggle for the Rebel River Forts

By January 1862 some 20,000 Federal troops under the command of General U. S. Grant had gathered near Cairo, Illinois, at the confluence of the Ohio and Mississippi Rivers. From his base of operations, Grant was ready and eager to strike at the northernmost outposts of General Johnston's Confederate forces. Fort Henry, the earthen bastion guarding the Tennessee River, seemed particularly vulnerable to assault. Grant believed that if Henry capitulated to the Union the 5,000-man garrison at Fort Donelson, on the Cumberland River, would soon follow suit.

Having earlier rejected the plan, Grant's superior, Major General Henry Halleck, changed his mind and on January 30 authorized a Federal offensive against the two forts. On February 3 Grant began shuttling 15,000 soldiers by transport up the Ohio, then south

A map prepared by Julius Pitzman of the U.S. Topographical Engineers in 1862 shows the terrain around Fort Henry in Tennessee. The surrender of the fort and the subsequent fall of nearby Fort Donelson opened the way for Grant's forces to penetrate even farther into Confederate territory.

up the Tennessee to the vicinity of Fort Henry. The Yankee troopships were escorted by a fleet of three timbered and four ironclad gunboats under the command of Flag Officer Andrew Foote. When the advance of the troops was delayed by a lack of transports and the heavy current of the rain-swollen rivers, Grant decided on February 5 to allow Foote to launch a naval assault on Fort Henry before the Rebel garrison could be reinforced.

Conditions at the fort could not have been worse. High river waters had flooded several batteries with two feet of water. Henry's commander, General Tilghman, decided to evacuate. Retaining his gun crews, he dispatched all but 150 of his 2,500-man garrison to Fort Donelson, a dozen miles to the east. On February 6 Foote's flotilla steamed to within 300 yards of the Southern earthwork, raking the defenders with deadly salvos. Despite the lopsided odds, Tilghman's gunners acquitted themselves well, damaging Foote's flagship, the *Cincinnati,* and putting the *Essex* out of action with an exploded boiler. But the outcome was a foregone conclusion; after 70 minutes of shelling, only four of Tilghman's 17 artillery pieces were still serviceable, and the Confederate commander surrendered to his naval counterpart. Without losing a single infantryman, Grant was able to telegraph the good news to Washington: "Fort Henry is ours."

Grant had hoped to be in position to invest Fort Donelson by February 8, but his plans were hindered by continued heavy rain that turned the roads to quagmires. It was February 12 before the Federal commander dispatched two divisions, marching on parallel roads, to cut off the Rebel bastion on the Tennessee River.

As Grant was closing in, Johnston was debating whether to unite his forces for a climactic battle at Donelson or to abandon the post altogether. In the end he settled for a compromise, opting to reinforce the garrison with 12,000 troops under the overall command of Brigadier General John B. Floyd, former U.S. secretary of war. With little hope that Donelson could sustain a protracted siege, Johnston hoped that Floyd would buy time for the remainder of the Southern army to withdraw from their precarious bases of operation at Columbus and Bowling Green and move southward.

Although he was now outnumbered by Fort Donelson's defenders, Grant on February 13 closed in on the outermost Rebel trenches with the divisions of Brigadier Generals Charles F. Smith and John A. McClernand. Hoping to match the success he had had at Fort Henry, Grant counseled his subordinates not to bring on a general engagement until Flag Officer Foote arrived with the gunboats. But despite their superior's orders, both Smith and McClernand permitted a series of disjointed assaults that were thrown back with heavy loss. That night both sides shivered in subfreezing temperatures as the icy rains became a blizzard.

On February 14 Grant was reinforced by 5,000 fresh troops, who were organized into a third division under the command of Brigadier General Lew Wallace. Foote was also now on hand with four ironclad and two wooden gunboats, and at 2:00 p.m., with cannons blazing, the flotilla steamed toward the river face of Fort Donelson. But Donelson was not to be so easily overcome; nearly half the Rebel shells found a target, and the battered ironclads were forced to withdraw. More than 50 sailors were dead or dying, and Foote himself was among the dozens of wounded.

Despite their success in repelling the naval assault, both Floyd and his second in command, Brigadier General Gideon J. Pillow, had little hope of sustaining a drawn-out siege. That night they settled upon a daring strategy. At dawn Pillow would lead a breakout through enemy lines nearest the river, and as the troops of General Buckner covered the rear, the Rebel garrison would cut its way through to Nashville, 75 miles to the south.

At first the gambit seemed to pay off. At 6:00 a.m., screaming the Rebel yell, Pillow's troops took the Yankees by surprise, pierced the line of McClernand's division, and gained the planned escape route on the Forge road. After repeated calls for assistance, Lew Wallace dispatched a portion of his division to McClernand's aid, but by 8:00 a.m. the Union right flank had been bent back at nearly a right angle to its initial position. Grant, who had been conferring with Flag Officer Foote when the unexpected blow struck, hurried to the scene of combat.

As the firing subsided, Grant determined to regain the initiative. Assuming that the enemy must have weakened their defenses in order to bolster their strike force, he ordered C. F. Smith, commanding the left, to launch an all-out assault on the trenches to his front. Smith personally led a bayonet charge that overran the outermost Confederate works, while Wallace and McClernand counterattacked and Foote's gunboats renewed their bombardment.

The advantage was lost for the Southern forces when General Pillow inexplicably brought his troops to a halt even as their breakout was succeeding. Floyd concurred with Pillow's decision, and by early afternoon the Confederates were pulling back into their fortifications. Floyd and Pillow then determined to avoid becoming prisoners of the Federals; they steamed south on transports with a handful of their command, leaving it to Buckner to open negotiations with the Federal commander for the surrender of Fort Donelson.

Grant's demand for "unconditional and immediate surrender" sealed the fate of the Confederate garrison. Nathan Bedford Forrest, the fiery cavalry colonel, managed to cut his way out with some 700 troopers, but nearly 15,000 Southern soldiers and 65 cannon fell into Yankee hands in the North's first great victory of the Civil War.

ORDER OF BATTLE   (Fort Henry and Fort Donelson)

ARMY OF CENTRAL KENTUCKY   (Confederate)

Floyd   21,000 men

Buckner's Division	Johnson's Command	Floyd's Division
Baldwin's Brigade	Heiman's Division	*Wharton's Brigade*
J. C. Brown's Brigade	*Davidson's Brigade*	*McCausland's Brigade*
	Drake's Brigade	

ARMY OF THE TENNESSEE   (Federal)

Grant   27,000 men

1st Division McClernand	2d Division C. F. Smith	3d Division L. Wallace	Navy Andrew H. Foote
Morrison's Brigade	*McArthur's Brigade*	*Cruft's Brigade*	*Carondelet*, Walke
Oglesby's Brigade	*Cook's Brigade*	*Thayer's Brigade*	*Conestoga*, Phelps
W. H. L. Wallace's Brigade	*Lauman's Brigade*		*Essex*, Porter
	Smith's Brigade		*Louisville*, Dove
			Pittsburgh, Thompson
			St. Louis, Paulding
			Tyler, Gwin

CAPTAIN JESSE TAYLOR
PORTER'S TENNESSEE BATTERY, BUCKNER'S DIVISION

The nephew of a Tennessee congressman and an honors graduate of the U.S. Naval Academy class of 1858, Taylor gave up a promising career in the Federal service to cast his lot with the Confederacy. As commander of Fort Henry's artillery, Captain Taylor won praise for the skill with which he waged a gallant fight against great odds.

On the 4th of February the Federal fleet of gun-boats, followed by countless transports, appeared below the fort. Far as eye could see, the course of the river could be traced by the dense volumes of smoke issuing from the flotilla—indicating that the long-threatened attempt to break our lines was to be made in earnest. The gun-boats took up a position about three miles below and opened a brisk fire, at the same time shelling the woods on the east bank of the river, thus covering the debarkation of their army. The 5th was a day of unwonted animation on the hitherto quiet waters of the Tennessee; all day long the flood-tide of arriving and the ebb of returning transports continued ceaselessly.

Commandeered for wartime service, the steamboat Aleck Scott unloads newly recruited Federal soldiers at Cairo, Illinois. Strategically situated at the confluence of the Ohio and Mississippi Rivers, the ramshackle community of Cairo became a Yankee stronghold and the principal staging area for General Grant's advance against the Confederate armies in Kentucky and Tennessee.

"Far as eye could see, the course of the river could be traced by the dense volumes of smoke issuing from the flotilla."

CORPORAL WILBUR F. CRUMMER
45TH ILLINOIS INFANTRY, W. H. L. WALLACE'S BRIGADE

An 18-year-old farmer from Elgin, Illinois, Crummer was promoted to corporal in January 1862, a month before the advance on Fort Henry. In May 1863, while serving as company first sergeant, he was severely wounded during a failed assault on the Rebel defenses at Vicksburg, Mississippi. Crummer recovered from his wound and was discharged at the end of his term of service in September 1864.

The next morning we took up our line of march toward Fort Henry. The rain had fallen the night before, making the roads very muddy. Many times we had to stop, stack arms, throw off knapsacks and put our shoulders to the wheels of the artillery and help them out of the mud holes. We came to several streams not bridged, but we were enthusiastic in our seeking the enemy and spoiling for a fight. Taking no time to build temporary bridges, we plunged into the water waist deep and pushed ahead. This made me think of what I had read of our Revolutionary fathers "wading swollen streams and toiling through almost impassable barriers to fight for their liberty and rights."

. . . In the distance the gunboats were hammering away at Fort Henry, and as the sound of the booming cannon came to our ears we wished we were there to attack from the land side. Commodore A. H. Foote, with five gunboats, had attacked the fort and the fight was a most thrilling picture; the whizzing of fragments of bursting shells; the deafening roar of the guns in the fort; the black sides of five gunboats belching fire at every port hole was something to be remembered a lifetime.

CAPTAIN JESSE TAYLOR
PORTER'S TENNESSEE BATTERY, BUCKNER'S DIVISION

Fort Henry's commander, General Lloyd Tilghman, evacuated the bulk of his garrison to Fort Donelson, leaving Captain Taylor in charge of a skeleton force of 150 men. Though outnumbered and outgunned, Taylor's artillery managed to inflict severe damage on several of the attacking Yankee gunboats.

The gun-boats formed line of battle abreast under the cover of the island. The *Essex*, the *Cincinnati*, the *Carondelet*, and the *St. Louis*, the first with 4 and the others each with 13 guns, formed the van; the *Tyler*, *Conestoga*, and *Lexington*, with 15 guns in all, formed the second

or rear line. Seeing the formation of battle I assigned to each gun a particular vessel to which it was to pay its especial compliments, and directed that the guns be kept constantly trained on the approaching boats. Accepting the volunteered services of Captain Hayden (of the engineers) to assist at the Columbiad, I took personal supervision of the rifle. When they were out of cover of the island the gun-boats opened fire, and as they advanced they increased the rapidity of their fire, until as they swung into the main channel above the island they showed one broad and leaping sheet of flame. At this point, the van being a mile distant, the command was given to commence firing from the fort; and here let me say that as pretty and as simultaneous a "broadside" was delivered as I ever saw flash from the sides of a frigate.

The action now became general, and for the next twenty or thirty minutes was, on both sides, as determined, rapid, and accurate as heart could wish, and apparently inclined in favor of the fort. The iron-clad *Essex,* disabled by a shot through her boiler, dropped out of line; the fleet seemed to hesitate, when a succession of untoward and unavoidable accidents happened in the fort; thereupon the flotilla continued to advance. First, the rifle gun, from which I had just been called, burst, not only with destructive effect to those working it, but with disabling effect on those in its immediate vicinity. Going to the Columbiad as the only really effective gun left, I met General Tilghman and for the first time knew that he had returned to the fort; I supposed that he was with his retreating army.

on the Tennessee river 8th 1862

Alexander Simplot, shown above seated beside his wife in an 1866 tintype, was working as an engraver in Dubuque, Iowa, when he got a job as a special artist for Frank Leslie's Illustrated Newspaper, a popular New York journal. He accompanied Flag Officer Andrew Foote's flotilla of ironclads, and he sketched the naval bombardment of Fort Henry (left). Simplot's wartime career was cut short in early 1863, when he fell ill with chronic dysentery and returned to his home in Iowa.

MASTER JAMES LANNING
U.S.S. ESSEX

As second master of the Essex, James Lanning commanded a section of guns in the actions at Forts Henry and Donelson. In October 1862 he received a volunteer commission as a lieutenant and was appointed superintendent of construction overseeing the outfitting of new ironclads at St. Louis.

A shot from the enemy pierced the casemate just above the port-hole on the port side, then through the middle boiler, killing in its flight Acting Master's Mate S. B. Brittan, Jr., and opening a chasm for the escape of the scalding steam and water. The scene which followed was almost indescribable. The writer . . . was met by Fourth Master Walker, followed by a crowd of men rushing aft. . . . I at once ran to the stern of the vessel, and looking out of the stern-port, saw a number of our brave fellows struggling in the water. The steam and hot water in the forward gun-deck had driven all who were able to get out of the ports overboard, except a few who were fortunate enough to cling to the casemate outside. On seeing the men in the water, I ordered Mr. Walker to man the boats and pick them up; Captain Porter, who was badly scalded, being assisted through the port from outside the casemate by the surgeon, Dr. Thomas Rice, and one of the men. When the explosion took place Captain Porter was standing directly in front of the boilers with his aide, Mr. Brittan, at his side. He at once rushed for the port-hole on the starboard side, and threw himself out, expecting to go into the river. A seaman, John Walker, seeing his danger, caught him around the waist, and supporting him with one hand, clung to the vessel with the other, until, with the assistance of another seaman, who came to the rescue, they succeeded in getting the captain upon a narrow guard or projection, which ran around the vessel, and thus enabled him to make his way outside, to the after-port, where I met him. Upon speaking to him, he told me he was badly hurt, and that I must hunt for Mr. Riley, the First Master, and if he was disabled I must take command of the vessel, and man the battery again. Mr. Riley was unharmed, and already in the discharge of his duties as Captain Porter's successor. In a very few minutes after the explosion our gallant ship (which, in the language of Flag-Officer Foote, had fought most effectively through two-thirds of the engagement) was drifting slowly away from the scene of the action; her commander badly wounded, a number of her officers and crew dead at their post, while many others were writhing in their last agony.

With seven of its crew killed, 20 wounded, and five unaccounted for, the ironclad gunboat Essex (right) sustained the heaviest loss of any Federal vessel at Fort Henry. The ship's captain, Commander William D. Porter (above), was among the most critically injured, scalded by steam escaping from a shell-torn boiler. Following his recovery, Porter was promoted to the rank of commodore and commanded the Essex in operations on the Mississippi River.

BRIGADIER GENERAL LLOYD TILGHMAN
COMMANDER, FORT HENRY

Born to an aristocratic Maryland family, Tilghman graduated from West Point in 1836 but left the army to pursue a career as a railroad engineer in Paducah, Kentucky. Exchanged six months after his surrender at Fort Henry, Tilghman assumed command of a brigade in the defense of Vicksburg. On May 16, 1863, he was killed by a Federal shell at the Battle of Champion's Hill, Mississippi.

The moment had arrived when I should join the main body of troops retiring toward Fort Donelson, the safety of which depended upon a protracted defense of the fort. It was equally plain that the gallant men working the batteries, for the first time under fire, with all their heroism, needed my presence. Colonel Heiman, the next in command, had returned to the fort for instructions. The men working the heavy guns were becoming exhausted with the rapid firing. Another gun became useless by an accident, and yet another by the explosion of a shell striking the muzzle, involving the loss of two men and disabling several others. The effect of my absence at such a critical moment would have been disastrous. At the earnest solicitation of many of my officers and men I determined to remain, and ordered Colonel Heiman to join his command and keep up the retreat in good order, while I should fight the guns as long as one man was left, and sacrifice myself to save the main body of my troops.

No sooner was this decision made known than new energy was infused. The enemy closed upon the fort to within 600 yards, improving very much in their fire, which now began to tell with great effect upon the parapets, while the fire from our guns (now reduced to seven) was returned with such deliberation and judgment that we scarcely missed a shot. A second one of the gunboats retired, but I believe was brought into action again.

. . . At 1:30 P.M. I took charge of one of the 32-pounders to relieve the chief of that piece, who had worked with great effect from the beginning of the action. I gave the flag-ship *Cincinnati* two shots, which had the effect to check a movement intended to enfilade the only guns now left me. It was now plain to be seen that the enemy were breaching the fort directly in front of our guns, and that I could not much longer sustain their fire without an unjustifiable exposure of the valuable lives of the men who had so nobly seconded me in this unequal struggle.

Several of my officers, Major Gilmer among the number, now suggested to me the propriety of taking the subject of surrender into consideration. Every moment I knew was of vast importance to those retreating on Fort Donelson, and I declined, hoping to find men enough at hand to continue a while longer the fire now so destructive to the enemy. In this I was disappointed. My next effort was to try the experiment of a flag of truce, which I waved from the parapets myself. This was precisely at 1:50 P.M. The flag was not noticed, I presume, from the dense smoke that enveloped it, and leaping again into the fort continued the fire for five minutes, when, with the advice of my brother officers, I ordered the flag to be lowered.

"Several of my officers, Major Gilmer among the number, now suggested to me the propriety of taking the subject of surrender into consideration."

Colonel Adolphus Heiman (above) of the 10th Tennessee Infantry took charge of the garrison evacuating Fort Henry when General Tilghman decided to remain at the fort. A week later Heiman was captured in the surrender at Fort Donelson.

Sporting the Zouave uniform of his prewar militia company, Marshall M. McIntire (right) took part in the advance on Fort Henry as a lieutenant in the 29th Illinois Infantry. Little more than a week later, he was mortally wounded at Fort Donelson.

CAPTAIN JESSE TAYLOR

PORTER'S TENNESSEE BATTERY, BUCKNER'S DIVISION

As Captain Taylor noted, high waters on the Tennessee River enabled Foote's fleet of Yankee gunboats to close within deadly range of Fort Henry. "An enemy had but to use their most common sense," General Tilghman reported, "to have complete and entire control of the position." During the one-sided fight both officers displayed an impressive indifference to danger, personally helping to load and fire the fort's artillery.

The flag-mast, which had been the center of fire, had been struck many times; the top-mast hung so far out of the perpendicular that it seemed likely to fall at any moment; the flag halyards had been cut by shot, but had fortunately become "foul" at the cross-trees. I beckoned—for it was useless to call amid the din—to Orderly-Sergeant Jones, an old "man-o'-war's man," to come to my assistance, and we ran across to the flag-staff and up the lower rigging to the cross-trees, and

by our united efforts succeeded in clearing the halyards and lowering the flag. The view from that elevated position at the time was grand, exciting, and striking. At our feet the fort with her few remaining guns was sullenly hurling her harmless shot against the sides of the gunboats, which, now apparently within two hundred yards of the fort, were, in perfect security, and with the coolness and precision of target practice, sweeping the entire fort; to the north and west, on both sides of the river, were the hosts of "blue coats," anxious and interested spectators, while to the east the feeble forces of the Confederacy could be seen making their weary way toward Donelson.

On the morning of the attack, we were sure that the February rise of the Tennessee had come; when the action began, the lower part of the fort was already flooded, and when the colors were hauled down, the water was waist-deep there; and when the cutter came with the officers to receive the formal surrender, she pulled into the "sally-port"; between the fort and the position which had been occupied by the infantry support was a sheet of water a quarter of a mile or more wide, and "running like a mill-race."

PRIVATE THOMAS F. MILLER
29TH ILLINOIS INFANTRY, OGLESBY'S BRIGADE

Miller had been in the army less than two months when he witnessed the gruesome aftermath of the Battle of Fort Henry. Promoted to corporal and acting as regimental sergeant major, Miller was captured during a Rebel raid on Holly Springs, Mississippi, in December 1862. Although he was exchanged a month later, Miller deserted rather than serve out his remaining term of enlistment.

Fort henry Tennessee feb 10th 1862

Mr. Bengamin Newton

we had a good time Searcing and pillfering their Camp they left all that they had there is Clothing Enough here to do a thousand men a life time as to the number killed on the Rebels Side I Could not Say for they buried their dead as fast as they ware killed we have dug up 25 or 30 that was buried in the fort and it is Suposed that they throwed a great many in the River I did not See but 4 men killed in the fort that was not buried but the Blood and Brains was Scattered all over the fort I am Satisfied that there was a great many killed our loss was but Small they Rebels did not kill more than five or Six but they throwed a ball in to one of the port holes of our gun boats and bursted the boiler which Scared them and Some of them Jumped over board and got Drowned Takeing the whole thing in Consideration it was one of the Completest victorys that has yet ben achieved.

Holding a fearsome "side knife" in one hand and a photographic case in the other, 23-year-old Private William J. Miles of the 27th Alabama posed for the camera shortly before the Rebel surrender of Fort Henry, where he was taken prisoner.

An engraving published in Leslie's Illustrated depicts Federal troops occupying the flooded earthworks of Fort Henry on the morning after its capture. The illustration was based on a sketch by artist Henri Lovie, one of several correspondents who accompanied Foote's expedition.

COLONEL WILLIAM H. L. WALLACE
BRIGADE COMMANDER, ARMY OF THE TENNESSEE

Colonel William H. L. Wallace of the 11th Illinois recounted the Union victory at Fort Henry in a letter to his wife, Ann. A successful attorney who had seen action in the Mexican War, Wallace was an efficient and highly regarded officer who was soon promoted to brigade command in McClernand's 1st Division. By April, Wallace was himself commanding the Army of the Tennessee's 2d Division, replacing the ailing General Charles F. Smith.

We are here, got in yesterday afternoon after the gunboats had shelled the enemy out. We (the Second Brigade) were some three or four miles out, on the march, when the cannonading ceased. It lasted about two hours and was tremendous. The effect of the fire on the fortifications here was terrible. Guns dismantled, earthworks torn up and the evidence of carnage meet the eye on every hand. It was a strong place and could have been held by a determined force for a long time. The enemy seemed to have been seized with a panic and the whole body, some four or five thousand, left, leaving one artillery company in the fort. General Lloyd Tilghman, who is in command of this district or division of the rebel forces, is among the prisoners. . . . The Eleventh didn't get under fire, but hope for better luck next time. . . . The men have been without tents most of the time since we started and were exposed to a tremendous rain the night before we reached here. The roads were horrible, but notwithstanding this they marched and took the heavy trains of artillery over the worst roads I ever saw.

LIEUTENANT HENRY G. HICKS
2D ILLINOIS CAVALRY, OGLESBY'S BRIGADE

With Fort Henry secured, Grant's army advanced on the far more formidable bastion of Fort Donelson, 12 miles away on the Cumberland River. Hicks rode with four companies of Federal cavalry screening Colonel Richard J. Oglesby's infantry brigade as it neared the outlying Rebel entrenchments. The panoply of war that so impressed young Hicks would later be tempered by grim experience. In November 1863 he was severely wounded during the fight for Chattanooga.

We passed the infantry about sunrise. Looking back over the long column in full view there was an army with banners marching to battle. This was no uncommon sight later in the war, but it was to me a most inspiring scene. The burnished arms glistened in the morning sunlight which seemed to make ruddy the faces, and rugged the forms, of the men in column. All were in the best of spirits. The air was balmy and betokened spring. Before noon of that day many an overcoat was thrown away as a useless burden, which two days later would have prevented suffering and preserved life. Soldiers were then, like generals, only learners in the science of war. Some two miles beyond the Peytonia furnace and shortly after noon our advance guard, consisting of Lieutenant Bennett with six men with whom I had obtained permission to ride, came upon the Rebel pickets who as soon as they saw us fired one volley and incontinently fled. About a mile further on, after crossing a little stream which, as near as I can now remember, must have been the headwaters of Hickman's creek, our vanguard —the Eighth Illinois Infantry and Companies A and B of the Second Illinois Cavalry—was attacked very vigorously for about fifteen minutes, until Dick Oglesby ordered forward Lieutenant Gumbart with one piece of artillery who sent two or three rounds of grape and canister into the enemy; thereupon they followed the example of their picket.

"He very good-naturedly said to me, 'Doctor, I believe I command this army, and I think I'll go first.' "

MAJOR JOHN H. BRINTON

STAFF, BRIGADIER GENERAL ULYSSES S. GRANT

Brinton—a member of a prominent Philadelphia family and first cousin to General George Brinton McClellan—was a graduate of the University of Pennsylvania with a medical degree from Jefferson College. During his tenure as surgeon on Grant's staff, the doctor saw no evidence of the heavy drinking often ascribed to his commander.

ly, he very good-naturedly said to me, "Doctor, I believe I command this army, and I think I'll go first."

When we reached Fort Donelson, our troops were extended and kept well in line, so as to be ready for any outburst of the enemy. Wandering off from the Staff to give some professional directions, I somehow or other got in front of this line, and it seemed to afford the men great pleasure to close up so as to keep me from getting through. I, and a solitary scared dog, were in front. After a while, when the men had had their joke at my expense, I passed through.

We met with no opposition on this march and finally arrived near Fort Donelson. Our line of investment was soon formed. We marched in battle order, ready for action. The actual luggage of the staff was represented by a few collars, a comb and brush and such toilet articles, contained in a small satchel belonging to me. General Grant had only a tooth brush in his waistcoat pocket, and I supplied him with a clean white collar. Of whiskey or liquor, of which so much has been said, there was not one drop in the possession of any member of the staff, except that in my pocket, an eight-ounce flask, which I was especially requested by the General to keep only for medical purposes, and I was further instructed by him not to furnish a drink under any pretext to any member of the Staff, except when necessary in my professional judgment.

T wo roads led from Fort Henry to Fort Donelson; the army moved along both, the cavalry watching the space between, so as not to allow any of the enemy to escape us. The Staff moved by the left-hand or low road. I rode near the General on my black horse, a strong powerful beast, which I had bought at Cairo. He was possessed of a fast walk, and moreover he would push in front of the other horses on the Staff. I could hardly keep him back; he particularly and persistently would pass the General who rode his old favorite stallion "Jack." Final-

CAPTAIN REUBEN R. ROSS

MAURY COUNTY ARTILLERY (TENNESSEE)

A graduate of West Point, Ross directed the fire of Fort Donelson's heavy artillery against Foote's gunboats. Taken prisoner when the garrison capitulated, Ross was exchanged only to be captured again in September 1864. En route to a Yankee prison camp Ross jumped from a train and escaped, but he was killed in a hand-to-hand fight with Federal soldiers on December 16, 1864.

General Pillow told me that men were wanted at the river batteries. I told the company what was desired and what was required of them, making a full explanation to them of the circumstances. I told them, as General Pillow had told me, that it was the post of danger, but the post of honor. Every man declared that the post of honor was the one he wanted. In a word, the Maury County (Tenn.) Artillery believed, when they went down to the river battery, that, in the desperate battle which was about to come on, they would not survive with more than one-fourth of their number. General Pillow had promised to have the guns protected by bomb-proof casements; but they were not yet constructed, and the battle was hourly expected. The companies in the batteries were under the same apprehension of the danger they incurred in doing that duty. Indeed, the whole army, from what I saw and heard, believed that the great danger lay in the gunboats; that the land forces were safe if only the gunboats could be driven back. The companies in the batteries were infantry, trained by Captain Culbertson (one of the first officers in the Confederate Army) to do work as artillerymen. . . .

Arriving at the river, I found the defenses were as follows: First, and lowest down, an 8-gun battery of 32 pdrs., with a 10-inch Columbiad on the left of them. These were placed in a strong but rough siege battery,

with natural earthen traverses, mostly revetted with hurdles of sapwood, capped between embrasures with sandbags, the embrasures lined as usual with rawhide. There were no bomb-proofs or roofs of any kind. The upper battery was a barbette battery without any traverses. During the several nights of the action embrasures were made, and greater safety secured, by filling in between muzzles with sandbags. . . .

. . . Only a single gunboat engaged us that morning. She appeared above the bend, took position, and opened fire on us. Though two and one-fourth miles off, her shot and shell reached us with perfect facility. We mostly answered her with the rifle, firing only a few rounds from the Columbiad. The rifle did fine service, striking, with an elevation of thirteen and one-half degrees, probably four or five times out of the twelve or fifteen shots fired. She drew off after about forty-minutes' bombardment, and we saw no more of them that evening. No one was killed or any damage done by this boat. Her object was, we suppose, to learn something of our guns and get the range.

Lieutenant Colonel James B. McPherson of the U.S. Topographical Engineers —later a Federal army commander—prepared a map (right) showing the disposition of the opposing forces at Fort Donelson. Protected on its northern flank by an impassable swamp, the fort was screened by an outer line of earthen defenses that guarded the approaches to the Confederate encampments.

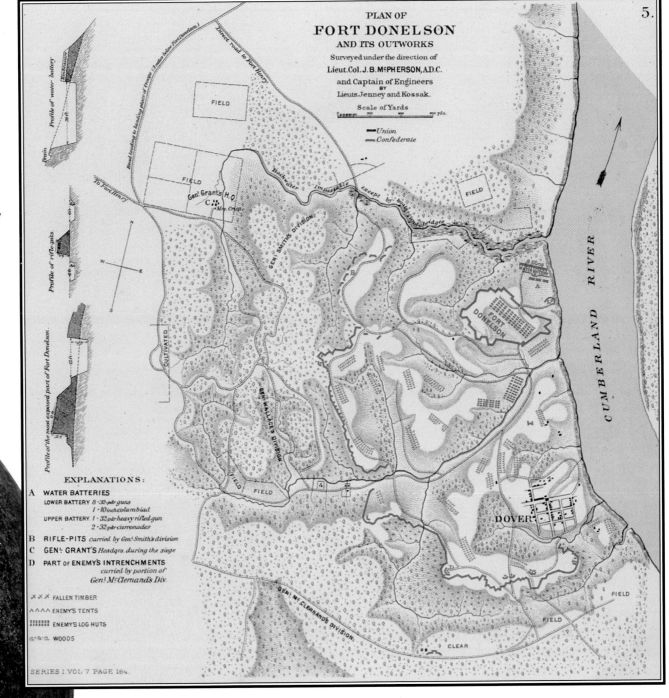

PLAN OF
FORT DONELSON
AND ITS OUTWORKS
Surveyed under the direction of
Lieut.Col.J.B.M^cPHERSON,A.D.C.
and Captain of Engineers
BY
Lieuts.Jenney and Kossak.

Scale of Yards

— Union
— Confederate

EXPLANATIONS:

A WATER BATTERIES
   LOWER BATTERY 8 -32-pdr guns
          1 -10inch columbiad
   UPPER BATTERY 1 -32-pdr heavy rifled gun
          2 -32-pdr carronades
B RIFLE-PITS *carried by Genl Smith's division*
C GEN^l GRANT'S *Headqrs. during the siege*
D PART OF ENEMY'S INTRENCHMENTS
        carried by portion of
        Genl McClernand's Div.

×××× FALLEN TIMBER
∧∧∧∧ ENEMY'S TENTS
▦▦▦▦ ENEMY'S LOG HUTS
🙵🙵🙵 WOODS

SERIES I.VOL.7 PAGE 164.

This 128-pound spherical solid shot, 10 inches in diameter, was recovered from the Fort Donelson battlefield. The Confederate batteries defending the fort mounted several 10-inch Columbiad cannon.

Brigadier General Gideon J. Pillow, second in command of the Confederate garrison at Fort Donelson, proposed that the defenders cut their way through the besieging Yankees. But when the decision to surrender was made, Pillow chose to avoid capture by taking a steamboat to Nashville with his commander, General John B. Floyd. Their escape was criticized by many in the South as cowardice in the face of the enemy.

ANONYMOUS CORRESPONDENT
Missouri Democrat

An unidentified reporter from a St. Louis newspaper, the Missouri Democrat, accompanied Federal skirmishers from C. F. Smith's division as they engaged the outermost Rebel works at Fort Donelson. The 7th Illinois and 52d Indiana of Colonel John Cook's brigade—supported by a detachment of sharpshooters commanded by Colonel John W. Birge—found their way blocked by felled trees, or an abatis, and came under heavy fire from Confederate artillery.

The operations of the day partook largely of the character of a series of reconnoissances. The artillery posted on the hill would send a ball across the valley on an enquiring errand, and in reply would get a solid ball or shell, which, lodging in close proximity to our artillerists, would be hunted up and examined, and inferences drawn as to the character of the batteries pitted against them. This practice resulted in no casualties on our side of importance, and revealed a good deal of information in regard to the position of their redoubts. The severest casualty of the morning was in the Seventh Illinois. In advancing down a road on a ridge connecting the two hills on which the opposing forces were drawn up, a battery of three guns, from the hill above, opened suddenly with grape and canister. Fortunately the battery had been discovered a moment before, and the men had to a great extent availed themselves of the protection of the neighboring trees, before the storm of iron hail was fairly among them. Your correspondent, who was advancing with the rest, has a very friendly recollection of a huge oak, but for whose protecting shelter the readers of the *Democrat* would probably have suffered the small loss of this imperfect narrative of subsequent scenes. . . .

In the mean time Birge's sharpshooters were doing good execution both to the right and left of this position. In squads of skirmishers they crawled up the ravines of the ridge on which the batteries and the rifle-pits of the enemy were located, and lying concealed behind stumps and logs, wo to the unwary rebel who dared to show his head above the intrenchments. The continual crack of the Dimmick rifle could be heard from these ravines all day, and at last became a perfect terror to the enemy. Lying in this position these men, for half a day, completely silenced the battery which covered the road over which the Seventh had advanced in the morning. In vain attempt after attempt was made to man the guns, but hardly had the gunners grasped their swabs ere a score of bullets would drop them in their tracks.

"Your correspondent . . . has a very friendly recollection of a huge oak, but for whose protecting shelter the readers of the *Democrat* would probably have suffered the small loss of this imperfect narrative of subsequent scenes."

Brothers Isa, Clark, Nelson, and Francis Collis (left to right) of Elgin, Illinois, hold the specially issued Dimick sporting rifles with which their unit, Birge's Sharpshooters, was armed. Officially known as the 14th Missouri, the Sharpshooters were transferred to the 66th Illinois later in 1862.

POSITION OF TAYLOR'S AND M'ALLISTER'S BATTERIES DURING THE BATTLE AT FORT DONELSON.—Sketched by Mr. Alexander Simplot.—[See Page 166.]

Emplaced behind an earthen breastwork, the guns of Captain Edward McAllister's Battery D, 1st Illinois Light Artillery, shell the western approaches to Fort Donelson with four 24-pounder howitzers. Published in Leslie's Illustrated, this engraving was based on Alexander Simplot's eyewitness sketch.

MAJOR JOHN H. BRINTON
Staff, Brigadier General Ulysses S. Grant

The hazards of waging a campaign in midwinter were brought home to Grant's Federal soldiers as they tightened the noose around Fort Donelson. Unaccustomed to long marches, many men had abandoned their overcoats and blankets to lighten their load while en route from Fort Henry. As Major Brinton noted, they soon regretted their decision. Snow and sleet began to fall on the afternoon of February 13 and continued for much of the siege.

The weather was terrible during almost the entire time, alternating between sleet and snow, especially at night. It was very cold, and the sufferings and deprivations of the men were excessive. As our lines extended close around the works, it was necessary to conceal the exact position of the soldiers as much as possible. Fires, therefore, on the front lines were not permitted, and I wondered at the time how our poor fellows could endure the long cold nights without fires and with insufficient coverings. This latter statement may seem strange, but the fact is that in the march across the country, many of the men had found their blankets and overcoats cumbersome, and had left them by the roadside, or placed them in wagons, which had failed to make a redistribution. As it was, very many of the troops laid on the ground at night, tentless, fireless, and with scanty covering. In spite of all this exposure, no cases of tetanus occurred among the wounded at Fort Donelson.

PRIVATE JOHN S. WILKES
3D TENNESSEE INFANTRY, J. C. BROWN'S BRIGADE

The 3d Tennessee—with 750 men the largest unit in General Simon Bolivar Buckner's division—arrived at Fort Donelson two days before the advancing Yankee army and was immediately put to work strengthening the Confederate defenses. Enemy sharpshooter and artillery fire soon forced the Rebels to pursue their labors under cover of darkness. For Private Wilkes and his comrades in the 3d Tennessee this was the first taste of combat in nine months of soldiering.

On the morning of the investment I was ordered to Dover with a train of a dozen wagons and a detail of thirty men to procure a week's rations. Our train was rolling slowly up the hill from our position toward Dover when the Federals far up the valley sent a shot at us. It passed through our train and struck in the opposite side of the hill. It was the first hostile shot the boys or I had ever heard. In less than one minute every mule was unhitched and mounted, and my detail were going at full speed back to the position in the fort. I followed as fast as my horse would carry, after vainly trying to stop them. When I reached the fort, they were around Colonel Brown explaining to him that they were not willing to be off on duty with a wagon train while a fight was raging, and they wanted to be in it. Colonel Brown assured them that the real fight had not begun, and that they must hurry to Dover and get the supplies before it did. In a few minutes they were all on the gallop back to the wagons. They went on to Dover, and never did I see such rapid work loading wagons, and soon they were at the fort again. They saw enough battles before the surrender, but they had no idea of being reported absent from the first fight on detached duty. So much for the spirit of the boys. They went out to fight, and did it.

LIEUTENANT SELDEN SPENCER
GRAVES' KENTUCKY BATTERY, LIGHT ARTILLERY, J. C. BROWN'S BRIGADE

A well-to-do native of Port Gibson, Mississippi, Lieutenant Spencer had uniformed a company of gunners at his own expense in July 1861 and tendered their services to General Buckner. On February 12 Spencer and his comrades in Graves' battery unlimbered their guns near the far right of the Southern line in time to confront the initial Federal threat. But it would be the following day before their enemy was ready to attack.

The enemy had driven in our pickets, but were advancing very cautiously. They soon placed a battery in position a little to our left, and sent a few shots to feel our position and provoke a reply. We did not answer. In about an hour they tried us again, sending some six-pound pills over our heads, but still we did not answer. Their battery was hidden from us by the undergrowth, and we did not intend that they should find us out until they were within good range and were visible. The enemy made no further demonstration that evening than to feel our position and to make preparation for the next day. In the afternoon an engineer, mounted upon a white horse, rode coolly down the valley to within six hundred yards of our line, and surveyed us with his field glass. A sharpshooter, having obtained permission, crept down the hillside to within three or four hundred yards of him and tried several shots at him without effect. He bowed gracefully, wheeled his horse, and rejoined his escort.

Enlisting as a private in 1861, John C. Brown was colonel of the 3d Tennessee Infantry by January of the following year and commanded a brigade in the defense of Fort Donelson. Severely wounded at the Battle of Franklin in November 1864, Brown finished the war as a major general and in the 1870s served two terms as governor of Tennessee.

CAPTAIN REUBEN R. ROSS
MAURY COUNTY ARTILLERY (TENNESSEE)

On February 13, with the bulk of Flag Officer Foote's flotilla yet to arrive, Commander Henry Walke advanced the Carondelet to within striking distance of Fort Donelson, shelling the Rebel defenses and drawing fire in return. The Carondelet was hit twice; six men were wounded by a shot that punctured the ship's steam heater. In the fort, Ross witnessed the effect of the gunboat's missiles.

We expected an attack from the fleet early on Thursday morning, but only a single boat came up again. She was armed with powerful rifles, and it was easy to see that she was taking advantage of knowledge gained by the boat of Wednesday; for, knowing where the rifle was situated, she fired fourteen rifle bombs in and about our battery in the course of about an hour and twenty minutes. Others she fired at the lower battery (I supposed at the Columbiad), and many promiscuously over the hill, on the top of which was situated the fort. These were elongated Parrot shells of 42 and maybe higher caliber. One of them dismounted a 32-pdr., by a bolt from which Captain Dixon was killed. Another plowed through the fortification on the hill above us, killing one infantry soldier and wounding two others. Still another ricochetted on the hilltop, passed through three strong cabins built of eight and ten-inch logs, mostly cutting their logs in two, then through a shanty, and finished by killing a mule. This, too, was at a distance from the huts of two and one-half miles.

COMMANDER HENRY WALKE
U.S.S. CARONDELET

A 30-year veteran of naval service, Commander Henry Walke was captain of the ironclad gunboat Carondelet. On February 14 the Carondelet joined three other ironclad and two wooden gunboats to engage the Confederate batteries at Fort Donelson, taking severe punishment before retiring downriver. Fifty-four sailors were killed or wounded, 33 of them aboard Walke's Carondelet.

On the 14th all the hard materials in the vessels, such as chains, lumber, and bags of coal, were laid on the upper decks to protect them from the plunging shots of the enemy. At 3 o'clock in the afternoon our fleet advanced to attack the fort, the Louisville being on the west side of the river, the St. Louis (flag-steamer) next, then the Pittsburgh and Carondelet on the east side of the river. The wooden gunboats were about a thousand yards in the rear. When we started in line abreast at a moderate speed, the Louisville and Pittsburgh, not keeping up to their positions, were hailed from the flag-steamer to "steam up." At 3:30, when about a mile and a half from the fort, two shots were fired at us, both falling short. When within a mile of the fort the St. Louis opened fire, and the other iron-clads followed, slowly and deliberately at first, but more rapidly as the fleet advanced. The flag-officer hailed the Carondelet, and ordered us not to fire so fast. Some of our shells went over the fort, and almost into the camp beyond. As we drew near-

"Still another ricochetted on the hilltop, passed through three strong cabins built of eight and ten-inch logs . . . then through a shanty, and finished by killing a mule."

During his sojourn with Foote's flotilla, artist Alexander Simplot sketched the gun deck of the U.S.S. Essex. Heavily damaged in the attack on Fort Henry, the Essex was at Cairo undergoing repairs while its sister ships battled at Fort Donelson. Two more gunboats were disabled in the unsuccessful Federal attack on February 14.

More than a foot in length and weighing 84 pounds, the Dyer pattern shell (right) was one kind of projectile that Foote's gunboats hurled at Fort Donelson's defenses.

er, the enemy's fire greatly increased in force and effect.

We heard the deafening crack of the bursting shells, the crash of the solid shot, and the whizzing of fragments of shell and wood as they sped through the vessel. Soon a 128-pounder struck our anchor, smashed it into flying bolts, and bounded over the vessel, taking away a part of our smoke stack; then another cut away the iron boat-davits as if they were pipe-stems, whereupon the boat dropped into the water. Another ripped up the iron plating and glanced over; another went through the plating and lodged in the heavy casemate; another struck the pilot house, knocking the plating to pieces.

"At the highest gun in my battery he stood perfectly straight, calm, cool, and collected. I heard him say, 'Now, boys, see me take a chimney.' The chimney and flag both fell."

CAPTAIN BELL G. BIDWELL
30TH TENNESSEE INFANTRY, DRAKE'S BRIGADE

At age 24, Bell G. Bidwell possessed degrees in both medicine and law, but he gave up a promising career in civilian life to become a company commander in the 30th Tennessee. Having volunteered his company for temporary duty as artillerymen, Bidwell displayed skill in supervising the fire that repelled the Yankee gunboats.

With cannon blazing, Foote's gunboats approach Fort Donelson's upper battery. The vessels depicted by Alexander Simplot are, from left to right, the Tyler, the Conestoga, the Carondelet, the Pittsburgh, the Louisville, and Foote's flagship, the St. Louis. Held back because they lacked iron siding, only the Tyler and the Conestoga escaped serious damage during the battle.

Our gunners were inexperienced and knew very little of the firing of heavy guns. They, however, did some excellent shooting. The rifled gun was disabled by the ramming of a cartridge while the wire was in the vent (it being left there by a careless gunner), and being bent, it could not be got out. But the two center boats were both disabled, the left center (I think) by a ricochet shot entering one of the port-holes, which are tolerably large. The right center boat was very soon injured by a ball striking her on top, and also a direct shot in the port-hole, when she fell back, the two flank boats closing in behind them and protecting them

from our fire in retreat. I think these two were not seriously injured. . . .

Our men all did well. I probably ought not to make any distinction, but will refer to the gallant conduct of John G. Frequa, a private and gunner. At the highest gun in my battery he stood perfectly straight, calm, cool, and collected. I heard him say, "Now, boys, see me take a chimney." The chimney and flag both fell. He threw his cap in the air, shouting to them defiance. "Come on, you cowardly scoundrels; you are not at Fort Henry," were his words to them. Very soon he sent a ball through a port-hole and the boat fell back.

CAPTAIN REUBEN R. ROSS
Maury County Artillery (Tennessee)

The determined nature of the Confederate response to the gunboats' onslaught was remarkable, considering that few of Fort Donelson's defenders had ever been in battle before. Despite tremendous incoming fire—the Pittsburgh alone loosed 111 shells—Captain Ross and the other battery commanders held their fire until the Yankee ships were nearly at point-blank range.

One of our balls refused to go down, stopping halfway in the bore; and all efforts to drive it down with rammers had proved unavailing. The boats were advancing, and things were looking serious. Ten or twelve men were ordered to leave the batteries and find a log long and large enough to fit the rifle. This they soon succeeded in doing, and in the midst of the fire they mounted the parapet and drove the ball home. After firing this load, these same men took the sponge, swabbed out the bore with copious water sufficient to soften the dirt already dried and stiffened by the heat; and then, applying the rifler, cut the dirt from each of the six grooves until loose; then sponged, thoroughly cleaning, and ended by greasing the sponge well and applying the same thoroughly to the entire bore. We were then able to resume the firing at any time. Several times before during the previous bombardments had the rifler been applied. Once again during the fleet attack, the rammer of the rifle was thrown over the parapet in suddenly jerking it out, when the No. 1 immediately jumped down into the battery. I told him that we must have the rammer. He mounted the epaulement and coolly walked over and returned it.

COMMANDER HENRY WALKE
U.S.S. Carondelet

So great was the carnage on the Carondelet that Flag Officer Foote felt compelled to send Commander Walke a letter expressing his sympathy for "the friends of the gallant dead." Walke had the note entered into the ship's logbook.

The "Louisville" was followed next by the flag steamer ("St. Louis") and then by the "Pittsburg." The latter, in attempting to turn, struck the "Carondelet's" starboard quarter and rudder, breaking off its hinges, thus compelling the "Carondelet" to retire after having nearly flanked the enemy's batteries. She was terribly cut up, not a mast or spar was standing. . . . In this condition the "Carondelet" drifted slowly out of battle without turning; and her bow guns were playing on the enemy as long as our shell could reach him. Our decks were so slippery with the blood of the brave men who had fallen, that we could hardly stand until we covered them with sand. While thus drifting we received a 32-pounder from the enemy on a ricochet in the starboard bow port, which beheaded two seamen and cut another in two, sending blood and brains over the captain, officers and men who were standing near them. The "Carondelet" with broken rudder, wheel and wheel ropes, was drifting on a point of the shore just below the fort, and thus receiving its concentrated fire, was obliged to steam up and away from it, in the rapid current.

SERGEANT HENRY O. DWIGHT
20th Ohio Infantry, Whittlesey's Brigade

Born in Constantinople, Turkey, where his father was a member of a mission, Dwight left Ohio Wesleyan University to enlist in the 20th Ohio in the fall of 1861. Newly arrived at the front, the regiment had yet to be assigned to a division when Dwight and his comrades witnessed the drama of the gunboat attack.

About 4 o'clock on the afternoon of the 14th someone said "Hark! There it is again!" Every heart beat quicker as we heard plainly enough the faint distant boom of cannon! We gathered in little groups and talked in low excited tones. We were for the first time within hearing of a battle! It was only a faint muttering, but as it increased in its rapidity of rhythm we became more excited and as it faded out of hearing or became less frequent we pictured to ourselves the victory that this slackened vehemence must forbode. But on which side was the victory?

Insensibly, the sound of the cannonade grew more distinct, and at last as we came around a bend in the river we saw a number of steamers tied up to the bank on our right. Farther on, at the next bend were

several other steamers, low and black, and hovering in midstream. The cottonwoods shut off the view beyond and indeed we had looked at them sometime before discovering that the white puffs of smoke which now and then appeared from their sides were the cannon shots. . . . The fleet was there under our eyes bombarding the fort! The rebels were just beyond! We were at the front at last! On the bank were hundreds of soldiers watching the fight and soon we began to see that it was not all play. "See that rebel shot throw up the water!" "That one burst on the gunboat!" Broken timbers, mattresses, and a mangled corpse floated by. Then one of the gunboats began to float helplessly on the stream. Soon another was disabled, and they all fell back out of range.

CAPTAIN WILLIAM F. WILDER
46TH ILLINOIS INFANTRY, THAYER'S BRIGADE

Wilder, whose regiment was held in reserve pending an infantry assault on Fort Donelson, was one of thousands of onlookers waiting to see if the navy would equal its earlier success at Fort Henry. The gore-stained splinter he saw was most likely from the battered Louisville, which lost four men killed and five wounded.

Soon we saw a puff of smoke at the fort and the ball, having passed over the gunboat flotilla, struck the water 200 yards beyond. This was the first shot fired. Soon the firing was general and rapid. The ironclads passed around a bend in the river and out of our sight, but the two wooden boats remained in full view, firing first the bow guns then swinging and giving the broadside, and turning fired the other broadside. This being steadily repeated was a grand sight. Missiles from the fort seemed constantly to go over them. The ironclads did not fare so well. They engaged the water batteries and were badly disabled and dropped back to their anchorage near the transports, the wooden boats following them. As I stood on the bank a splinter of wood about five feet long from one of the ironclads was brought ashore. It was covered entirely with blood and said to have caused the death of four men.

The fight at Fort Donelson was but one of dozens of fierce engagements the ironclad U.S.S. Carondelet witnessed in four years of war. Built in 1861 by the brilliant naval contractor James B. Eads, the Carondelet was formidably armed with 13 guns that ringed its 175-foot hull. By the end of the war the ship had fired more salvos and seen more action than any other vessel in the Western Flotilla.

LIEUTENANT SELDEN SPENCER
Graves' Kentucky Battery, Light Artillery, J. C. Brown's Brigade

Under cover of darkness on the morning of February 15, the guns of Graves' battery were moved forward to support the Confederate infantry's attempted breakthrough on the right flank of the encircling Yankee lines. The artillerymen performed heroically under a cross fire from enemy cannon.

About two o'clock we were roused by marching orders. The horses were soon geared to the guns. We marched back through the town to our left wing, and took up our position there. The distance was about three miles, and we accomplished it in three hours. Down the hill we went, on across the little valley, and up the hill leading to the town, the hills slippery with ice, requiring all the strength of the cannoneers at the wheels and the drivers' spurs to get the battery up one hill in an hour. From the town we went down another long hill and up the steep side of the opposite one, and at daylight found ourselves there on our left wing. It then appeared that we were to be the attacking party in the next day's fight. Gen. Floyd had taken his division, a part of Buckner's Division, and B. Johnson's Brigade, and Saturday at daylight we attacked the enemy on our extreme left. The battle had opened when we gained position. The Seventh Texas was next to us on the right wing of this new line of battle, next to it the Eighth Kentucky, the First Mississippi, Third Tennessee, Twentieth Mississippi, Fifty-sixth Virginia, etc. The enemy fought gallantly, contesting the ground inch by inch, but we were not to be cool spectators of the scene. As soon as we gained our position the enemy opened on us from a battery about eight hundred yards to our right with rifled ten-pound Parrott and James rifled guns and well handled, while we had to fight them with smooth-bores, except one rifled ten-pound Parrott gun in our battery.

COLONEL JOHN GREGG
7th Texas Infantry, Davidson's Brigade

Despite confusion, delays, and stiff resistance, the Southern onslaught rapidly gained ground against the Federal right, largely because of the leadership of regimental commanders such as Colonel Gregg. A fiery advocate of states' rights, Gregg resigned his seat in the Confederate Congress in order to recruit a regiment for wartime service. He was killed in 1864 while commanding the Texas Brigade.

In about half an hour their line broke, and we pursued them to the next ridge, upon which a fresh line was drawn up. I caused the regiment to continue our forward movement and keep up a continuous fire, and in a short time the second line broke and fled, leaving in our hands one 6-pounder, with ammunition and horses. We continued to press them until a third force was seen drawn up in a ravine near a clearing; and upon this we pressed and continued to fire until it also broke and fled, and, although the slaughter of the enemy had before been very great, their difficulty in getting through the felled timber caused our fire to be much more destructive upon them at this place.

Many of the Rebel soldiers fighting at Fort Donelson were armed with antiquated flintlock smoothbore muskets like the D. Nippes Model 1840 shown here.

COLONEL JOSEPH B. PALMER
18TH TENNESSEE INFANTRY, J. C. BROWN'S BRIGADE

Advancing on the Confederate left, three regiments of J. C. Brown's brigade— including Colonel Palmer's 18th Tennessee—deployed from column into line and charged the Federal positions. In heavy fighting the Rebels managed to secure the vital Wynn's Ferry road, but they came to a halt rather than pursue the retreating foe. Although he initially opposed secession, Palmer would rise to general's rank in the Confederate service and sustain four wounds.

"The enemy fought gallantly, contesting the ground inch by inch, but we were not to be cool spectators of the scene."

*M*any of my arms (flint-lock muskets), by coming in contact with the melting snow, had become too inefficient for further use until they could be dried and put in proper order. My ordnance wagons were more than a half mile distant, and the men only had a few rounds of ammunition each remaining in their boxes. I marched my regiment therefore back to a better position, a distance of, say, 150 paces, ordered the men to put their pieces in order by drying them as rapidly as possible, sent for an additional supply of ammunition, made details to have my wounded taken from the field and properly cared for, and threw out a small number of skirmishers in connection with Colonel Cook, to notice the movements and position of the enemy, who reported that he had gone back beyond the Wynn's Ferry road, and could not be seen at all from the position of our late engagement.

With 546 men the largest regiment in Davidson's brigade, the 23d Mississippi Infantry took part in the attack on McClernand's Federal division. The above flag was carried in the action by the regiment's Company A, which had been organized in 1861 by Captain J. C. Blount.

Alexander Simplot sketched the exterior of Fort Donelson in the aftermath of the five-day siege. The fort itself was a stronghold within a surrounding network of earthworks, rifle pits, and batteries. Grant's chief of staff, Colonel Joseph D. Webster, admitted that "our army approached the place with very little knowledge of its topography."

SERGEANT HENRY O. DWIGHT
20TH OHIO INFANTRY, WHITTLESEY'S BRIGADE

Marching at a double-quick to shore up the faltering line of McClernand's division, Sergeant Dwight and his comrades came upon the stragglers and walking wounded of Colonel Richard Oglesby's brigade, which had borne the brunt of the Confederate assault. Oglesby's line was broken, and more than 800 of his men killed, wounded, or captured, but even so the Confederates failed to exploit their success.

Finally we came out into an open woods on a hill where a number of Regiments were lying at rest. Farther down the road seemed to be a deep valley shrouded in thick forest, whence came the most deafening sound of musketry. My lips began to be very dry and [I] knew that I was considerably frightened at this sudden entrance upon the skirts of the battlefield. It is the unknown that terrifies and our feeling our way into this battle in the way that we did was to all of us one of the most trying experiences of the whole war. Where we were, what we were going to do, what the bearing upon our army or the rebels of the tremendous roar of sound in our front—all these problems were constantly coming before our minds and as constantly being referred to the future for an answer.

Then came an order for us to lay aside our heavy knapsacks and pile

them under care of a guard. Next we discovered that as we moved on, the air was full of objects that flew like birds, and seemed to whisper softly as they went. When once or twice we heard these flying objects hit trees with a sharp crack, it occurred to us that they were bullets from rebel guns. Wounded men were pouring toward us in streams from all directions, some with a bleeding arm or shoulder, some with a finger gone, some carried on stretchers by four or five men. With them were numbers of stragglers, who with pretence of caring for the wounded were getting off the field as fast as possible.

"The 31st Indiana is no more a regiment, only 50 men are left," said one. "The 18th Illinois is all hacked to pieces," was the story of another, and one Dutch man pale and out of breath declared, "Die batterie Schwartz is all taken and kilt but six and dat ish me!" "Boys, it is no use, they are driving us all the time," was often repeated in our ears, and we did not know that the rascals had not been near enough the front to see who was driving and who was being driven. Staff officers were dashing about in every direction with contagious anxiety trying to find Regiments for which they had been sent. Suddenly we were ordered out of the road in haste and a battery of artillery came galloping by with a thundering roar and clank and rattle. It went down into the abyss beyond, and soon added its roar to the ear-splitting sound that came up from the thicket. There was a rushing swish through the air and an explosion behind us, and we knew that we had encountered our first shell from the enemy.

"We discovered that as we moved on, the air was full of objects that flew like birds, and seemed to whisper softly as they went."

BRIGADIER GENERAL LEWIS WALLACE
DIVISION COMMANDER, ARMY OF THE TENNESSEE

Already hard-pressed, Colonel W. H. L. Wallace's brigade came under a heavy cross fire when Oglesby's troops withdrew from their right. With ammunition running dangerously low, Colonel Wallace ordered his embattled regiments to fall back to a new position half a mile in the rear. The colonel was leading his disorganized units when he met reinforcements under General Lew Wallace.

I saw, finally, an officer riding slowly toward me, one leg thrown over the horn of my saddle, and four or five hundred men with a flag behind him. I galloped to meet him.

"Good morning," I said, "May I ask who you are?"

"My name is Wallace," he returned, stopping.

"Oh, you are Colonel W. H. L. Wallace. Well my name is Wallace."

"Lew Wallace, of the Eleventh Indiana?"

"The same."

We shook hands, he saying: "Our names and the number of our regiments—mine the Eleventh Illinois—have been the cause of great profanity in the post-office."

"Mixture of letters, I suppose?" "Yes."

I noted him hurriedly, a man above medium height, florid in face, wearing a stubby, reddish beard, with eyes of a bluish cast and a countenance grave and attractive.

"I take it, Colonel, you are getting out of a tight place."

"Yes, we are out of ammunition." "That's bad," said I, "But I can help you. Down the road by the big tent, which is mine, and at your service, you will find two wagons. They, too, are mine and loaded with ammunition. Help yourself, and tell McClernand to do the same!"

"Thank you, I will do it." His men were halted; facing them, he called out in a cheerful voice, "Forward!" "A moment Colonel," I said, "Are the enemy following you?" "Yes." "How far are they behind?" Just then the head of my column hove in view. The Colonel saw it. "Are those yours?" "Yes." "Well"—his face took on an expression of calculation,—"you will about have time to form a line of battle here." "Is that so? Then please give my men room to come—and good-by, Colonel, I'll see you again."

A French-made .69-caliber smoothbore, the Model 1862 musket was rebored and rifled before being issued to Federal troops serving in the western theater.

PRIVATE GEORGE D. CARRINGTON

11TH ILLINOIS INFANTRY, W. H. L. WALLACE'S BRIGADE

A Connecticut-born farmer, Carrington was serving as a drummer with the 11th Illinois when he found himself in the midst of the bloody battle on February 15. His regiment was nearly surrounded. The men won praise from their commander for fighting their way through the Rebels with "all the coolness and precision of veterans."

Scattering fire now commenced off to the right, and in our immediate front. As I was a drummer up to this time, I was only a spectator, and remained near my company. My drum was covered with snow and became the spoil of war, as I never saw it afterwards. About this time a German boy in Co. I was hit just under one eye. He was sitting in the snow and looking very dismal. I took his cartridge-box, buckled it around my waist, and also grasped his musket. I was now fully armed and equipped. The Captain pointed with his sword and I took my place in line with the file-closers. We were armed with French rifled-muskets, caliber 69; the bullet was elongated, pointed, with a hollow in the back end and weighed one and a half ounces. One of these missiles crashing through a man's ribs, would make a wreck of the human frame.

Our uniforms were gray. We changed to blue on the battlefield. We all had on long blue overcoats with capes; hence the rebels afterwards said that they fought the "long-tailed blues."

Our line was rather in semicircle to conform with the brow of the hills we were to defend. Pretty severe musketry began to roar all along our front. The right regiments were fully engaged and gradually forced back by the pressure of the rebel infantry. The heaviest firing drew nearer, showing our lines were giving way.

Bullets were cutting through our ranks, but we were returning the fire. The rebels knowing the ground, could evidently see us better than we could see them. However, we loaded and fired into the smoke and at the enemy when we could catch a glimpse of a butternut uniform or a gray hat. The wounded drifted down the hill and to the rear, while the dead lay just as they fell. . . .

By 2 P.M. Forrest's cavalry cut out and got away through the gap in the lines. The rebel infantry at the same time charged, and they were so earnest in the matter that we broke (having no supports) and got over the next hill without stopping to consider the order of our going. No orders were given by any of our officers to retreat that I heard of; it was every man for himself. However, we brought our bullet-slitted flag with us. The Color-Bearer had been hit three times, and was down but not dead; all the color-guard had been wounded and were left on the field.

While slipping in the snow and climbing the opposite hill, I looked back once, and there on the crest of the hill, where our dead and some of the wounded lay, the position we had so long defended and with such fearful loss, the rebels stood shoulder to shoulder and every man in the act of firing. Bullets cut the snow at my feet, cut off twigs and branches about my ears; one went through my overcoat and bruised the point of the hip-bone, not even breaking the skin. I felt the sting, but never stopped until over and out of range.

Based on a sketch by Henri Lovie, this Leslie's Illustrated engraving depicts a Federal counterattack by troops of the 8th Missouri and the 11th Indiana.

LIEUTENANT JAMES O. CHURCHILL

11TH ILLINOIS INFANTRY, W. H. L. WALLACE'S BRIGADE

As Lieutenant Churchill's regiment turned to cut its way through the Rebels back to the rest of their brigade, they were charged in flank and rear by Lieutenant Colonel Nathan Bedford Forrest's Confederate cavalry. Churchill was among 339 casualties suffered by the 11th Illinois—the heaviest loss of any Federal regiment in the battle.

efore reaching the cavalry line I selected the point at which I would go through, and when within ten feet of it, on turning my eyes to the right, saw a cavalryman with his rifle pointed at, and within six feet of me; I threw my revolver (which was in my left hand), round, but before I got a "bead" on him, he fired and I fell on, and among a pile of dead and wounded. In falling, my right wrist struck a sharply pointed stub, my hand opened and my sword flew beyond reach. This time it was a "minie" ball that had struck me in the center of the right hip-socket from above, splitting off the outer half, and passing down by the thigh bone, fractured it four inches below the head, and lodged above the knee. The sensation was the same as the first, this time, as before, I could not tell in which hip or thigh I had been hit.

I attempted to get up, but could only raise my head—my hips and lower limbs were as of lead. In a moment the enemy's infantry were passing over me, and in less than five, only their stragglers could be seen. They commenced robbing and tearing the clothing from the dead and wounded. I remonstrated, and told them that it was not in accordance with civilized warfare; that there was no objection to their stripping the dead, but the wounded required all they had to keep them from freezing. The stragglers of an army are usually the worst men in it, and purposely fall to the rear to rob the dead and wounded. Its general character should not be judged by them.

COLONEL ROGER W. HANSON

2D KENTUCKY (C.S.)
INFANTRY,
J. C. BROWN'S BRIGADE

Colonel Hanson showed great initiative in the fight of February 15. In the absence of clear instructions from his superiors Hanson continued to press forward, breaking the line of McClernand's division. Promoted to brigadier general, he was fatally wounded a year later at the Battle of Stones River.

The blue silk regimental flag carried by the 11th Indiana Infantry at Fort Donelson had been presented to the regiment by the citizens of Indianapolis in a ceremony held on May 9, 1861. "That banner," stated the Indianapolis Journal, "will be bravely sustained by the gallant regiment to which it has been entrusted, and brave hearts will remember the ladies of Indianapolis who presented it."

Colonel McCausland, of Virginia, arrived, and said that unless they were re-enforced the enemy would retake what they had gained; that after four hours of hard fighting the enemy were bringing forward new troops and in overwhelming numbers. I examined the state of the contest. I saw Colonel Forrest make two gallant but unsuccessful charges. I saw that the enemy were gradually driving us back. My men were eager for the fight. I felt confident that I could dislodge the enemy and drive them from their position. I sent for General Buckner. He had gone to the right and was conducting another movement. There was no time for delay. I concluded to take the responsibility and make the effort. I marched the regiment across the abatis, a distance of more than a quarter of a mile. When I reached the little ravine where Forrest was with his cavalry I halted the regiment, and was joined by the two detached companies. In front of us was an open space, which had formerly been occupied as a camp. This space was about 200 yards in width. Beyond the space in the timber and thick undergrowth the enemy were posted. I directed the regiment, when the command was given, to march at quick-time across the space and not to fire a gun until they reached the woods in which the enemy were posted. The order was admirably executed, and although we lost 50 men in killed and wounded in crossing the space, not a gun was fired until the woods were reached. The enemy stood their ground until we were within 40 yards of them, when they fled in great confusion, under a most destructive fire.

PRIVATE LORENZO A. BARKER
Birge's Sharpshooters (Missouri), Lauman's Brigade

A 22-year-old private in Birge's Sharpshooters, five-foot three-inch "Ren" Barker was among the troops who advanced on the Rebel earthworks on the Federal left north of Fort Donelson. The charge was led by their division commander, C. F. Smith, whose indifference to danger inspired the Yankee soldiers as they forced a way through the abatis and gained the enemy lines.

Little disposed as the Western volunteers were to favor what they called the millinery features of the Regular Army, they now saw them displayed to the best advantage upon the stalwart, soldierly form of their white-haired, white-mustached old General, who, wearing everything which the regulations assigned to his rank, placed himself in their center, sitting rigidly erect upon his horse, with his face toward the enemy. He gave the command "Forward," and rode on in alignment with their colors. He was a grand sight, and inspired every man who looked upon him. The instant that he came in range of the rebel sharpshooters the air around him became sibilant with their bullets. He rarely turned his head, and then only to see that the alignment was kept up, but rode straight down into the deep ravine and then up the long slope through the abatis. His horse picked his way as best he could through the jagged branches, and his men, tearing aside the obstructions at times, pressed on after him.

Two months shy of his 55th birthday and with more than three decades of military service behind him, Brigadier General Charles F. Smith was the most experienced soldier in Grant's army. One officer recalled that Grant and Sherman "never quite got over the sense of awe which they felt in his presence."

PRIVATE JOHN T. BELL

2D IOWA INFANTRY, LAUMAN'S BRIGADE

Bell, shown at left in a postwar image, was 19 years old when he took part in the attack on Fort Donelson. After capturing one position, the 2d Iowa was mistakenly fired upon by a Federal unit to their rear. The Iowans lost nearly 200 men to enemy and friendly fire, including three soldiers who fell while carrying the regimental colors.

The regiment is formed behind our stacked muskets, the command "take arms!" given, the line is dressed right and left on the colors, the colonel explains that we are to charge on the enemy's breastworks and take them at the point of the bayonet, particular instructions being given that not a shot is to be fired until we are inside the works; the left wing of the regiment to go in advance under command of Colonel Tuttle, the right to follow as a support under Lieutenant Colonel Baker.

Our first line of battle thus formed, the left wing (which includes our company), with the colors, moves forward, the right a short distance to the rear. We cross an open meadow, then a gully, tear down and clamber over a rail fence, and commence the ascent of a hill covered with abattis, or fallen trees. The line is well preserved, considering the nature of the obstructions, and thus far not a shot has been fired by the enemy. On we go, when suddenly we reach a point on the hill where a full view is obtained of the rebel rifle pits in front, and as far as we can see to the right and left of us. "Crash!" and the yellow clay of the pits is covered by a flame of fire which leaps from the rifles of the Mississippians and Tennesseeans, by whom they are manned, and who are evidently anticipating an assault. The volley passes over our heads, cutting twigs and limbs off the trees. We give a hearty cheer and rush forward, and then the shots of the enemy begin to tell.

LIEUTENANT JAMES O. CHURCHILL

11TH ILLINOIS INFANTRY, W. H. L. WALLACE'S BRIGADE

When Floyd and Pillow called off the attempt to break through the Federal lines south of Fort Donelson, the Rebel units pulled back into the defenses, leaving behind hundreds of wounded from both armies. Many, like Churchill, would lie unattended through a night of subfreezing temperatures. In addition to 70 soldiers of the 11th Illinois killed outright, 32 men succumbed to their wounds.

Some with boyish voices were calling "Mother," others shrieking as though in great agony, many groaning, and occasionally one was swearing like a Spanish trooper. Presently along came three Confederate surgeons, who commenced to examine the wounded, selecting those they thought would live. These they turned over to the ambulance corps, to be taken off as prisoners of war. They gave me a thorough examination, after which I asked them what they proposed to do with me. They told me my right hip and thigh were both broken, that the blood was fast dripping from the left leg, that it was no use to haul me off, as I would peg out before morning. I had fallen between the legs of a wounded man, my head resting on his stomach. They dragged him from under me, and my head fell to the ground in the snow.

I told one of the surgeons that I would like to be taken to the hospital. He appeared to be a very pleasant gentleman. He said, "To tell you the truth, we haven't the facilities to get our own men off. We are taking as prisoners now only those of you we think will live. If I can return and take you, I will."

A dead man lay at right angles to my position, his head against my right side, and another so that his head was against mine; to avoid it, I had to turn my neck to the left. The head of a third was against my left breast. This man was not yet dead, groaning occasionally. I asked him where he was wounded; he was unable to reply. Seeing blood on his coat, I reached over, and found, and put my finger into a large bullet hole in the left breast.

I now felt a very severe cutting pain just above the hips; on reaching down I found I was lying on a two inch limb of a neighboring fallen tree, my body being suspended as if over a swing rope about six inches from the ground.

Seeing several Confederates near by I called them; they came to me, when I told them I desired to be lifted from the limb, and away from the dead man at my right, so I would not be obliged to turn my head to one

side. The head occupied nearly two inches of the space where mine would be if lying straight. One man took hold of my head, another my feet, and one my shoulders. The one at my feet lifted them first, fully three feet high. I could feel the broken thigh bone cutting its way through the muscles below. I gave such a piercing shriek that he dropped my legs as though frightened. I told them to try it again, and to all lift together. The one at my hips lifted first this time, and I felt the sharp cutting bone coming through the flesh. I put my hand down and could feel the end just under the skin. I gave another yell, with the same result as before. Then I told them that would do, and they left in the direction of Dover.

. . . It seemed as though the battle lasted an hour, when both parties stopped firing, and the enemy retired towards Dover. I could hear no noise now, except the cries and groans of the wounded. Some of those near by, I could individually recognize as they grew fainter and fainter, and finally ceased altogether. The soldier on my left had stopped groaning before the last battle, and putting my hand on the forehead, found it was cold. The heads of the other two felt like pieces of ice. I was bareheaded, having lost my cap when I fell the first time. I could feel that it was growing very cold; judged it must be 15 or 20 degrees below freezing; the trees snapped, and the branches and twigs moved with a sharp, crispy sound. Night had come, and I was evidently between the respective picket lines. All hope of being taken from the field vanished, and I was left to my reveries. My mind was unusually active, and involuntarily ran to subjects singularly appropriate to the surroundings.

After a time I began to feel great pain, which was caused by the limb upon which I was lying, apparently cutting into my side and back. My head was resting against that of the dead man on my right, and was getting very cold. In attempting to raise it, I found it stuck fast; my hair had frozen to the ground. I worked my hand under it and by using my fingers as a lever pried it out, and turned my neck so as to bring my head against the shoulder of the dead man on my left. I did not forget to change its position every few minutes during the rest of the night, so it would not freeze down again. I then got out my knife, and bringing it across to my left side, tried to cut off the tree limb. After cutting at it for nearly an hour, I found I had made no impression upon it. It was of very hard, half-seasoned oak, and my position was such that I could but just reach it.

I was now seized with an intolerable thirst, and commenced reaching about me and filling my mouth with snow. Putting my hand under me, where the central part of my body was held up by the limb, I found the snow had been melted under my hips by the hot blood from my wounds. But now there were several small icicles of blood from my leg injuries, and the wounds had apparently frozen up. This undoubtedly saved my life; otherwise I probably would have bled to death.

In reaching back of my head for snow, I felt a metallic substance. It proved to be a canteen filled with something frozen solid; it evidently belonged to the soldier who had been pulled from under me. I took it by the strap, and pounded it against the log, reaching over the face of the dead man at my left, until I had broken the contents in pieces. Then, taking my knife, I cut out one side of the canteen. What should I find the contents to be but frozen coffee, and what a feast I had! Ask any soldier what he prefers when worn out after a long fatiguing march, and he will answer "Hot coffee," without sugar or milk to demoralize it. Mine was cold, but good and strong. I ate it until the last fragment was gone.

During the night I gave an occasional mighty yell, to see if my voice was growing fainter. Strange, but I could discern no change. Finally welcome streaks of light began to appear in the east.

BRIGADIER GENERAL
SIMON BOLIVAR BUCKNER
DIVISION COMMANDER, ARMY OF CENTRAL KENTUCKY

Buckner graduated from West Point in 1844, a year after his friend Grant, and was a veteran of the Mexican War. Leaving the army in 1855, Buckner lived in Chicago for several years before becoming Kentucky's adjutant general. Despite close ties to the North—his wife's brother was a Union officer—Buckner declined a commission in the Federal service and joined the Confederacy.

The troops had been worn down with watching, with labor, with fighting. Many of them were frosted by the intensity of the cold; all of them were suffering and exhausted by their incessant labors. There had been no regular issue of rations for a number of days and scarcely

Buckner's pleated fatigue blouse, adopted before the war by the Kentucky State Guard, bears on its collar the wreath and stars of a Confederate general. The comfortable garment became popular among Southern officers.

any means of cooking. Their ammunition was nearly expended. We were completely invested by a force of nearly four times the strength of our own. In their exhausted condition they could not have made a march. An attempt to make a sortie would have been resisted by a superior force of fresh troops, and that attempt would have been the signal for the fall of the water batteries and the presence of the enemy's gunboats sweeping with the fire at close range the positions of our troops, who would have thus been assailed on their front, rear, and right flank at the same instant. The results would have been a virtual massacre of the troops, more disheartening in its effects than a surrender.

In this opinion General Floyd coincided, and I am certain that both he and I were convinced that General Pillow agreed with us in this opinion. General Pillow then asked our opinion as to the practicability of holding our position another day. I replied that my right was already turned, a portion of my intrenchments in the enemy's possession—they were in position successfully to assail my position and the water batteries—and that, with my weakened and exhausted force, I could not successfully resist the assault which would be made at daylight by a vastly superior force. . . . I expressed the opinion that it would be wrong to subject the army to a virtual massacre when no good could result from the sacrifice, and that the general officers owed it to their men, when further resistance was unavailing, to obtain the best terms of capitulation possible for them. General Floyd expressed himself in similar terms, and in this opinion I understood General Pillow to acquiesce.

For reasons which he has stated, General Floyd then announced his purpose to leave, with such portions of his division as could be transported in two small steamers, which were expected about daylight. General Pillow, addressing General Floyd, then remarked that he thought that there were no two persons in the Confederacy whom the Yankees would prefer to capture than himself and General Floyd, and asked the latter's opinion as to the propriety of his accompanying General Floyd. To this inquiry the latter replied that it was a question for every man to decide for himself. General Pillow then addressed the inquiry to me, to which I remarked that I could only reply as General Floyd had done, that it was a question for every officer to decide for himself, and that in my own case I regarded it as my duty to remain with my men and share their fate, whatever it might be. General Pillow, however, announced his purpose to leave; then General Floyd directed me to consider myself in command.

> ## "I expressed the opinion that it would be wrong to subject the army to a virtual massacre when no good could result from the sacrifice."

Buckner's stoic decision to remain with his troops stood in marked contrast to his superiors' abandonment of Fort Donelson's doomed garrison. In an unseemly display of favoritism, General John Floyd (above)—a former Virginia governor and U.S. secretary of war—permitted only his Virginia brigade to leave with him. The following month President Davis removed Floyd from command.

" 'I admire your loyalty, but d—— your judgment!' "

LIEUTENANT COLONEL NATHAN BEDFORD FORREST
FORREST'S REGIMENT OF CAVALRY

Having battled so fiercely on February 15, Forrest declined to surrender his battalion of Tennessee cavalry with the rest of Fort Donelson's garrison. With the sanction of his commanding officers, the intrepid horseman led some 700 men on a daring escape through enemy lines.

About 12 o'clock at night I was called in council with the generals who had under discussion the surrender of the fort. They reported that the enemy had received 11,000 re-enforcements since the fight. They supposed the enemy had returned to the positions they had occupied the day before.

I returned to my quarters and sent out two men, who, going by a road up the bank of the river, returned without seeing any of the enemy, only fires, which I believed to be the old camp fires, and so stated to the generals; the wind, being very high, had fanned them into a blaze.

When I returned General Buckner declared that he could not hold his position. Generals Floyd and Pillow gave up the responsibility of the command to him, and I told them that I neither could nor would surrender my command. General Pillow then said I could cut my way out if I chose to do so, and he and General Floyd agreed to come out with me. I got my command ready and reported at headquarters. General Floyd then informed me that General Pillow had left, and that he (Floyd) would go by boat.

I moved out by the road we had gone out the morning before.

When about a mile out we crossed a deep slough from the river, saddle-skirt deep, and filed into the road to Cumberland Iron Works. I ordered Major Kelley and Adjutant Schuyler to remain with one company at the point where we entered this road, where the enemy's cavalry would attack if they attempted to follow us. They remained until day was dawning. Over 500 cavalry had passed, a company of artillery horses had followed, and a number of men from different regiments, passing over hard-frozen ground. More than two hours had been occupied in passing. Not a gun had been fired at us. Not an enemy had been seen or heard.

PRIVATE JOHN S. WILKES
3D TENNESSEE INFANTRY, J. C. BROWN'S BRIGADE

More than 200 men from various units chose to accompany Forrest's cavalry on the hazardous passage through the besieging Yankee army, and many others would have joined them had their officers granted them permission. Although Private Wilkes believed that the entire force could have escaped, freezing temperatures and waist-deep water would probably have proved fatal to many.

The first time I ever saw General Forrest was in the gray dawn of the morning of the surrender. He was waiting on his horse in front of the old cemetery, just above Dover, gathering his boys around him. He saw I was mounted, and called to me and asked if I did not want to go out with him. I told him I did not think I ought to leave my command, but ought to share their fate. He turned with the remark: "All right; I admire your loyalty, but d—— your judgment!"

In a short while I saw him at the head of his command passing out of the fort over the Wynn's Ferry road, where but for the incompetency of our generals all the garrison could have gone.

David E. Lusby, a private in Graves' Mississippi Light Artillery, was captured in the surrender of Fort Donelson. Three months later he escaped from a Yankee prison camp.

BRIGADIER GENERAL BUSHROD R. JOHNSON

DIVISION COMMANDER, ARMY OF CENTRAL KENTUCKY

An Ohio-born Quaker and the son of abolitionists, Johnson would appear to have been an unlikely Confederate general. But a prewar career in Kentucky and Tennessee cemented his loyalty to the South. Following his escape from Fort Donelson, Johnson became a division commander in Johnston's army.

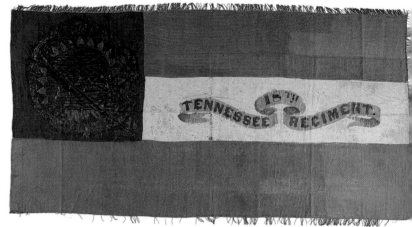

The flag of the 18th Tennessee, a regiment in J. C. Brown's brigade, was among dozens of colors surrendered to the Federals at Fort Donelson. The regiment's commander, Joseph Palmer, praised his troops' "glorious spirit of self-sacrifice."

Many of the men and officers commenced to leave Fort Donelson as soon as they were aware of the proposed surrender, and hundreds of them no doubt have made their way to their homes and to the Army. I have not learned that a single one who attempted to escape met with any obstacle.

Almost immediately upon discovering that steps had been taken towards surrendering our forces, the question occurred to me whether the example of our commanding general was an appropriate one, under the circumstances in which I was placed, to be followed, especially as I had no part in the surrender, and had only on an emergency taken command of the troops with which I had not been previously identified. I, however, concluded to stay with the men, promote their comfort as far as possible, and share their fate.

By Tuesday, February 18, the troops of my command had been separated from me, having been sent down the river on board of steamers, and I concluded that it was unlikely that I could be of any more service to them. I, however, formed no purpose or plan of escape.

In the afternoon, towards sunset, of February 18 I walked out with a Confederate officer and took my course towards the rifle pits on the hill formerly occupied by Colonel Heiman, and finding no sentinel to obstruct me, I passed on and was soon beyond the Federal encampments.

MAJOR WILLIAM N. BROWN

20TH MISSISSIPPI INFANTRY, BALDWIN'S BRIGADE

Major Brown, whose gray hair belied his 32 years, was ordered to keep hundreds of anxious Confederate soldiers at bay while General Floyd and his escort boarded the steamboats that would carry them beyond reach of the victorious Yankees. Brown's men fulfilled their duty but were denied passage on the boats and compelled to surrender. Three months later Brown was exchanged for Union surgeon Edward Revere, a grandson of the famous Revolutionary War patriot.

At 1 o'clock on Saturday night I was sent for to report to General J. B. Floyd, which I did promptly, and received notice from him that the place was to be surrendered, but that he would not surrender himself, and would cut his way out with his immediate command. To carry out this determination he ordered me to form my regiment on the left of our line, as the previous morning, with the Virginia regiments. While executing this order an aide-de-camp of General Buckner brought an order countermanding this arrangement, and directing me to the steamboat landing, to embark on one of the two boats then momentarily expected.

I went immediately to General Floyd, so as better to understand the movement, and from him learned the authenticity of the instructions, and also that we would embark according to the rank of commanding officers (Colonel Wharton's brigade and Colonel McCausland's brigade would precede me in order). I was further directed to place a strong guard around the steamboat landing, to prohibit stragglers from going aboard. The boats being detained until nearly daylight and the news of a surrender spreading through the camp, caused many to flock to the river, almost panic-stricken and frantic, to make good their escape by getting aboard. In all this confusion I am proud to say that the Twentieth Mississippi Regiment stood like a stone wall, which, as the necessity had required, I had thrown in a semicircle around the landing, to protect General Floyd and his Virginia regiments while embarking; and, when the last hope had vanished of getting aboard according to the orders and promises of General Floyd, and we realized the sad fate that we had been surrendered, the regiment stacked arms in perfect order, without the least intimidation, but full of regret.

I am not able to state why we were not taken aboard the boat; there were about 200 men and officers between my regiment and the boat and General Floyd was aboard. I sent my adjutant to inform him we were ready to go aboard. I did not get a satisfactory answer, but learned that the general was fighting off the men in my front, who I thought belonged to one of the Virginia regiments, commanded by Maj. Thomas Smith, who has since informed me that some did not go.

There seemed to me to be room enough on board for us all, and if he had wanted them out of the way I could have cleared the bank in a moment's time. When the boat left there did not seem to me to be 50 men on deck. It is, perhaps, unbecoming in me to say whose fault it was that my regiment was not embarked, but I certainly owe it to myself to show that it was not mine. While this excitement was going on General Buckner sent for me and informed me that unless the steamboat left the landing immediately he would have a bomb-shell thrown into it; that he had sent word to the boat to that effect. He made some further remarks of an explanatory character, among others that we were in danger of being shelled by the gunboats of the enemy, as he had surrendered the place, and the gunboats were or might be at the fort; that his honor as an officer and the honor and good faith of the Confederacy required that at daylight he should turn over everything under his command agreeably to the terms of capitulation with General Grant, of the Federal Army. I returned to the boat to make every effort to get aboard, but it had shoved off and was making up the river, with very few persons aboard.

Thomas P. Gooch, a 19-year-old private in Company C of the 20th Mississippi, was among the 454 men of that regiment who surrendered at Fort Donelson.

Thomas Gooch's brother, Alphonso S. Gooch—a fellow soldier in the 20th Mississippi—was also captured at Fort Donelson on February 16.

" 'What answer shall I send to this, General Smith,' asked Grant. 'No terms to the damned rebels,' replied Smith."

BRIGADIER GENERAL ULYSSES S. GRANT
COMMANDER, ARMY OF THE TENNESSEE

With Floyd and Pillow gone, ammunition running perilously low, and the Confederate defenders exhausted by days of strain and exposure, Buckner deemed his forces to be in "confusion, amounting almost to a state of disorganization." Seeing no choice but to open negotiations with the Federal commander, Buckner ordered all outlying troops back to their trenches and dispatched a courier to Grant.

Before daylight General Smith brought to me the following letter from General Buckner: "Sir:—In consideration of all the circumstances governing the present situation of affairs at this station, I propose to the Commanding Officer of the Federal forces the appointment of Commissioners to agree upon terms of capitulation of the forces and fort under my command, and in that view suggest an armistice until 2 o'clock today."

Buckner selected Major George B. Cosby (above) of his staff to carry the request for proposed terms of surrender to Grant. A former instructor of cavalry tactics at West Point, Cosby won Buckner's praise for "gallant and intelligent discharge of his duties."

MAJOR JOHN H. BRINTON
STAFF, BRIGADIER GENERAL ULYSSES S. GRANT

Rejecting Buckner's request for a cease-fire and formally negotiated terms of surrender, Grant insisted upon "unconditional and immediate surrender" lest the Federals "move immediately" against Fort Donelson's defenders. The stern demand—which, according to Brinton's account stemmed in part from the views held by the crusty old veteran C. F. Smith—would assume near legendary status.

The night was inclement. Our troops slept on their arms, General C. F. Smith's division being absolutely within the lines of defense around Fort Donelson. All apparently passed quietly enough, no sorties were made by the enemy and no attack by us. General Grant slept at his headquarters in a feather bed in the kitchen, and I remember that I was curled up on the floor near the fire with my head resting in the seat of my saddle. Early, very early, an orderly entered, ushering in General C. F. Smith, who seemed very cold, indeed half frozen. He walked at once to the open fire on the hearth, for a moment warmed his feet, then turned his back to the fire, facing General Grant who had slipped out of bed, and who was quickly drawing on his outer clothes. "There's something for you to read, General Grant," said Smith, handing him a letter, and while he was doing so, Smith asked us for something to drink. My flask, the only liquor on the Staff, was handed to him, and he helped himself in a soldier-like manner. I can almost see him now, erect, manly, every inch a soldier, standing in front of the fire, twisting his long white moustache and wiping his lips. "What answer shall I send to this, General Smith," asked Grant. "No terms to the damned rebels," replied Smith. Those were his actual words. General Grant gave a short laugh, and drawing a piece of paper, letter size, and of rather poor quality, began to write. In a short time, certainly, not many minutes, he finished and read aloud as if to General Smith, but really so that we understrappers could all hear, his famous "Unconditional surrender" letter, ending with, "I propose to move immediately upon your works." General Smith gave a short emphatic "Hm!" and remarking, "It's the same thing in smoother words," stalked out of the room to deliver the letter, which was shortly followed by the return answer of surrender.

BRIGADIER GENERAL SIMON BOLIVAR BUCKNER
Division Commander, Army of Central Kentucky

Buckner was taken aback by Grant's brusque reply to his proposal for negotiations, but he believed a refusal of the Yankee commander's terms would "have led to the massacre of my troops without any advantage resulting from the sacrifice." Despite his prewar friendship with Grant, Buckner reflected his anger in an equally curt response.

Headquarters Dover, Tenn.,
February 16, 1862.
To Brig.-Gen. U. S. Grant, U.S.A.:

Sir: The distribution of the forces under my command, incident to an unexpected change of commanders, and the overwhelming force under your command, compel me, notwithstanding the brilliant success of the confederate arms yesterday, to accept the ungenerous and unchivalrous terms which you propose. I am, sir, your very obedient servant,

S. B. Buckner
Brig.-Gen. C.S.A.

The day after the surrender of the fort, Lieutenant Horace Lurton of the 5th Tennessee managed to scrawl a brief note to his mother letting her know that he had survived the battle. Following his parole Lurton signed on with a Kentucky cavalry unit. He was captured again, at Buffington, Ohio, in August 1863.

With defiance in their eyes, captured Confederates pose for a Northern photographer soon after their arrival at Camp Douglas, Illinois, the prison for most of Fort Donelson's former garrison. The Rebels wear prisoner of war identity tags about their necks and are clad in Federal overcoats, which were issued to them following the surrender.

LIEUTENANT ISRAEL P. RUMSEY

BATTERY B, 1ST ILLINOIS
LIGHT ARTILLERY,
W. H. L. WALLACE'S BRIGADE

Serving as acting assistant adjutant general on the staff of W. H. L. Wallace, Rumsey shared his commander's surprise and elation at the Rebel surrender. Wallace had reason to be proud of his brigade: 547 of his men had fallen in the fight for Donelson, nearly 20 percent of the total Federal loss.

Sunday morning we expected a general charge, but report came that the enemy had surrendered. General Wallace ordered me to form the brigade and move it forward down the road toward the enemy's lines while he went forward to satisfy himself as to the truth of the report. When I met him at the enemy's works he said, "Rumsey, it is true; their arms are stacked and they stand behind them," and the look on his face showed a feeling far deeper than words could express; seldom have I seen a more expressive face than his.

At the head of our brigade General W. H. L. Wallace moved through the works, and on toward the river fort, when several staff officers were sent to him trying to halt him; one with great assurance and pomp rode up in great haste, and saluting, stated that he was from General Smith, who ordered him to halt his brigade; General Wallace moved on with great dignity, remarking to the officer, "General Smith is not my commander" and to me he said, "I am going to the fort; I commenced this battle, and it is my right."

PRIVATE THOMAS W. MOFFATT

12TH ILLINOIS INFANTRY, OGLESBY'S BRIGADE

Two days after the surrender, General Buckner noted, "Our camps have been a scene of almost indiscriminate pillage by the Federal troops." But as Private Moffatt's account indicates, the blue-clad soldiers, having been on short rations for over a week, were more interested in food than in trophies.

The rations over which I stood guard consisted of raw smoked bacon, hard tack, sugar and coffee and notwithstanding a deep sense of responsibility which I felt, I was unable to prevent passing soldiers from appropriating and eating some of the raw bacon and other delicacies. Fighting all day on an empty stomach makes one not too particular about the "mine and thine" aspects of food. And why wait for the cook to fuss interminably over things which a hearty appetite accepts as is.

By sundry unofficial foraging operations we were able to add to the above bill of fare. A barrel of pickles and one of sauerkraut came bouncing in and I also saw a few live geese from a neighboring farmhouse. By this it will be seen that the demands of the inner man were beginning to be heard above the excitement of the battle.

The rations were soon served and it was proposed to cook the bacon but most of the boys looked upon this formality in the light of a piece of ridiculous red tape and proceeded to dispose of it without further fuss. And it was not so bad that way if you ask me. . . .

I saw thousands of knives and swords that had been rudely and hastily fashioned out of files and other instruments of peace. Large quantities of provisions were piled on every hand. Some attempt had been made to destroy these. Heads had been knocked out of barrels of flour and their contents strewn upon the ground. Hams had been thrown in the dirt.

That cook was a prince of his profession.

Imagine if you can a pan at least four feet long lying upon stones with a fire under it and our glorious cook nearby slicing hams captured from the enemy with a sword also from the same source. Hams were dissected with a lavish hand—no fussing with the little slices from the hock end. As soon as ten or a dozen slices were removed and the slices began to get small, the bone, with meat enough on it to feed a good sized family, would go sailing through the air and a new one would be handed to him—too much work cutting the little slices.

Occasionally this cook would take a smaller grocer's scoop and walk to where a barrel of flour had been overturned, remove the exposed portions which had been dampened by the melting snow, and plunge his scoop into the dry flour. Returning to the fire he would then majestically sprinkle this into the sizzling grease. Oh, the heavenly odors that arose from that humble pan to be wafted hither and thither on the vagrant breeze. How our mouths watered and how sanctified the cooks homely face appeared to us that day.

The meal, when ready, was truly a feast for the Gods. Ham smothered in beautiful brown flour gravy, sauerkraut, a barrel of which mysteriously appeared in our midst. Apple sauce appeared in tubs where a moment before was nothing. Syrup even appeared at the command of our Aladdin of the frying pan. A large bundle of home cured tobacco came bumping into camp propelled by willing hands and feet. In a few moments uncouth cigars having the general size, shape and appearance of ears of corn in November were the reigning fashion.

The fame of our cook and his assistants spread rapidly through the camp and our company began to grow in numbers in an astonishing manner. Men whom we had never seen before would come and swear by their God that they belonged to our company. But there was enough for all and as soon as everyone was satisfied our ranks began to dwindle from desertions as amazingly as they had been recruited a short time before.

SERGEANT HENRY O. DWIGHT
20TH OHIO INFANTRY, WHITTLESEY'S BRIGADE

Grant's terms permitted Confederate officers to retain their side arms and private property, while the captured enlisted men were allowed whatever blankets and other belongings they could conveniently carry. Each prisoner was issued two days' rations before boarding transports that would carry them to Cairo, and eventually to confinement in the North. Sergeant Dwight was among those assigned to escort the prisoners.

Our Regiment was detailed to take charge of the prisoners and carry them north. So we marched up through the rebel works to the landing at Dover. The rebels were a very rough looking lot, their long uncombed hair and their butternut colored homespun clothes giving them a dirty appearance which we deemed evidence of inferior qualities. Yet there is no doubt of their pluck in the fight. If they had been well commanded they would have got off free through the gap made in our line on Saturday morning. Six thousand men were placed in the charge of the 20th Regt. and some four thousand were given to another Regt. to take to the north. Altogether the prisoners numbered about 12,000.

Brothers Calvin and James Walker of the 3d Tennessee shared confinement at Camp Douglas, where they were photographed in a group of Southern prisoners (right). Calvin (top row, center) and James (middle row, second from left) were eventually exchanged. James was severely wounded in May 1863; Calvin was killed in the Atlanta campaign in June 1864.

The Push to Pittsburg Landing

The capture of Forts Henry and Donelson by Grant's Federal army broke the back of the Confederate defensive line in northern Tennessee and Kentucky. As the Yankees prepared to continue their advance southward, Confederate commander A. S. Johnston was shocked by the magnitude of the disaster, lamenting, "We lost all."

With the victorious Federal troops poised on the Cumberland and Tennessee Rivers, threatening to sever the rail link between Memphis and Nashville, Johnston realized that he must quickly pull back the widely separated elements of his army lest they be cut off and destroyed in detail. He would have to abandon his northern outpost at Bowling Green, yielding the crucial border state of Kentucky to the enemy. Even worse, the Southern commander knew that Nashville—a vital transportation and supply cen-

Troop transports carrying Negley's Pennsylvania brigade steam down the Ohio River in this drawing from Leslie's Illustrated. Part of Buell's Army of the Ohio, the Pennsylvanians rushed to Pittsburg Landing in time for the second day of fighting at Shiloh.

ter—must also soon be given up. Johnston saw no choice but to regroup, concentrate, and reinforce his scattered contingents. Only then could he give battle to his powerful enemy.

Some 14,000 Rebel soldiers under Johnston's personal command withdrew from Bowling Green to Nashville, with General Buell's 50,000-man Army of the Ohio in slow but relentless pursuit. Nearly a third of Johnston's army had fallen sick campaigning in the frigid rains, and with the odds more than 3 to 1 against him, the Southern commander dared not risk a battle for the Tennessee capital. On February 18 Johnston began to evacuate Nashville, continuing his retreat southeastward toward Murfreesboro. As Buell closed in on the city, its inhabitants were seized with panic, and hundreds of civilian refugees followed in the wake of the bedraggled and dispirited Rebel columns.

Nashville surrendered to Buell's army on February 25, and that same day, some 150 miles to the northwest, General Polk began withdrawing his Confederate troops from their base at Columbus, Kentucky. Polk had been effectively blocking a Federal advance down the Mississippi. But as his men fell back across the state of Tennessee, a vital stretch of the great river was opened to the enemy; Major General John Pope led 25,000 Federal troops to capture the outnumbered Southern garrisons at New Madrid, Missouri, and Island No. 10, on the Mississippi.

General Johnston was under bitter attack in the Confederate press, his abilities now questioned by the Southern public as well as by many of his most trusted subordinates. But President Davis stood by his western commander, and the retreat continued. Murfreesboro was abandoned on February 28, and Johnston led his men south into Alabama, his troops reaching the town of Decatur on March 15. Along with Kentucky, most of central Tennessee was now under Federal control. Johnston knew he had to somehow reverse the deteriorating situation.

General Pierre Gustave Toutant Beauregard, the ambitious Louisianan whose victories at Fort Sumter and Manassas had made him a Confederate hero, had been dispatched to the western theater early in February. Johnston assigned Beauregard the task of marshaling reinforcements from garrisons throughout the lower South. Their rendezvous point would be the strategic rail hub of Corinth, Mississippi—just south of the Tennessee border, 25 miles west of the Alabama line. Johnston, Polk, and the other retreating columns would join them there.

Though nursing a severe bronchial infection, Beauregard energetically carried out his orders. Brigadier General Daniel Ruggles arrived at Corinth with 5,000 troops from the defenses of New Orleans, and Major General Braxton Bragg brought 10,000 men from Mobile. By March 24 both Polk and Johnston had the last of their regiments encamped in the environs of the town, bringing the concentrated strength of the Army of the Mississippi to 40,000 soldiers. Determined to hold Corinth, Johnston assessed the dispositions of his enemy and began to consider the possibility of launching a counteroffensive.

Despite Federal triumphs at Henry and Donelson, Johnston's principal opponent—newly promoted Major General U. S. Grant—had been experiencing his share of trouble in the month following his victory. Relations between Grant and his superior officer, General Halleck, had become strained, with Halleck characterizing Grant's administration as one of "neglect and inefficiency." Envious of his subordinate's newfound fame, and believing allegations that Grant had resumed the heavy drinking that so marred his prewar military career, Halleck removed Grant from field command on March 4 and placed General C. F. Smith in charge of active operations.

Halleck ordered Smith to continue up the Tennessee to the vicinity of Savannah, a town on the river's east bank. There Smith would link up with a division newly arrived from Paducah, Kentucky, led by General Sherman. Halleck wanted Smith to establish a base of operations and launch a series of raids on enemy lines of communication, but not to attempt a major engagement. "It would be better to retreat," Halleck advised, "than to risk a general battle."

Smith arrived at Savannah on March 11 but injured his leg in a fall the following day. What had at first seemed a minor cut and abrasion turned life threatening with the onset of tetanus, and Smith would die of the infection five weeks later. With Smith out of action, Halleck—newly designated commander of the Department of the Mississippi—turned again to Grant. Two weeks after being shelved, the hero of Fort Donelson was back in charge of active operations on the Tennessee.

Following Halleck's instructions, Grant gathered Federal forces along the banks of the Tennessee in the vicinity of Savannah, where the river made a sweeping loop to the west. On March 16, the day before Grant arrived at Savannah, the last of Sherman's division had moved 10 miles downstream to Pittsburg Landing, a rustic moorings on the Tennessee's west bank. Only 22 miles northeast of the Rebel stronghold at Corinth, Pittsburg Landing seemed an obvious point of concentration from which to resume the offensive against Johnston's army. Though he continued to maintain his headquarters at Savannah, over the following days Grant deployed five divisions at Pittsburg Landing, with a sixth—commanded by Lew Wallace—at Crump's Landing, six miles to the north.

With nearly 40,000 troops on hand, the Yankee camps sprawled across the rugged, wooded countryside west and south of Pittsburg Landing, some near a one-room log meeting house called Shiloh Church. Freed from the confines of the river transports, the Federal soldiers enjoyed their respite from active campaigning, and despite the nearby presence of an enemy army, evidently no one considered erecting defensive earthworks and rifle pits. As Sherman later admitted, digging in was thought to be "evidence of weakness."

While his troops relaxed, Grant was eager to make a move against Johnston's growing force to the west. Believing enemy morale to be low, the Federal commander thought the time right for a decisive strike. But Halleck insisted that Grant await the arrival of substantial reinforcements before risking battle. On March 16 Buell's army had started from Nashville on the 120-mile march to Savannah. Once Buell linked up with Grant, the Yankees would have better than 2-to-1 odds in their favor, and Halleck would be confident of a Union victory.

But the methodical Buell was moving with characteristic caution, his column hampered by bad weather, muddy roads, and the destruction the retreating Confederates had left in their wake. When Buell's vanguard reached Columbia, 35 miles southwest of Nashville, the Federals found the bridge that spanned the rain-swollen Duck River in ruins. Buell himself did not leave Nashville until March 25, a week after his lead division had arrived at Columbia. His troops had neither the skill nor the tools necessary to quickly rebuild the bridge, and it was April 2 before subsiding water allowed the Army of the Ohio to cross the Duck and continue their march for Savannah. Three days later the first of Buell's divisions arrived at Savannah, only to find that no transports were on hand to ferry them upriver across the Tennessee to Pittsburg Landing. The division commander, Brigadier General William "Bull" Nelson, was told it would be April 8 before the move could be undertaken.

Realizing that Federal strength was increasing by the day, Johnston decided that his army would have to strike before Buell's forces linked up with Grant. Not all the desired reinforcements had arrived, but for the time being the Confederate troops at Corinth were nearly equal in number to their opponents at Shiloh Church and Pittsburg Landing. Functioning as Johnston's second in command, Beauregard had organized the army into four corps led by Generals Bragg, Polk, Hardee, and Breckinridge. And it was Beauregard who devised the daring strategy that his superior now embraced.

Johnston accepted Beauregard's plan on April 2 and the following day began shifting his troops to their staging area at Monterey,

Tennessee, a point halfway between Corinth and Shiloh Church. The Southern leaders hoped to launch their assault at dawn on April 5. But heavy rains and the inevitable confusion of marching large numbers of troops from widely scattered locations over rugged terrain made it necessary to delay the attack until the following day, April 6. After two months of retreat and humiliation, Johnston intended to drive the complacent Yankees into the Tennessee River and turn the tide of war in the West.

After capturing Forts Henry and Donelson in February 1862, Grant moved his army south on the Tennessee River to Pittsburg Landing, where he and Sherman waited for Buell's force to arrive from recently captured Nashville. The Confederate commander, A. S. Johnston, reinforced by Ruggles and Bragg, marched out from Corinth, hoping to strike Grant and Sherman before Buell could join them.

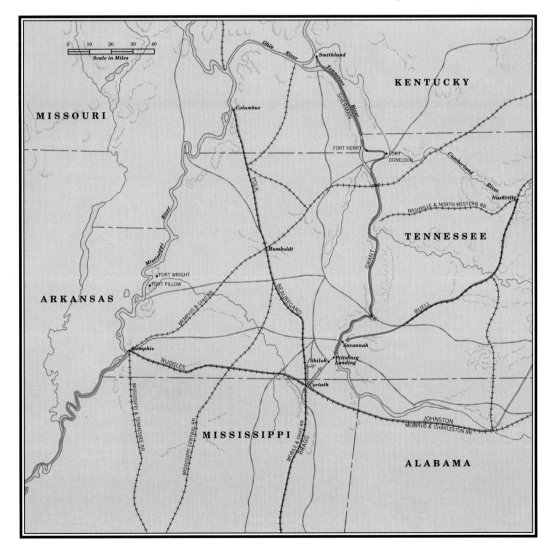

SARAH JANE HILL

RESIDENT OF ST. LOUIS

Sara Jane Full emigrated from England in 1838 at the age of 12. Settling in St. Louis, she married Eben Marvin Hill in 1858. When her husband joined the Missouri Volunteer Engineers in 1861, she frequently braved the hardships of wartime travel to visit him at the front. While at home in St. Louis in the winter of 1862, Sara Hill recorded the news from Forts Henry and Donelson in her diary.

Soon after this came the news of the fall of Fort Henry and the battle of Fort Donelson, in which the Union Army was victorious. It was almost the first success of our army, and was a hard fought and desperate battle, and the little gray man with his bull dog grip had compelled victory after three days hard fighting. How anxious we all were, and when word came that our flag floated over both forts, the city went wild with excitement and rejoicing. Men and women went up and down the streets waving flags and singing, glad of the opportunity to at last have something to rejoice over. But soon the steamboats came with their loads of maimed and wounded and we had the dread side of war.

SOPHIA MCCLELLAND

ADMINISTRATOR, U.S. SANITARY COMMISSION

On hearing news of the fighting at Henry and Donelson, a determined Sophia McClelland, wife of a St. Louis physician, pressured General Nelson to grant a pass permitting her team of volunteer doctors and nurses to travel on government steamers to the battlefield. On February 22, 1862, General Sherman placed the steamboats Hastings and Fannie Bullitt under McClelland's charge, with orders to evacuate the wounded. In her memoirs, McClelland described her arrival at Cairo with a load of wounded—Federal and Confederate.

I was becoming impatient and restless in waiting, therefore determined to take the boat that first arrived, and trust to chance to have the other one overtake us. We brought on board about sixty prisoners; half of them were wounded men, the others were suffering from the effects of measles and colds from exposure. They coughed almost incessantly, and there was not an ounce of opiate or sedative to be found this side of Cairo. It was in the evening and nearly dark when we reached Cairo. We had very few provisions and our needs were extremely pressing. In order to get our order on the commissary honored it was necessary to report at headquarters at once. Then, to make matters still more desperate, our boxes of sanitary stores, containing bedding, clothing, and bandages, had gone astray; we had been placed in such straits for the bandages that some of us had taken our underclothing and torn it into strips to bind up the wounds of the suffering soldiers.

A long line of cars from Chicago had just come in, and for fifty minutes continued drilling back and forth until it was quite dark. There were no lamps or lights on the wharf, save here and there what seemed a flaming torch of some resinous substance, which only partly lighted up the vicinity. As soon as the cars stopped long enough, I climbed through and over them to the other side. The mire was knee deep. At every step I was obliged to extricate one foot before I could plant the other down. I lost one congress gaiter in the mire, and was obliged to present myself at headquarters with one shoe on and the other foot covered with a badly soiled stocking. I received a pair of heavy army shoes, and endeavored to hunt up the representative of the Sanitary Commission of the Northwest. I worked all that Sunday morning—war knows no Sabbath—packing boxes with needful articles that brought comfort and life to many who were well nigh ready to despair.

Crowds assembled at the wharves of the several towns as our boats passed, and we were greeted with cheers. Deputations of ladies were allowed to come on, who brought many needed delicacies—milk, fresh butter, and home-made biscuits. Oh, what a feast it was for the wounded and sick when the ladies distributed it to all, Federal and Confederate alike!

"We had been placed in such straits for the bandages that some of us had taken our underclothing and torn it into strips to bind up the wounds of the suffering soldiers."

In this sketch by Alexander Simplot, a Federal ambulance delivers wounded to a temporary field hospital set up in a hotel in Dover, Tennessee, after the fall of Fort Donelson. Dover, a small river port adjacent to the captured Rebel fort, served as the evacuation point for most of the 3,500 Federal and Confederate wounded.

ANONYMOUS CORRESPONDENT
RICHMOND DISPATCH

Word of the fall of the river forts spread panic in the Confederate cities and towns along the Tennessee and Cumberland Rivers, which were now vulnerable to the attentions of the Federal ironclad gunboats. An article printed in the Richmond Dispatch on February 27 described the reaction among citizens of the manufacturing city of Nashville.

The enemy are represented to have fought nobly, far better than the Northern soldiers have ever fought before; but most, if not all of them, were from the West, sturdy farmers and backwoodsmen, and, like ourselves, accustomed to the use of arms. . . . Had reinforcements been sent forward, so that eight or ten thousand fresh men could have stood the brunt of the battle of Saturday afternoon, instead of our jaded soldiers, Fort Donelson would not have fallen. . . . The news of the surrender reached Nashville, Tenn., by telegraph, on Sunday morning about church time, while many of the citizens were on their way to their accustomed places of worship. Instantly, of course, every other consideration gave place to the thought of personal safety. Every means of transportation at hand was employed to remove furniture and valuables; and children, anxious to leave the city; train after train was put in motion; Government stores were thrown open to all who chose to carry them away, and negroes, Irish laborers, and even genteel looking persons, could be seen "toting" off their pile of hog, clothing, or other property belonging to the army, though, by order of the military authorities, much of this was recovered on the ensuing day. In a single word, the city was crazy with a panic. All the rolling stock of the railroads converging in Nashville was brought into requisition, and the machines in the Armory, guns, and much valuable provisions, were removed. Seven trains, loaded with women and children inside and crowded with frightened men on the top left the city in one day. On Sunday, the army evacuating Bowling Green passed through Nashville, en route to Murfreesboro, or some other locality in that vicinity—a heterogeneous mixture of artillery, cavalry, infantry, ambulances, wagons, and negroes, all worn down with their long forced march of eighty miles.

A giant hand seizes a diminutive General Simon B. Buckner while his ragged Confederate soldiers, led by a pillow and cannon representing his commanding officers Gideon Pillow and John Floyd, stream toward Nashville. The cartoon, printed on the advertising page of Harper's Weekly on March 8, 1862, satirized the flight of the two senior Confederate generals as well as Buckner's reply to General Grant's demand for the unconditional surrender of Fort Donelson.

"Tears filled the eyes of many at the depot when these poor fellows were taken from the cars, so chilled and benumbed that a majority of them were helpless."

MAJOR CHARLES W. ANDERSON
QUARTERMASTER, CHATTANOOGA, TENNESSEE

With the approach of the Federal forces, more than a thousand sick and wounded Confederate soldiers from the military hospitals in Nashville were hurriedly evacuated by rail to Chattanooga. Lacking government resources, Major Charles W. Anderson, the staff officer in charge of rail transportation at Chattanooga, was forced to call upon civilian physicians and authorities in order to deal with the crisis.

While a Quarter-Master of Transportation and on duty at Chattanooga in February, 1862, a telegram was received, announcing the surrender of Fort Donelson, the retreat of Albert Sidney Johnston's Army, and the evacuation of Nashville. The seats and aisles of all the cars arriving at Chattanooga were literally "packed" with refugees; the platforms were crowded also, and numbers were seated on the steps, clinging to the hand railings for safety.

The weather was cold, and all cars from over the mountain were covered with frozen snow. Amid the excitement that such news and the advent of so many fleeing refugees was likely to produce, my consternation may be imagined on receiving another telegram, which was in substance as follows:

"Prepare as best you can for the reception of some thousand or twelve hundred sick and convalescent soldiers from this Army and from the hospitals at Nashville. They will be sent forward as fast as cars can be supplied.

A. S. Johnston, General."

At this time there was not an organized body of troops of any kind at Chattanooga, nor a man or officer there whose services I had a right to command. More than all, there was not a dollar of Government funds at the Post. Under such circumstances, to care for so great a number of men seemed to me an utter impossibility. Calling to my assistance some old citizens of Chattanooga, the work of preparations was begun at once. Three large buildings were taken possession of and a force of negro men and women put to work cleaning them up. Two bakeries were contracted with for bread, and coffee, sugar and other supplies were purchased. Fuel was provided at all the buildings, and arrangements made for conveying to the hospitals all soldiers unable to walk, and a special contract was made with a reliable man to put up temporary stands at the depot and serve each soldier with hot coffee and fresh bread as the trains arrived.

When the first train arrived with some three hundred on board, they were in a most pitiable condition. They had been stowed away in box and cattle cars for eighteen hours, without fire, and without any attention other than such as they were able to render each other. Tears filled the eyes of many at the depot when these poor fellows were taken from the cars, so chilled and benumbed that a majority of them were helpless. Two other trains came the following day with men in the same condition. Three soldiers were found dead in the cars, one died in the depot before removal, and another died on the way to the hospital. . . .

Getting these men from the cars into warm, comfortable rooms was a great improvement in their condition, but they were without beds and were compelled to lie on the bare hospital floors. Carpenters were set to work making cot frames, and every bale of brown cotton cloth in Chattanooga was purchased.

CAPTAIN GEORGE W. LENNARD

STAFF, BRIGADIER GENERAL THOMAS J. WOOD

A physician, newspaper editor, and real estate attorney, George Lennard enlisted at age 37 as a private in the 36th Indiana in September 1861. He was rapidly promoted to captain and soon after was appointed aide-de-camp to General Wood. In a letter to his wife, Clarinda, Lennard recounted his impressions of Tennessee's slave population as his command marched on Nashville at the end of March 1862.

After a very hard days march of fiften miles over a very dry dusty road, I sit in my open tent with a light on a camp stool and a book on my knees to pen a few lines for my dear wife, but when it will reach you, or when I will have a chance to mail it is more than I know at this time. We are now twenty six miles from Nashville and I believe about fiften or sixteen from Columbia. The Country on every side is most beautiful The farms are large and in a high state of cultivation. The farms are generally from 500 to 1.000 acres, with from ten to 50 slaves. The negros look very clever at us and want to go along. I could get 50 every day to go with me, but we have nothing to do with them. The General forbids them coming into camp and if they do get in they must be given up to their masters, or turned over to the civel authorities wich means putting them in jail. I do pity the poor creatures. After the "white folks" have told them all kinds of stories about us taking them to Cuba and selling them and taking them out and shooting at them for fun, they still flock to us, and I do assure you it is pretty hard to put the poor cretures off, but we have it to do. I think if a John Brown was to get among them now it would not be such a failure as it was at Harpers Ferry. All they want is a leader, when I have no doubt they would rise and destroy every thing before them.

COLONEL JOHN BEATTY

3D OHIO INFANTRY, SILL'S BRIGADE

A successful banker from Columbus, Ohio, Beatty organized a company of the 3d Ohio Infantry in 1861. He served in most of the major engagements of the Army of the Ohio before resigning in January 1864 with the rank of brigadier general. After the war he served three terms in Congress before returning to the banking business. In 1879 Beatty published his diary under the title The Citizen Soldier. He died in 1914 at the age of 86.

Routed out at daylight and ordered to make Nashville, a distance of thirty-two miles. Many of the boys have no shoes, and the feet of many are still very sore. The journey seems long, but we are at the head of the column, and that stimulates us somewhat. Have sent my horse to the rear to help along the very lame, and am making the march on foot.

The martial band of the regiment is doing its utmost to keep the boys in good spirits; the base drum sounds like distant thunder, and the wind of Hughes, the fifer, is inexhaustible; he can blow five miles at a stretch. The members of the band are in good pluck, and when not playing, either sing, tell stories, or indulge in reminiscences of a personal character. Russia has been badgering William Heney, a drummer. He says that while at Elkwater Heney sparked one of Esquire Stalnaker's daughters, and that the lady's little sister going into the room quite suddenly one evening called back to the father, "Dad, dad, William Heney has got his arm around Susan Jane!" Heney affirms that the story is untrue. Lochey favors us with a song, which is known as the warble. . . .

General Nelson's command came up the Cumberland by boat and entered Nashville ahead of us. The city, however, had surrendered to our division before Nelson arrived. We failed simply in being the first troops to occupy it, and this resulted from detention at the river-crossing.

"The rebels evacuated Bowling and Nashville like a flock of sheep chased with dogs. They burn bridges and destroy property and then run like the devil."

SERGEANT MICHAEL S. BRIGHT
77TH PENNSYLVANIA INFANTRY, NEGLEY'S BRIGADE

Orphaned in childhood, Michael Bright was raised on the farm of his uncle in Penn Township, 15 miles east of Pittsburgh. In 1861 he enlisted in the 77th Pennsylvania, one of only three regiments from his state assigned to the Army of the Ohio in 1862. Bright fought at Shiloh and Stone's River; he was killed in action on September 19, 1863, at Chickamauga.

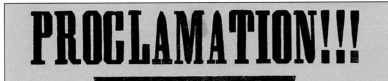

PROCLAMATION!!!

To the inhabitants of Clarksville, Tenn.:

At the suggestion of the Hon. Cave Johnson, Judge Wisdom, and the Mayor of the city, who called upon me yesterday, after our hoisting the Union flag and taken possession of the forts, to ascertain my views and intentions towards the citizens and private property, I hereby announce to all peaceably-disposed persons, that neither in their persons nor in their property, shall they suffer molestation by me or the naval force under my command, and that they may in safety resume their business avocations with the assurance of my protection.

At the same time I require that all military stores and army equipments, shall be surrendered--no part of them being withheld or destroyed---and farther, that no secession flag, or manifestation of secession feeling, shall be exhibited, and for the faithful observance of these conditions, I shall hold the authorities of the city responsible.

ANDREW H. FOOTE,
Flag Officer, Com'dg Naval Forces Western Waters.
U. S. Flag Steamer "Conestoga," Clarksville, Tenn., Feb. 20, 1862.

On February 20, 1862, Flag Officer Foote accompanied the gunboats Conestoga and Cairo on an expedition up the Cumberland River to Clarksville, Tennessee, only to find that Rebel forces had fled the city, abandoning their fortifications and burning the railroad bridge over the river. Observing that Clarksville was "in a state of the wildest commotion from rumors that we would not respect the citizens either in their persons or in their property," Foote issued the proclamation above at the request of the city's mayor.

*D*ear Uncle. . . .
Three days after I went back there was a general movement of the Army, and every man that was not able for duty was left behind. I remained behind from the 14th of Feb to the 3rd of March, when I heard that our Brigade was encamped 5 miles south of Nashville, one hundred and twenty miles from Camp Wood. Six of the 77th Regt and myself took the cars for Bowling green on Monday last. We were very much pleased with the place and we concluded to remain there to Wednesday. On Wednesday at 2 oclock we took the cars for Nashville. We arrived there at 12 P.M. So my sickness saved me 120 miles march.

The rebels evacuated Bowling and Nashville like a flock of sheep chased with dogs. They burn bridges and destroy property and then run like the devil. Our boys had a pretty hard march. They marched 72 miles in three days and it was bitter cold. They were pretty well used up when they arrived in Nashville.

"With cheers the old flag was hoisted and Nashville's capitol was thenceforth under American colors."

The 79th Pennsylvania Infantry, part of Brigadier General James S. Negley's brigade, carried the national colors (above) when the regiment marched from Bowling Green, Kentucky, to occupy Nashville on March 3, 1862. The silk flag bears the Pennsylvania coat of arms in the center of the field of stars.

Federal troops of the 51st Ohio Infantry, Army of the Ohio, form for a dress parade in the shadow of the Tennessee state capitol building in Nashville on March 4, 1862. A correspondent for the New York Times reported that "at present an air of gloom hangs heavily over the whole city. The stores are closed almost without exception, and the inhabitants gather in sullen knots to talk over the new order of things." After its capture, Nashville became a major supply base and headquarters for Federal operations in the western theater.

LIEUTENANT HORACE N. FISHER

STAFF, BRIGADIER GENERAL WILLIAM NELSON

Lieutenant Horace Fisher arrived in Nashville on a riverboat with the first Federal occupation forces on the morning of February 25, 1862. In his postwar memoirs, Fisher recalled events of the day, including a ceremony to raise the Union flag over the Tennessee state capitol.

At 8:00 A.M., February 23rd, the fleet started for Nashville by the Cumberland River, convoyed by the ironclad gunboats, Tyler and Lexington. Part of the voyage, especially the latter part, was in two columns—the *"Diana"* (Nelson's Flagship) leading the left and the "Woodward" (General Jacob Ammen's) the right, each preceded by a gunboat. During the night, about 10:00 o'clock, we reached Fort Donelson where General Grant came aboard the Diana and had a conference with General Nelson. About midnight the fleet moved on and reached Clarksville at 8:00 A.M., February 24th—then held, but not in force, by General C. F. Smith. At noon we moved forward again, during the night with great care; and daybreak found us in sight of Fort Zollicoffer, on a high bluff 5 miles below Nashville, commanding a long straight reach of the river for a good mile. General Ammen landed a strong reconnoitering party to develop the enemy's position. The gunboats moved forward to support Ammen's advance, while the fleet waited with anxiety the developments of the reconnaissance. The guns were made out with field glasses, but no garrison or flag observed. The fort was well located and armed with 12 heavy guns and, if well defended, would have caused us much trouble. But it had been evacuated and the guns disabled when General Johnston abandoned Nashville.

At 7:00 A.M., February 25th, the fleet reached Nashville; the gunboats took position commanding the landing. The Diana, Nelson's flagship, was the first to land her troops. Five companies of the 6th Ohio were sent forward on the double quick to the main square under a good guide; the rest of the regiment advanced part way, to cover the landing of the rest of the command, which proceeded rapidly. As we approached, the high ground above the landing was crowded with people, silent and anxious; many houses had hoisted the yellow hospital flag, as if they feared bombardment.

Arriving at the City Hall, General Nelson demanded the presence of the Mayor and Council. He ordered them to continue their civil functions, assuming to himself the preservation of the public peace. By his order the banks were opened at 1:00 P.M. for business with a Sergeant's guard at each bank. By nightfall Nashville was more orderly and safe than it had been for two weeks.

The 6th Ohio hoisted its flag at the Capitol about 9:00 o'clock, before Nelson arrived. Soon after he reached the Capitol about 9:00 o'clock, a man, pushing through the crowd with a bedquilt on his arm, asked who was the commanding officer. He introduced himself as Captain Driver, a Salem, Mass. sea captain and a solid Union man. When satisfied that General Nelson was the commanding officer, he began to rip open the bedquilt he carried and, pulling out an American flag, he exclaimed, "Here is the flag that the rebel, Governor Harris, pulled down from the State Capitol and which I have prayed to see put back there again. It has covered my wife and me; for a year we have slept under the Stars and Stripes." With cheers the old flag was hoisted and Nashville's capitol was thenceforth under American colors.

EMILY TODD HELM

VOLUNTEER NURSE

Half sister to first lady Mary Todd Lincoln and wife of Colonel Benjamin H. Helm of the 1st Kentucky Cavalry, Mrs. Helm was one of the last refugees to escape from Nashville when the city fell to the Federals. She wrote of her adventures in an 1896 letter published in Confederate Veteran magazine. When her husband was mortally wounded at Chickamauga in 1863, Mrs. Helm, then a resident of occupied Chattanooga, was invited to stay at the White House in Washington.

I left Nashville on the evening of the day that the army passed through, and, I think, on the very last train. It was that which carried the railroad President. Mr. Stevenson, and his belongings, and who kindly allowed me and my children and servant to get on

"The refugees came from the trains into the little dingy reception room to wait, sometimes for hours, for a room, looking so worried, with baskets, bundles and dilapidated valises surrounding them."

The domed state capitol dominates the Nashville skyline (upper left) in this prewar photograph. A booming war-fueled economy in the city bred an unsavory element characterized by the Nashville Daily Press as "thugs, highwaymen, robbers and assassins."

board. I reached Chattanooga in time to secure a room in the only hotel there. Mr. Chauncey Brooks, of Louisville, afterwards of West Virginia, a brother-in-law of Rev. Stuart Robinson of Louisville, and an old friend of mine, took charge of me from Nashville, and it was due to his humanity and tenderness for those poor, sick soldiers, that anything was done for them outside of official duty. Mr. Brooks cut out the material, assisting me and a lady at the hotel, whose name I cannot recall.

The refugees came from the trains into the little dingy reception room to wait, sometimes for hours, for a room, looking so worried, with baskets, bundles and dilapidated valises surrounding them. Sometimes there would be a mother with a sleeping child in her arms, and others on the hard floor, with little or nothing to eat, ennuied to death. As they waited, I would go in, with brass thimbles, needles and thread and cotton sacks on my arm and enquire if there was anyone among them who would sew a little on the cots so much needed for the suffering soldiers. Every fagged woman would brighten up at the idea of being useful, and sew diligently until time for them to continue their journey. A great deal was thus accomplished. Among the ladies who passed through, I remember Miss Henrietta Johnston, daughter of Gen. Albert Sidney Johnston, and his daughter-in-law, Mrs. William Preston Johnston, on their way to Virginia, who willingly lent helping hands. A lady in the hotel helped greatly, I am so sorry I cannot remember her name—I went to her room one morning to cut out the sacks; the little stove room, combined with the poor food I had tried to eat for breakfast, made me faint. There was no stimulant at hand, but Mr. Brooks, after tearing around the hotel in great fashion, found a man with a bottle of Hostetter's Bitters, which, without the ceremony of adding water, they poured down my throat. It would have resuscitated the dead. I think we cut out about 1,200 sacks. The hospital, I think, was on a hill, or one had to go over a hill to reach it. Mr. Brooks told me of a pathetic trip he took over this hill. Meeting a poor, sick soldier going to the hospital, and looking so ill, he offered to help him along. After reaching the brow of the hill, the man told him he could go no further. Placing him as comfortably as he could, with his back against a tree for support, Mr. B. went to the hospital for assistance. When he returned with a stretcher, the poor man was dead.

Nashville's graceful suspension bridge over the Cumberland River, shown in this painting by an unknown artist, was designed by Prussian immigrant Adolphus Heiman in the early 1850s. In February 1862 retreating Rebel forces cut the cables and dropped the span into the river. They also burned the nearby railway drawbridge.

CORPORAL JOHN G. LAW

154TH (SENIOR) TENNESSEE INFANTRY, JOHNSON'S BRIGADE

A resident of Memphis, Law joined Company I of the 154th Tennessee, the Hickory Rifles, in 1861. In March 1862 he was on duty in Columbus, Kentucky, when the order came to destroy all military supplies and evacuate the town. Later he was slightly wounded at Shiloh but survived the war to become a Presbyterian minister in Darlington, South Carolina.

March 3d.—Jackson, Tennessee. On last Thursday I was detailed for picket duty. Soon afterwards the regiment was ordered to pack up baggage, and be ready to move at a moment's notice. I passed a miserable night, sleeping in the open woods with only one blanket to protect me from the chilling blasts of winter. Returned to camp at 3 o'clock Friday evening, and was detailed to go on the cars with the regimental baggage, expecting to leave that night. A long weary night passed away, and no train. Saturday, March 1st, dawned cold and cheer-

less, and we were doomed to wait another day and night for the expected train, with nothing to eat, save a few hard, indigestible crackers. On that day, our army burnt their cabins, and evacuated Columbus. I walked over the deserted town in the evening; it was a grand and gloomy sight, the lurid flames were shooting into the air from thousands of log cabins, and in some instances, private dwellings were consumed by the devouring element. Ere night the work of destruction was well nigh complete, and what had the day before been the homes of thousands of Confederate soldiers, now lay a heap of smouldering ruins. At two o'clock, our baggage was all on board the train, and we were ready to consign Columbus to the tender mercies of the Lincolnites. I made my bed on the top of a box car, and with one blanket slept soundly and sweetly, although the rain fell in heavy showers. Sunday morning I awoke feeling badly, and as the rain was still falling, I sought shelter in a car attached for the sick. At half past two o'clock, we started at a snail's pace, and reached Humboldt at seven o'clock this morning having travelled seventy-nine miles in nineteen hours. I suffered greatly from hunger and thirst. At Humboldt I got a good breakfast, and at nine o'clock, we were off for Jackson. I was obliged to ride in an open platform car, and notwithstanding Miss Fackler's comfortable helmet, Mrs. Pope's gloves, and mother's overcoat, I suffered intensely from the cold. Enjoyed a fine dinner at the Jackson City Hotel; but had to borrow money to pay for it, as I had loaned my last cent to my hungry comrades to get breakfast at Humboldt. Such is my experience of the retreat from Columbus.

ISAAC N. RAINEY
RESIDENT OF MAURY COUNTY, TENNESSEE

In the spring of 1862, 17-year-old Isaac Rainey, standing at left with his parents, six of his seven brothers, and one sister, lived on his father's farm in Maury County, Tennessee, six miles from Columbia. His father, Winfield Scott Rainey, a Democrat and supporter of secession, acted as a guide for Confederate cavalry operating in the area. On reaching his 18th birthday, Rainey joined the 7th Tennessee Infantry and served for the rest of the war.

One morning Pa was aroused at about 2:00 o'clock. Col Scott of the 4th La. Cavalry told him that he understood my father knew the country along Duck River, on which was Columbia, and that he wanted his guidance to the several bridges on the river which he was instructed to burn to retard the enemy on his march south from Nashville. Pa went with them and several of the bridges were destroyed.

Money was scarce with us about that time and I had been clerking in a hardware store for some little time. One afternoon Laws White came into the store much excited and said to me: "Nelse, the Yankees are coming! They are on the Major Brown place across the river." I got permission and he and I ran about half a mile to the bluff above the town. On the other side we saw a skirmish line of blue coats, about one-fourth mile of us. White jumped on a log and yelled at them in language not very nice, calling them ugly names. One of those fellows got behind a stump, took aim and shot at us. That was the first shot fired at Columbia, the first angry bullet I ever heard. I dodged down behind the log. White put away from there. I suppose he did for I saw him no more for a week. I had not been behind my log long when an unorganized band of town boys 50 strong came galloping up and from behind boulders for an hour wasted many shots from shot guns and hunting rifles. . . .

The next morning the Federals managed to cross the bridgeless river and took possession of the town. About 8 A.M. a friend came out and warned my father to get away. An informer had kindly reported his part in destroying the bridges. He was proclaimed an outlaw and squads sent in all directions to apprehend him. He had a pair of fine Claybank horses which he had put to a light buggy. He drove out the Mt. Pleasant turnpike. About six miles out he met a squad who stopped and asked him if he knew W. S. Rainey? If he had seen him this morning? Pa said: "I saw him in town on yesterday." "Well we are after him and are going to get him too," their officer said, and galloped off. He was an exile for several months, but managed to communicate with Mother. Slipped in a few times, piloted through the pickets by Mother's faithful house servant, Emeline. Only Mother and the servant knew of these visits, not even the children. One day an officer rode out and told Mrs. Rainey that if her husband would come in and take the oath the ban of outlawry would be removed. He refused to take the oath. After several months more he was sent word to come in anyhow without conditions. He came home and was not molested. But he never took that oath.

*The Lexington, a commercial side-wheel steamer converted into a gunboat, was armed with four eight-inch Dahlgren smoothbores and two 32-pounder cannon.
After the capture of Fort Henry, the vessel, teamed with the Tyler and Conestoga, swept the Tennessee River of Confederate vessels.*

BRIGADIER GENERAL WILLIAM T. SHERMAN
DIVISION COMMANDER, ARMY OF THE TENNESSEE

*After the capture of Columbus, Kentucky, on March 3, Sherman's division
joined General Charles F. Smith's fleet of 63 transports in the advance up the
Tennessee River. Escorted by gunboats, Sherman's command pressed up the
river as far as Eastport, Mississippi, on the Alabama border, where strong
Confederate fortifications forced the expedition to return to Pittsburg Landing.*

General C. F. Smith arrived about the 13th of March, with a large fleet
of boats, containing Hurlbut's division, Lew. Wallace's division, and that
of himself, then commanded by Brigadier-General W. H. L. Wallace.
General Smith sent for me to meet him on his boat, and ordered me
to push on under escort of the two gunboats, Lexington and Tyler,
commanded by Captains Gwin and Shirk, United States Navy. I was
to land at some point below Eastport, and make a break of the Memphis & Charleston Railroad, between Tuscumbia and Corinth. General
Smith was quite unwell, and was suffering from his leg, which was
swollen and very sore, from a mere abrasion in stepping into a small-boat. This actually mortified, and resulted in his death about a month
after. . . . I immediately steamed up the Tennessee River, following
the two gunboats, and in passing Pittsburg Landing, was told by Captain Gwin that, on his former trip up the river, he had found a rebel regiment of cavalry posted there, and that it was the usual landing-place
for the people about Corinth, distant thirty miles. I sent word back to
General Smith that, if we were detained up the river, he ought to post
some troops at Pittsburg Landing. We went on up the river cautiously,
till we saw Eastport and Chickasaw, both of which were occupied by
rebel batteries and a small rebel force of infantry.

LIEUTENANT SILAS T. GRISAMORE

18TH LOUISIANA INFANTRY, POND'S BRIGADE

A native of Illinois, Grisamore ventured to Louisiana and enjoyed a successful career there as a merchant. In 1861, at the age of 36, he joined the Lafourche Creoles, a company of the 18th Louisiana. On March 1, 1862, his regiment fought a skirmish near Pittsburg Landing with a Federal landing party.

About 12 o'clock N., the report was circulated that "Gun boats were coming," and upon looking down the river two columns of black smoke curling over the tree tops attested the correctness of the statement. As they advanced up the river, apparently unconscious of any enemy, the pieces on the bluff above us opened on them. They made a few shots which were doubtless well aimed, but which fell short of their mark some 200 or 300 yards. As soon as the position of the battery was exposed, the boats prepared for action. We were immediately called to arms, and whilst the officers were endeavoring to form their companies the shells where whizzing over our heads, causing every one of us to bow down just at the moment we were commanded to "eyes right," to jump backwards at the command of "right dress." Our Captain who seldom lost the equilibrium of his mind, became a little excited on the occasion, but the line was finally formed. It was the first time any of us had ever heard the peculiar music of a bomb shell, and I believe without exception every man thought he was going to be hit just below the ear; at least every fellow first bowed his head and then came down on his knee. Solemn as the affair was likely to be, I know that several of us could not keep from laughing at the sudden and uniform movement of everyone as a shell passed over our heads.

A few well directed shots from the boats caused the battery above to fall back, whilst the two howitzers, from not being properly prepared, were not fired at all, and all fell back into the woods.

Col. Mouton, who was absent at the beginning, came up and assumed command. Our company was ordered to a rifle pit that was being made on the bank of the river in front of our camp, but not being completed, we were unable to protect the men in it and being too far from the boats to have any effect upon them with our arms, and visible to the gunners who were now firing upon us, we were withdrawn to the rear, not however until two or three shots passed so close to us that we could feel the wind raising the hair on our heads. Had one of the shots been a couple of feet lower it would have enfiladed the company and settled up the accounts of a good many of us.

The troops were then all withdrawn to the woods behind the field and concealed. The enemy, after shelling the woods in every direction, sent a detachment of about 100 men on shore. Having never seen but our company and the battery, it is presumed that they imagined the force on land to be small and to have retreated. As soon as they reached the top of the hill, forming into line, they advanced towards the woods, where they were met by the fire of the whole regiment. The enemy precipitately rushed to their boats, our men following them closely, and as they were obliged to embark on small crafts, the gun boats not being able to get nearer than 50 yards of the shore, they became good marks for our men, who could fire from the top of the steep banks and step back out of their sight whilst they were reloading their pieces. The gun boats were wooden affairs, and our riflemen silenced their pieces easily. Had the battery been present then we could have sunk them or compelled a surrender. As it was, they floated off down the river and did not use their engines until the current had carried them a mile or more below the scene of action. Our loss was about a dozen killed and wounded. The enemy report 12 killed and 60 odd wounded and missing. The missing with three exceptions were all in the Tennessee River.

. . . The engagement lasted three hours. The shells of the enemy being thrown promiscuously throughout the woods played havoc with the branches of trees, frequently cutting them off over our heads. Once whilst we were posted in the road some distance back, Lieutenant Gautreaux remarked that whilst we were doing nothing, he might as well stand behind a tree which was close by, and he accordingly took that position, but no sooner had he posted himself than a shot cut off a limb which came tumbling down at his feet and caused him to so completely change his mind that he was satisfied the open road was the safest place.

The Major had a servant who was mounted and had directions to watch his master and be near with his horse in case of necessity. It would be difficult to tell how many positions Eugene assumed in order to keep in view of his master and not come in contact with a shell, and how little time it took him to do it.

As we were falling back from the rifle pit one of the members of our company who was over six feet high stopped behind a tree which was not quite so large as his body, and the way in which he extended his arms over his head so as to make his size as diminuitive as the tree was ludicrous in the extreme. When it was ascertained that the shots were all flying over our heads, we could look with wonder and admiration upon the scene, and although it was a small affair to what we subsequently experienced, it was one of intense interest to us all.

Orderly Sergeant David W. Messick was part of a detachment from the 32d Illinois landed by the gunboat Tyler at Pittsburg Landing on March 1, 1862. Messick was killed in action, one of two fatalities out of the 11 casualties suffered by the Federal forces that day.

PRIVATE E. T. LEE
41ST ILLINOIS INFANTRY, WILLIAMS' BRIGADE

Throughout March, Federal forces of the Army of the Tennessee arrived at Pittsburg Landing and nearby Savannah, massing for the expected advance on the Confederate base at Corinth, Mississippi. In an article published in the National Tribune in 1887, E. T. Lee, then secretary of the 41st Illinois' veterans association, recalled the scene as the host of Federal steamboats transported troops up the Tennessee River.

Never was a grander sight presented to human eye than the old Army of the Tennessee loaded on the steamers, with flags floating and bands playing. As they started up the river the steamers Glendale and Silver Moon, with their steam calliopes, joined in the chorus—one playing "Dixie" and the other "The Girl I Left Behind Me."

Amid all our rejoicing an order arrived from Gen. Halleck directing Gen. Grant to turn over his command to Gen. C. F. Smith, and to remain on a boat at Fort Henry. Halleck claimed that Grant had exceeded his authority by taking Nashville, and claimed he had not reported the strength of his army; when Grant had sent a full report each day, and had only done what everyone said was right. Halleck

PRIVATE JOSEPH W. RICH

12TH IOWA INFANTRY, TUTTLE'S BRIGADE

Rich served with the 12th Iowa from October 1861 until he was discharged in 1863 for physical disability. Having participated in both days of battle at Shiloh, Rich was asked to assist in a survey of the battlefield for the Shiloh National Military Park Commission in 1908. In a 1911 article he described the terrain behind Pittsburg Landing.

Shepherded by the ironclad St. Louis, steamers carrying Federal troops prepare to leave Mound City, Illinois, in the spring of 1862. The stern-wheel riverboats, chartered or purchased by the army, were prewar commercial vessels whose shallow draft and powerful engines made them well suited to navigate the swift currents and shifting channels of the great western waterways.

was afraid Grant would put down the rebellion before he got down from his headquarters in St. Louis. We felt it was unjust to our commander to be thus left behind, but he did as ordered, and we had to go up the river without him.

On the way up the faster boats would pass the slower ones, and cheer after cheer would rend the air as we glided by. We were lucky to be on the Alexander Scott, which was afterward made the ram Queen of the West, on account of her speed. We passed every boat on the river except Gen. Hurlbut's headquarters boat, and arrived at Pittsburg Landing in advance of the others. We loaded our guns on the steamer and deployed as skirmishers up the bank and out into the timber, but found no rebels there at that time.

The plateau, rising eighty to one hundred feet above the Tennessee on the east, was surrounded by almost impassable barriers on all sides—except an opening to the southwest, two and a half to three miles in width. The plateau sheds its waters west, north, and east—west and northwest into Owl Creek; north into Snake Creek; and east into the Tennessee. The creeks were effectually guarded by swampy margins and heavy timber, or by a combination of the three—timber, under-brush, and swamp. They admitted of no crossing except by bridges, of which there was one on each of the streams leading to and from the battle field. The Tennessee could be crossed only by boat, as the army had never been supplied with pontoons.

This plateau, bordered as described, was cut into numerous gullies and ravines by small spring-branches, running to all points of the compass in finding their tortuous ways to the larger streams. Most of these spring-branches ran through marshy ground—impassable in the early spring except where bridged. Some of the ravines were deep, miry, and so densely choked with briers and brambles as to defy invasion by anything much larger than a rabbit. The hillsides and the ridges were covered with timber and underbrush, except where small farms were under cultivation. There was not an elevation anywhere on the three miles square from which a general view could be had. Wide flanking movements were impossible to either army, and cavalry was practically useless. The Landing itself was a mud bank at the foot of a steep bluff, a single road winding around the bluff and up the hillside to higher ground. At a distance of about a half-mile from the Landing the road forked and a little further on struck the Hamburg and Savannah road, running nearly parallel with the river. Still further on the Corinth road crossed the Hamburg and Purdy road and struck the Bark road, one branch three miles out and the other branch four miles out. Besides these main roads shown on the map, there were numerous farm roads winding around on the ridges, and the needs of the army made many new roads—all were deep in mud made of the most tenacious clay, so that the unloading of boats and the hauling to camp was a slow and laborious process for both man and mule.

PRIVATE JOHN T. BELL
2D IOWA INFANTRY, TUTTLE'S BRIGADE

Nineteen-year-old John Bell joined the 2d Iowa in December 1862 and fought in the battles at Fort Donelson and Shiloh. While in the service he made a study of shorthand and acted as a military court reporter. After the war he worked as stenographer for the district court in Omaha, Nebraska. Ever restless, Bell lived in California and Oregon before dying in Seattle in 1918.

On the 12th of March we embarked on the "Champion No. Four," and proceeded up the river and after a good deal of steaming up and down past a long line of heavily loaded boats, finally on the 9th disembarked at Shiloh, or Pittsburg Landing. While our boat was tied up and we were still on board, a soldier belonging to the Seventh Iowa, on a steamer a couple of hundred yards further up stream, fell off the crowded hurricane deck and was swept down past us by the swift current. He had on a heavy overcoat and was encumbered with belt, cartridge box and bayonet, but managed to keep afloat quite a distance. The cry was heard "man overboard!" and the deck hands on our steamer hurriedly launched a boat and rowed out to his rescue. As the poor fellow passed us he gave us an imploring look and probably saw the efforts that were being made in his behalf, but the odds were too strong against him; his heavy woolen clothing absorbed a great weight of water and he sank in full view of ten thousand men, his hat floating down stream as his body disappeared forever.

SERGEANT HENRY O. DWIGHT
20TH OHIO INFANTRY, WHITTLESEY'S BRIGADE

Sick with a fever, Henry Dwight found the steamboat trip up the Tennessee anything but exhilarating. Bad weather, overcrowding, and officious officers combined to make his journey miserable. After the Battle of Shiloh, Dwight was promoted to lieutenant and served on the staff of Major General Manning Force, another veteran of Shiloh. He mustered out of the service in July 1865 with a captain's brevet.

Gen. Sherman was a passenger on our steamer, and as the impression was widely circulated at that time that he was crazy, we watched him askance, seeing in all of his quick and nervous motions signs that the Government had made a mistake in trusting him in the field. Perhaps he felt this suspicious scrutiny. At all events he enraged us all very much by sharp criticism of the manners and customs of our regiment. He said that we were a bunch of dandies!

I was still sick, and could get nothing to eat that tasted good. Hard bread and fat pork is pretty poor diet for one who is sick with the camp fever. I lay on the deck of the steamer rolled in my blanket, homesick enough, and wishing for some face that was truly a home face to look down at me. The men were kind and helpful enough in their rough way, but they were after all strangers, and their interest in me was the interest that one has to take in suffering anywhere. In good weather my place on the deck was good enough, but one night it rained and was very cold and I was shivering in terrible chills. I would go and shove my way to the smoke stack and stand there until too weary to stand up any longer, and then go back and lie down until too cold to endure that any longer, and so the dreary night passed away. In the morning I was wet and cold and one of the men advised me to go into the cabin and dry off by the stove. I went in and revelled in the unwonted warmth. But I could not sit up for any length of time and therefore lay down in a retired corner. There I was dozing in bliss, when the officer of the guard came in. He was a First Lieutenant, and I only a Sergeant, and his lofty soul was horrified on discovering that that place was polluted by the presence of one of "the men."

"We can't allow men to come in here," said he, in a tone of surprise and indignation. "Guard, put this man out."

I gathered up my blanket and went out of the cabin holding onto the walls for support. The officer then sat down to calm repose and reflection on his satisfactory performance of his duty. It was always a cause for content to me that one year from that time I was an officer in a position where that Lieutenant more than once had occasion to come to me for favors.

After entering the Tennessee River the weather became more reasonable and I could lie on the deck in the sun and dream that I was in fairy land, with the ever changing colors of field and forest, of broad valley and of beetling bluff sweeping by me. Or sometimes I could stand on the deck and look at the fleet. For we were but one steamer out of some seventy-five or eighty that were bearing troops by this route into the heart of the Confederacy. It is almost enough to make a sick man well to see this grand display of force directed upon the one object of putting away all the rebellious folly that is threatening the Union. At evening the bands on all the steamers play sweet melodies of home and of the homeland, or give the dwellers by the river a strain from their own Dixie Land. Even the steamers themselves take up the contagious feeling of exhilaration, and give vent to their feelings in the bass bellowing of the "Calliope." If ever an elephant tried to sing he performed in the unwieldy style of these great chests of steam whistles. Ever and anon the exuberant spirits of the men burst forth in cheers, and then from boat to boat the shout was taken up, until the whole army was shouting from sheer joy at the indescribable sense of power which belongs to the sight of masses of troops in a time of triumphant progress.

CORPORAL LEANDER STILLWELL

61ST ILLINOIS INFANTRY, MILLER'S BRIGADE

After helping bring in the autumn harvest in 1861, 18-year-old Leander Stillwell left his father's Jersey County, Illinois, farm and enrolled in the 61st Illinois. After fighting at Shiloh, his first battle, the young noncommissioned officer served the remainder of his three-year term in Tennessee, Arkansas, and Vicksburg. Stillwell below describes the vicissitudes of life at Pittsburg Landing.

I shall never forget how glad I was to get off that old steamboat and be on solid ground once more, in camp out in those old woods. My company had made the trip from St. Louis to Pittsburg Landing on the hurricane deck of the steamboat, and our fare on the route had been hardtack and raw fat meat, washed down with river water, as we had no chance to cook anything, and we had not then

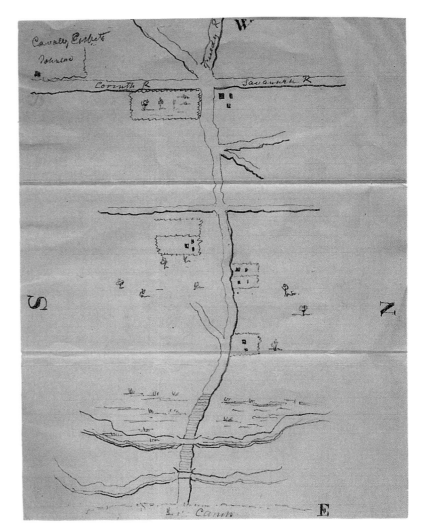

The sketch above, created by an unidentified Federal officer, records the route of the Bark road to the west of Owl Creek and Pittsburg Landing. A note at upper left marks a Federal cavalry outpost along the Corinth road. During the Federal buildup at Pittsburg Landing, Federal outposts in this area suffered constant harassment by small parties of Confederate cavalry.

learned the trick of catching the surplus hot water ejected from the boilers and making coffee with it. But once on solid ground, with plenty of wood to make fires, that bill of fare was changed. I shall never again eat meat that will taste as good as the fried "sowbelly" did then, accompanied by "flapjacks" and plenty of good, strong coffee. We had not yet got settled down to the regular drills, guard duty was light, and things generally seemed to run "kind of loose." And then the climate was delightful. We had just left the bleak, frozen north, where all was cold and cheerless, and we found ourselves in a clime where the air was as soft and warm as it was in Illinois in the latter part of May. The green grass was springing from the ground, the "Johnny-jump-ups" were in blossom, the trees were bursting into leaf, and the woods were full of feathered songsters. There was a redbird that would come every morning about sunup and perch himself in the tall black-oak tree in our company street, and for perhaps an hour he would practice on his impatient, querulous note, that said, as plain as a bird could say, "Boys, boys! get up! get up! get up!" It became a standing remark among the boys that he was a Union redbird and had enlisted in our regiment to sound the reveille. . . .

Owing to improperly cooked food, change of climate and of water, and neglect of proper sanitation measures in the camps, camp diarrhea became epidemic at Pittsburg Landing, especially among the "green" regiments like ours. And for about six weeks everybody suffered, more or less, the difference being only in degree. The fact is, the condition of the troops in that quarter during the prevalence of that disorder was simply so bad and repulsive that any detailed description thereof will be passed over. I never saw the like before, and never have seen it since. I always thought that one thing which aggravated this trouble was the inordinate quantity of sugar some of the men would consume. They would not only use it to excess in their coffee and rice, but would frequently eat it raw, by handfuls.

CORPORAL ABNER DUNHAM

12TH IOWA INFANTRY, TUTTLE'S BRIGADE

A farmer from Delaware County, Iowa, Abner Dunham signed up in 1861 for the "duration of the war." He was captured at the Battle of Shiloh and held in prisons in Alabama, Georgia, and Virginia before he was finally exchanged in December 1862. After his return to service, Dunham rose through the ranks and was commissioned a lieutenant in April 1865.

*P*ittsburg Landing Tennessee March 28 1862
This is as beautiful a spring morning as I ever saw. the sun shines out in his splendor. the grass is growing trees budding out peach trees in full bloom & the little birds singing their sweet songs cannot help but be pleasing to the soldier as it is here at the present time. it does look beautiful to see the peach trees in full bloom. the warm weather wilts us down a little as it always does in the spring but to go out and have a good game of ball and take a sweat seems to drive the old diseases out of our system and we are growing as tough and hearty as when at Camp Union. I believe that in a few days our Regt will hardly have a man unfit for duty. every day the sick list becomes smaller.

PRIVATE GEORGE S. RICHARDSON

6TH IOWA INFANTRY, McDOWELL'S BRIGADE

Private Richardson's regiment reached Pittsburg Landing in late March after an uncomfortable voyage in poor weather on the steamer Crescent City. The only noteworthy occurrence on board was the issue of new Springfield rifles. In a letter to his parents, Richardson described the situation and morale of the Federal army.

*P*ittsburg Landing
March 29th, 1862
Dear Father and Mother,
Here we are in Dixie Land looking forward with great anxiety to what we expect will prove to be a successful victory in favor of the Federal forces who are now in Tennessee. We were on the boat 10 days and when we received orders to march out and camp, we did it cheerfully. The boys are all well and in fine spirits.

You would be surprised to see the different camps which now line the woods in southern Dixie. There are about 80,000 troops in the

90

vicinity and more coming all the time. What the movements will be in the future is more than I can say, for there is no one allowed to know anything about what is going on except as the movements are executed.

There are a great many deserters from the Rebel Army coming to seek protection from the Union troops and according to their stories there are about 40,000 rebels 18 miles from here on the R.R. that runs from Memphis to Charleston. The roads are so bad at present that it will be impossible to get artillery over the roads until they are fixed, but the roads will be ready to move over in a few days and then God keep the Rebel soldiers for the Lincolnites will not.

"But the roads will be ready to move over in a few days and then God keep the Rebel soldiers for the Lincolnites will not."

PRIVATE LIBERTY INDEPENDENCE NIXON

26TH ALABAMA INFANTRY, GLADDEN'S BRIGADE

While the Yankee host assembled around Pittsburg Landing, the Confederate commanders continued to concentrate their forces at Corinth, Mississippi, 20 miles to the southwest. Private Nixon, a 38-year-old farmer in the 26th Alabama, made the long journey by rail from Mobile, Alabama, with the other units of Major General Braxton Bragg's corps.

We lay at the Depot all day and until 12 oclock at night when we got on flat cars for Corrinth. There were another Regiment on the train besides ours. So we traveled verry slow. It commenced thundering lightning and raining about 2 oclock in the night. We got verry wet and cold and to add to our misfortunes the trains got stalled going up grade. The Engineer seemed to do all in his power to get on but could not move. Some of us thought he was doing it on purpose so as the Yankees might take us all prisners. After we had got thoroughly wet another Engine arrived and assisted in pushing us up the hill. I looked around to see if I could discover my friend Donnell on the cars. At length I saw him seated on a large box, by a flash of lightning he looked like a statue. He is naturally an unassuming man and seemed to be indeferent about the scene that was going on around him. It was broad daylight before we got over the hill. . . . We arrived at Corrinth at 8 oclock and pitched our tents exactly in the same place that we had left them. The sun shone out about 12 oclock. We commenced drying our clothes and blankets.

PRIVATE BENJAMIN A. SHEPHERD

154TH (SENIOR) TENNESSEE INFANTRY, JOHNSON'S BRIGADE

On March 16 Private Shepherd and his comrades in the 154th Tennessee Infantry were loaded into boxcars and dispatched from Corinth to garrison Bethel, a stop on the Mobile & Ohio Railroad 17 miles west of Pittsburg Landing. Their mission was to block Federal incursions against the rail lines. At Bethel, Shepherd encountered his first Yankees, prisoners captured from the Federal picket lines by Confederate cavalry.

The trip up was very disagreeable. We were in box cars, the floors an inch thick with wet sawdust and crowded to excess. I put on my coat & blanket and roosted "on top" all day Sunday and at night sat crowded to death in the seats made for us with my feet nearly frozen, for it was very cold. Haitsfield just declared he *should* certainly freeze. At Corinth, which place we reached about 6 p.m., we switched off and on about a dozen times, and at last switched on to the Mobile & O. road with 32 cars full of soldiers and 3 locomotives to draw us.

When we reached B., I was partially asleep, and did not know that we had arrived here until someone on the bank shrieked out, Bethel! Then the order was given, get on your "dud" and "evacuate" the place. The first jump I went into the clay bank, and Dan Flournoy helped me out. D. has been quite kind, showing me around generally. At 10 a.m. he started out on the "scout." The Yanks are some 20 miles from here and do not disturb us yet.

Sixteen prisoners were sent to Corinth today. One of them said to some soldier gazing at him (for he was 7 ft. high): "You need not stare at me so hard, for before you eat 8 meals more, you will see plenty of them." And this scout expedition went to see those "tall fellows."

Surprise Attack at Shiloh Church

In spite of the mud, disorder, and nagging delays, by the evening of April 5 most of A. S. Johnston's 40,000-man Confederate army was in position to attack the Yankee camps at Shiloh Church. On the very eve of the offensive, however, Johnston's second in command, General Beauregard, expressed grave doubts about the wisdom of carrying out the attack. The troops were exhausted by the confused marching and countermarching that had brought them to their jumping-off point. Most of the soldiers were nearly out of food, and the men of Braxton Bragg's division had consumed their five-day allotment of rations two days earlier than planned. Worst of all, Beauregard feared the Yankees were well aware of the Southern soldiers to their front. For two days Hardee's division—the first of Johnston's units to take position—had been skirmishing with Federal pickets and

A sketch by Confederate soldier-artist William L. Sheppard depicts the charge of Braxton Bragg's Confederates into a camp of Benjamin Prentiss' startled Federals at dawn on April 6, 1862— the beginning of the Battle of Shiloh.

scouting patrols. The enemy, Beauregard thought, must be "entrenched to the eyes," ready and waiting for the impending assault. But Johnston was adamant: The attack would proceed as planned.

The Confederate commander had initially intended to carry out an assault in echelon— a series of carefully timed blows that would commence with Polk's division on the left, followed at intervals by Bragg in the center and Hardee on the right. Brigadier General John C. Breckinridge's division would be held in reserve, to be used as needed. In the final hours before the attack, Johnston apparently agreed to Beauregard's suggestion that the assault be made in three successive waves, rather than in echelon. The change in tactics would prove to be an unfortunate decision. But Johnston was correct in his belief that the Federal high command was unaware of the Confederate army massed just south of Shiloh Church. "The main force of the enemy is at Corinth," Grant informed General Halleck. "I have scarcely the faintest idea of an attack being made upon us."

One Yankee officer was convinced that something was up, however. At 3:00 a.m. on the morning of April 6, Colonel Everett

Peabody—a brigade commander in Benjamin Prentiss' division—took it upon himself to dispatch five companies drawn from the 25th Missouri and the 12th Michigan on a reconnaissance beyond Shiloh Church. Shortly after 5:00 a.m. the Federal patrol ran into the advanced pickets of Hardee's Confederate division. Their exchange of fire marked the beginning of the great battle, which quickly escalated as Hardee sent forward the brigades of Thomas C. Hindman and Sterling A. M. Wood, and Peabody brought his brigade into line to defend their threatened encampment.

At 6:30 a.m. Johnston gave the order for a general advance and 10 minutes later rode to the front with his staff to take personal charge of the attack. Beauregard was left behind at headquarters to shuttle troops forward as needed. Any doubts Johnston may have entertained about his subordinate's ability to oversee the operation were swept aside in the enthusiasm of the moment. "Tonight," Johnston remarked to a staff officer, "we will water our horses in the Tennessee River."

With the brigade of Patrick R. Cleburne in the vanguard, Hardee's and Polk's divisions slammed into the Yankee right flank, held by Sherman's division. For several days Sherman had blithely dismissed warnings of a Rebel presence just beyond his camps as the false alarms of jumpy volunteers. "Oh, tut, tut!" he scoffed at one subordinate. "You militia officers get scared too easily." But now the magnitude of the threat was all too clear, as Sherman galloped through a hail of bullets in a desperate attempt to steady his wavering lines.

Cleburne's initial attack was stymied by Colonel Ralph Buckland's brigade of Sherman's division. But when Bragg's division swept forward in the second wave of the Con-federate onslaught, Colonel Jesse Hildebrand's brigade on Sherman's left was hit in front and flank, and gave way. For a time, elements of Sherman's division made a determined stand near the crossroads at Shiloh Church, but soon even the most stalwart soldiers were forced to take to their heels lest they be killed or captured.

While Sherman's line unraveled, the Confederate juggernaut was forcing back the troops of Prentiss' division in the Federal center. Colonel Madison Miller's brigade was hit in the front and flank, and Peabody's brigade was virtually destroyed in a vain endeavor to defend their campground against Hardee's assault. Colonel Peabody was shot dead from his horse, and his surviving soldiers joined the chaotic retreat northward. By 8:45 a.m. the entire Federal front had given way, and the Union reserves were beset with throngs of fugitives, stragglers, and walking wounded making their way toward Pittsburg Landing and the river.

But not all the Federal troops were stampeded. Prentiss succeeded in rallying about a thousand of his men along a wooded crest edged by a sunken road that seemed a promising defensive position. At 9:00 a.m. Prentiss drove back a Rebel charge, and his men regained a measure of confidence. As the Federals caught their breath, they were bolstered by reinforcements from the divisions in the rear that had yet to be engaged. Bolstered by a brigade from John McClernand's division, and another from Stephen Hurlbut's, Sherman was able to patch together a line along the road that led east to Pittsburg Landing. Sherman held out on Prentiss' right until 10:00 a.m., when the attack of Polk's division compelled the Yankees to continue their fighting retreat north of the Corinth-Pittsburg road.

While McClernand covered the withdrawal of Sherman's battered division, other units moved forward to assist Prentiss. Two of Hurlbut's brigades and three from the division of Brigadier General William H. L. Wallace—who had replaced the injured C. F. Smith—came into position alongside Prentiss' troops in the sunken road. Batteries unlimbered their guns in support, and the Federals prepared to breast the coming storm.

While his army tottered on the brink of disaster, General Grant was making his way to the sound of the guns from his headquarters in Savannah. Nursing a severely sprained ankle from a recent riding accident, Grant stopped briefly at Crump's Landing, where Lew Wallace was ordered to hold his division in readiness to march to the battlefield. Disembarking at Pittsburg Landing, Grant and his staff rode to the front, through crowds of stragglers whose demoralization showed all too clearly the extent of the crisis that gripped the embattled Union army. Grant realized that unless his lines held and Buell's Army of the Ohio could be hastened to the field, defeat was all but inevitable.

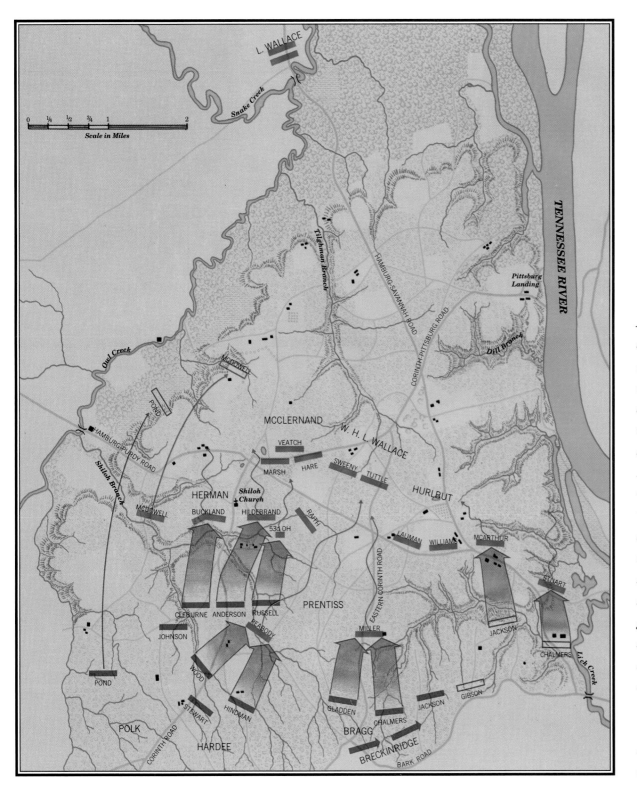

At dawn on April 6, Confederate brigades under Polk and Hardee (red arrows) smashed their way into Union camps, sending Hildebrand's and Buckland's brigades reeling. At the same time, Bragg's brigades hit scattered units of Prentiss' inexperienced division, which also retreated northward. The Federals refused to collapse completely, however, and Sherman managed to cobble together a makeshift defensive line on the crest of a small hill. Most of Prentiss' men, giving ground but still fighting stubbornly, threw up a temporary line two miles to the rear. From camps farther to the north, the Union troops of McClernand and W. H. L. Wallace joined the fight and helped slow the now badly disorganized Confederate assault.

Two days before the battle, A. E. Mathews of the 31st Ohio Infantry sketched the humble log meeting house known as Shiloh Church. Following the engagement, Mathews' drawing was published in the form of a lithograph (above)—one of the few contemporary illustrations of the battlefield.

PRIVATE JAMES A. JONES
23D TENNESSEE INFANTRY, CLEBURNE'S BRIGADE

Advancing just west of the Corinth-Pittsburg road, a brigade of six regiments commanded by Irish-born Brigadier General Patrick Cleburne was slated to spearhead the initial Confederate assault on Sherman's encampments. As Private Jones recalled, Cleburne sought to galvanize his men with the notion that they were fighting to liberate Tennessee from Yankee occupation.

The first night after we left Corinth Gen. Cleburne addressed our regiment, telling us that we were soon to be engaged in a great battle, and that if we did our duty as good soldiers he was satisfied we should gain a great victory, and that we should regain Tennessee and be in a measure restored to our families and homes. He said that we, as Tennesseeans, had more to fight for than he or his own Arkansans, as we were to make the "fight for our homes and firesides." "Old Pat" was an eloquent talker when aroused, as well as a good fighter when the battle was on.

GENERAL ALBERT S. JOHNSTON

COMMANDER,
ARMY OF THE MISSISSIPPI

Despite his retreat from Tennessee and the loss of Forts Henry and Donelson, General Albert Sidney Johnston retained the admiration of the army as a skilled strategist and dedicated commander. On the eve of his daring offensive, Johnston issued a general order, urging his troops to turn the tide of war in the western theater in favor of the Confederacy.

On April 3, 1862, General Johnston penned this rough draft of a note to inform President Jefferson Davis of his plans.

H eadquarters Army of the Mississippi
Corinth, Miss., April 3, 1862.
Soldiers of the Army of the Mississippi:

I have put you in motion to offer battle to the invaders of your country. With the resolution and disciplined valor becoming men fighting, as you are, for all worth living or dying for, you can but march to a decisive victory over agrarian mercenaries, sent to subjugate and despoil you of your liberties, property, and honor. Remember the precious stake involved. Remember the dependence of your mothers, your wives, your sisters, and our children on the result. Remember the fair, broad, abounding land, the happy homes, and ties that will be desolated by your defeat. The eyes and hopes of 8,000,000 of people rest upon you. You are expected to show yourselves worthy of your valor and lineage; worthy of the women of the South, whose noble devotion in this war has never been exceeded in any time. With such incentives to brave deeds and with the trust that God is with us your generals will lead you confidently to the combat, assured of success.

A. S. Johnston,
General, Commanding.

LIEUTENANT EDWIN L. DRAKE

2D TENNESSEE INFANTRY, CLEBURNE'S BRIGADE

Edwin L. Drake, whose bravery at Shiloh would win him promotion from private to lieutenant, wrote that many Rebels feared that their advance on the night before the battle had been discovered. In fact, the Federals remained unaware of the proximity of Johnston's army.

T he wishes of General Johnston to move quietly were not generally regarded; and, at one point on the march, the presence of a wild deer, which ran along the lines, evoked a yell among Hardee's men which could have been heard for miles. Hard showers fell. There was great uneasiness among the men lest their guns should fail fire; and many pieces were discharged on the route, and on Sunday morning as the lines were forming for the attack. It seems to be certain that our presence was disregarded by the enemy up to a late hour Saturday night. Their bands were serenading at different headquarters until after midnight. This I have since learned from a Federal officer who was present. At the time, the object of the music was misunderstood by the Confederates, being attributed to the arrival of reënforcements to take up positions for the morrow's battle. This idea was strengthened by an occasional cheer, which rang out in that direction.

PRIVATE SIMEON GILLIS
68TH OHIO INFANTRY, THAYER'S BRIGADE

A six-foot, teenage farmer from Marion, Ohio, Private Gillis could plainly hear the opening of the battle from his picket post near Crump's Landing, six miles to the north. His regiment was attached to Lew Wallace's division, which made a sluggish advance to the field and did not see action till the following day. In May 1863 Gillis would lose a leg at the Battle of Champion's Hill in Mississippi.

Just at the break of day there rang out on the morning air a single shot, which, though two or three miles from our post, sounded as if but a few furlongs away. This shot was followed almost instantly by another, then others followed in rapid succession . . . as if a picket post had fired; then came other shots singly and in light volleys, each moment adding to the number; soon it appeared that companies and regiments had entered the fray. Now the rattle of musketry became constant and terrific. It seemed to me that the fight had been raging for a half or three-quarters of an hour, when the first spiteful report of the field gun was heard. Like the small-arms, the cannon dropped into action singly, then by battery, and it was not long until reports could not be distinguished, the roar of cannon became continuous, and the small-arms could only be heard as a low rumble under the billowing wave of the cannon.

CAPTAIN ANDREW HICKENLOOPER
5TH INDEPENDENT BATTERY, OHIO LIGHT ARTILLERY, PRENTISS' DIVISION

Youthful Captain Andrew Hickenlooper noted the ominous words of Rebel prisoners whose bravado reflected the Southern army's assurance of victory. Destined to play a gallant role in some of Shiloh's bloodiest fighting, Hickenlooper would finish the war a brevet brigadier general and would later serve as Ohio's lieutenant governor.

While returning to my own quarters I encountered several detachments of troops escorting squads of prisoners, who, though indifferently clad and unkempt in appearance, generally bore a determined and defiant air, and who, in response to the taunts and jibes of our boys, sent back as good as they received. One such fellow, in response to the inquiry as to whether there were enough "Graybacks"—the favorite term at that time applied to our enemies—left out in the woods from whence they came to make interesting hunting, replied: "Yes, more than you'ns have ever seen, and of a new kind that hunts men, and if you all ain't mighty careful, they'll run you into hell or the river before to-morrow night."

A Mexican War veteran, lawyer, and Republican politician, Brigadier General Benjamin M. Prentiss commanded a Federal division that bore the brunt of the Confederate assault. Both Prentiss and his inexperienced troops performed valiantly during the day's fighting.

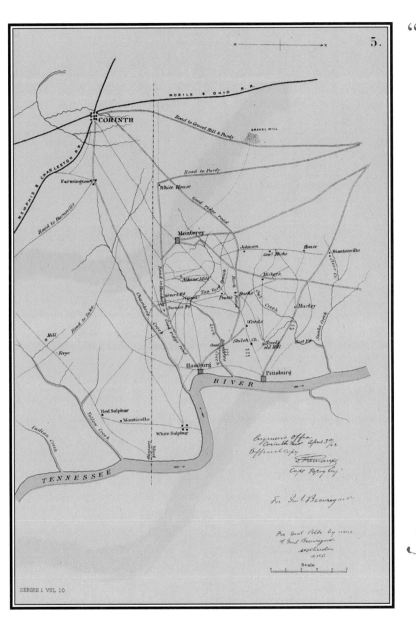

SERIES 1 VOL 10.

At the order of General Beauregard, Captain L. J. Fremaux plotted the approaches to Pittsburg Landing on a map that was distributed to the Confederate corps commanders. The copy above was given to General Leonidas Polk, whose troops were initially intended to advance on the Rebel left. In the revised plan, Polk would be the second wave in a succession of assaults.

" 'If you all ain't mighty careful, they'll run you into hell or the river before to-morrow night.' "

LIEUTENANT COLONEL THOMAS JORDAN
Staff, General P. G. T. Beauregard

Shown here as a brigadier general, Virginia-born Thomas Jordan had been William T. Sherman's roommate at West Point. A talented staff officer, he won promotion for his bravery at Shiloh and served with General Beauregard for much of the war.

Gen. Johnston and his staff were already at the same point, in occupation of a house at which we dismounted just as some cavalry brought from the front a soldierly young Federal volunteer officer, Major Crockett, of the 79th Ohio, who had just been captured a few hours before in a skirmish in close proximity to the Federal lines brought on by a Confederate reconnoitering force pressed most indiscreetly from Gen. Bragg's corps almost upon the Federal front line. As this officer rode beside his captors through the mass of Confederate infantry and batteries, and his eyes rested intelligently on the warlike spectacle, he exclaimed, "This means a battle"; and he involuntarily added, "They don't expect anything of this kind back yonder." He was taken in charge by myself, and, assisted by Major Gilmer, chief engineer on the staff, I interrogated him with the least possible semblance of so doing, with the result of satisfying me, as I reported to Gens. Johnston and Beauregard, that we should have no earthworks to encounter, and an enemy wholly unaware of what was so near at hand.

The flag of the 6th Arkansas Infantry of General Thomas Hindman's brigade bears the so-called silver moon insignia, which was distinctive to units serving in General William Hardee's division.

PRIVATE LOT D. YOUNG
4TH KENTUCKY (C.S.) INFANTRY, TRABUE'S BRIGADE

Their spirits fired by the patriotic airs of a military band, Private Young and his mates moved forward as part of General Breckinridge's Reserve Corps in the fourth wave of the Confederate assault. Two days of combat cost the 4th Kentucky 213 men—the heaviest regimental loss in their brigade. Young survived and the following month was promoted to the rank of lieutenant.

Just at early dawn we were quietly awakened by our officers—many a noble and brave boy from his last sleep on earth; the bugle not sounding the reveille, for fear of attracting the attention of the enemy, it being part of the great general's plan to take him by surprise, which succeeded admirably, notwithstanding the oft repeated denials of General Grant to the contrary. Quickly arranging our toilets and having hastily despatched breakfast from our haversacks we formed in double column by company, the band in front leading, playing "Dixie," which sounded upon the early morning stillness in this deep wildwood, as it never before sounded, soul-stirring and inspiring. What patriotic soldier could fail to be moved by its charm and pathos? The veil of caution and silence now removed by the band, down through the woods of massive oaks we moved at quick-step, every man doubtless believing himself the equal of half a dozen Yankees. A very erroneous notion indeed, soon dispelled by hard and stubborn facts to the contrary. But on we moved stopping but once to unsling knapsacks, which with our Sunday clothes and precious jewels we never saw again. Ah, some of those precious jewels! Still on we moved.

" 'Perhaps the Yanks won't shoot me if they see me wearing such flowers, for they are a sign of peace.' "

PRIVATE HENRY M. STANLEY

6TH ARKANSAS INFANTRY, HINDMAN'S BRIGADE

Later famed as a journalist and African explorer, Stanley fought at Shiloh as a teenage volunteer in the Dixie Grays—Company E of the 6th Arkansas. The illegitimate son of a Welsh farmer and a butcher's daughter, he had immigrated to the United States three years before the outbreak of the war.

Next to me, on my right, was a boy of seventeen, Henry Parker. I remember it because, while we stood-at-ease, he drew my attention to some violets at his feet, and said, "It would be a good idea to put a few into my cap. Perhaps the Yanks won't shoot me if they see me wearing such flowers, for they are a sign of peace." "Capital," said I, "I will do the same." We plucked a bunch, and arranged the violets in our caps. The men in the ranks laughed at our proceedings, and had not the enemy been so near, their merry mood might have been communicated to the army.

We loaded our muskets, and arranged our cartridge-pouches ready for use. Our weapons were the obsolete flintlocks, and the ammunition was rolled in cartridge-paper, which contained powder, a round ball, and three buckshot. When we loaded we had to tear the paper with our teeth, empty a little powder into the pan, lock it, empty the rest of the powder into the barrel, press paper and ball into the muzzle, and ram home. Then the Orderly-sergeant called the roll, and we knew that the Dixie Greys were present to a man. Soon after, there was a commotion, and we dressed up smartly. A young Aide galloped along our front, gave some instructions to the Brigadier Hindman, who confided the same to his Colonels, and presently we swayed forward in line, with shouldered arms. Newton Story, big, broad, and straight, bore our company-banner of gay silk, at which the ladies of our neighbourhood had laboured.

As we tramped solemnly and silently through the thin forest, and over its grass, still in its withered and wintry hue, I noticed that the sun was not far from appearing, that our regiment was keeping its formation admirably, that the woods would have been a grand place for a picnic; and I thought it strange that a Sunday should have been chosen to disturb the holy calm of those woods.

Before we had gone five hundred paces, our serenity was disturbed by some desultory firing in front. It was then a quarter-past five. "They are at it already," we whispered to each other. "Stand by, gentlemen," —for we were all gentlemen volunteers at this time,—said our Captain, L. G. Smith. Our steps became unconsciously brisker, and alertness was noticeable in everybody. The firing continued at intervals, deliberate and scattered, as at target-practice. We drew nearer to the firing, and soon a sharper rattling of musketry was heard. "This is the enemy waking up," we said. Within a few minutes, there was another explosive burst of musketry, the air was pierced by many missiles, which hummed and pinged sharply by our ears, pattered through the tree-tops, and brought twigs and leaves down on us. "Those are bullets," Henry whispered with awe.

BRIGADIER GENERAL WILLIAM T. SHERMAN

DIVISION COMMANDER, ARMY OF THE TENNESSEE

Although Sherman—seen above in a rare civilian portrait—later sought to excuse his division's unpreparedness to meet the Rebel attack at Shiloh, his failure to construct earthworks indeed contributed to the near disaster. Following the battle, Sherman was subjected to severe criticism by the Northern press.

always acted on the supposition that we were an invading army; that our purpose was to move forward in force, make a lodgment on the Memphis & Charleston road, and thus repeat the grand tactics of Fort Donelson, by separating the rebels in the interior from those at Memphis and on the Mississippi River. We did not fortify our camps against an attack, because we had no orders to do so, and because such a course would have made our raw men timid. The position was naturally strong, with Snake Creek on our right, a deep, bold stream, with a confluent (Owl Creek) to our right front; and Lick Creek, with a similar confluent, on our left, thus narrowing the space over which we could be attacked to about a mile and a half or two miles.

> "We did not fortify our camps against an attack, because we had no orders to do so, and because such a course would have made our raw men timid."

On April 5, the day before the Confederates struck, Sherman sent a dispatch to Grant in which he assured his commander, "All is quiet along my lines." Sherman appended the message with an additional paragraph that concluded, "I do not apprehend anything like an attack."

PRIVATE HENRY M. STANLEY
6TH ARKANSAS INFANTRY, HINDMAN'S BRIGADE

Private Stanley's regiment was among the first Confederate units to be engaged, surging forward against the troops of Colonel Peabody's Federal brigade. But the Yankees fought hard and for a time brought Hindman's brigade to a standstill in front of the Union encampments.

We trampled recklessly over the grass and young sprouts. Beams of sunlight stole athwart our course. The sun was up above the horizon. Just then we came to a bit of parkland, and overtook our skirmishers, who had been engaged in exploring our front. We passed beyond them. Nothing now stood between us and the enemy.

"There they are!" was no sooner uttered, than we cracked into them with levelled muskets. "Aim low, men!" commanded Captain Smith. I tried hard to see some living thing to shoot at, for it appeared absurd to be blazing away at shadows. But, still advancing, firing as we moved, I, at last, saw a row of little globes of pearly smoke streaked with crimson, breaking-out, with spurtive quickness, from a long line of bluey figures in front; and, simultaneously, there broke upon our ears an appalling crash of sound, the series of fusillades following one another with startling suddenness, which suggested to my somewhat moidered sense a mountain upheaved, with huge rocks tumbling and thundering down a slope, and the echoes rumbling and receding through space. . . .

. . . we heard the order to "Lie down, men, and continue your firing!" Before me was a prostrate tree, about fifteen inches in diameter, with a narrow strip of light between it and the ground. Behind this shelter a dozen of us flung ourselves. The security it appeared to offer restored me to my individuality. We could fight, and think, and observe, better than out in the open. But it was a terrible period! How the cannon bellowed, and their shells plunged and bounded, and flew with screeching hisses over us! Their sharp rending explosions and hurtling fragments made us shrink and cower, despite our utmost efforts to be cool and collected. I marvelled, as I heard the unintermitting patter, snip, thud, and hum of the bullets, how anyone could live under this raining death. I could hear the balls beating a merciless tattoo on the outer surface of the log, pinging vivaciously as they flew off at a tangent from it, and thudding into something or other, at the rate of a hundred a second.

General Hardee, whose division led the Confederate attack, was former commandant of cadets at West Point and a highly regarded tactician in the prewar Regular Army.

A Harvard graduate who hailed from a prominent Boston family, Colonel Everett Peabody was shot dead from his horse while supervising the Federal defense.

CAPTAIN VIRGIL H. MOATS
48TH OHIO INFANTRY, BUCKLAND'S BRIGADE

Commanding a company in one of the three Ohio regiments of Colonel Ralph Buckland's brigade, Captain Moats recalled the shock of the sudden Rebel onslaught. Buckland's men offered stiff resistance to Cleburne's Rebel brigade but were forced to retreat when the Federal troops on their left gave way. A little more than a year later, Moats was mortally wounded in an attack on Vicksburg.

We, I mean our tent, had breakfast very early & soon after the rebels commenced firing on our pickets & drove them in. We were immediately formed in line & marched out into the woods & had been there but a short time until on came the secesh pell mell firing at us at a distance of 20 rods. They having crossed through a deep hollow with thick underbrush which was the reason of their getting so close to us before we saw them, but our men took them as they came, each man jumping behind a tree log or anything else that came handy & then they commenced in earnest.

CORPORAL LEANDER STILLWELL
61st Illinois Infantry, Miller's Brigade

Stillwell, shown here in December 1863 following his promotion to first sergeant, remembered the surprise that swept through the camps of the Federal soldiers, who had no inkling of an impending attack. A member of Prentiss' division, Stillwell was destined to be in the thick of the action.

We had "turned out" about sunup, answered to roll-call, and had cooked and eaten our breakfast. We had then gone to work, preparing for the regular Sunday morning inspection, which would take place at nine o'clock. The boys were scattered around the company streets and in front of the company parade grounds, engaged in polishing and brightening their muskets, and brushing up and cleaning their shoes, jackets, trousers, and clothing generally. It was a most beautiful morning. The sun was shining brightly through the trees, and there was not a cloud in the sky. It really seemed like Sunday in the country at home. . . . The wagons were silent, the mules were peacefully munching their hay, and the army teamsters were giving us a rest. I listened with delight to the plaintive, mournful tones of a turtle-dove in the woods close by, while on the dead limb of a tall tree right in the camp a woodpecker was sounding his "long roll" just as I had heard it beaten by his Northern brothers a thousand times on the trees in the Otter Creek bottom at home.

Suddenly, away off on the right, in the direction of Shiloh church, came a dull, heavy "Pum!" then another, and still another. Every man sprung to his feet as if struck by an electric shock, and we looked inquiringly into one another's faces. "What is that?" asked every one, but no one answered. Those heavy booms then came thicker and faster, and just a few seconds after we heard that first dull, ominous growl off to the southwest, came a low, sullen, continuous roar. There

was no mistaking that sound. That was not a squad of pickets emptying their guns on being relieved from duty; it was the continuous roll of thousands of muskets, and told us that a battle was on.

What I have been describing just now occurred during a few seconds only, and with the roar of musketry the long roll began to beat in our camp. Then ensued a scene of desperate haste, the like of which I certainly had never seen before, nor ever saw again. I remember that in the midst of this terrible uproar and confusion, while the boys were buckling on their cartridge boxes, and before even the companies had been formed, a mounted staff officer came galloping wildly down the line from the right. He checked and whirled his horse sharply around right in our company street, the iron-bound hoofs of his steed crashing among the tin plates lying in a little pile where my mess had eaten its breakfast that morning. The horse was flecked with foam and its eyes and nostrils were red as blood. The officer cast one hurried glance around him, and exclaimed: "My God! this regiment not in line yet! They have been fighting on the right over an hour!" And wheeling his horse, he disappeared in the direction of the colonel's tent.

LIEUTENANT SAMUEL T. CARRICO
61st Illinois Infantry, Miller's Brigade

Having arrived at Pittsburg Landing only four days earlier, the 400 men of the 61st Illinois were about to receive their baptism of fire. Recently promoted from private to second lieutenant, Carrico noted that his unit had been issued muskets only a few days before the battle.

This position was in the edge of the woods, with considerable underbrush. In a few minutes the Johnnies could be seen marching in column of fours to our left. As soon as they came opposite each company of our regiment, our men commenced firing, the rebels

"There was no mistaking that sound. That was not a squad of pickets emptying their guns on being relieved from duty; it was the continuous roll of thousands of muskets, and told us that a battle was on."

being within easy range. They made no reply until far enough to the left to outflank us, when they came to a front and the fun began.

I did not realize a sense of danger until a man named Robinett, in Co. G, a few feet to my right, fell dead with a bullet through his brain, for I had for some time been looking for bees, not knowing, being a "green" soldier, that the buzzing and "zips" were made by bullets.

PRIVATE LIBERTY INDEPENDENCE NIXON
26TH ALABAMA INFANTRY, GLADDEN'S BRIGADE

Thirty-eight years old and nearly six feet in height, Private Nixon was one of the oldest and tallest men in his company. The 26th Alabama and the four other regiments of Brigadier General Adley H. Gladden's brigade moved to the attack on the Confederate right and struck Miller's Federal brigade at the southern edge of a clearing known as the Spain Field. General Gladden was among the first to fall, struck from the saddle by an exploding shell.

$\mathcal{I}$ was in the front rank close to our battle flag. A verry dangerous position as the enemy directed the most of their fire at the flag. Three of our men fell dead and several were wounded the first fire. Our Officers ordered us to fall back to a Ravine some 30 or 40 steps

in our rear. We only Stayed here a few minutes when we were ordered to charge which we did with a shout. We ran up near enough to be certain that our balls would reach them. We than fired a tremendous volly which seemed to have a considerable effect on them. We then fell flat to reload. By this time the times got too hot for the Yanks and concluded I have no doubt that self preservation was the first law of nature and acted accordingly.

They gave way in great discord. While we rushed up to their tents with a great shout. The Yankees had left every thing they had which consisted of Corn Oats Pants Vests Drawers Shirts Shoes and a great many other thing in great abundance and of the finest quality. We stoped to rest a few minutes. I walked around to look at the dead and wounded which lay thick over the camp ground. They were mangled in every conceivable form. Some were in the last agonies of death. I could not pass a wounded man without saying "God have mercy on him." I noticed a dead Yankee whose coat pocket was riped open with a ball a deck of cards had fallen out of the rent. I could not help believing that God was determined to expose his true character. One poor fellow was shot through the hips. He beged me to do something for him. I asked him why he had left his home to come here to destroy people who had never harmed him. He replied that he was sorry for it and if he was spared he would not do so any more. I told him to look to a higher power and then left him.

LIEUTENANT HORACE N. FISHER
STAFF, BRIGADIER GENERAL WILLIAM NELSON

The first of Buell's Army of the Ohio to arrive at the Tennessee River was the brigade of brawny, hot-tempered Bull Nelson, which had gone into camp on the outskirts of Savannah on the evening of April 5. The sound of battle aroused the camp early the following morning, as Nelson's aide, Horace Fisher, recalled.

Our tents were on a little knoll, on the other side of the meadow from the wagons. While ascending the knoll from the meadow, I heard skirmish fire up the river. When I got in front of the tents, I heard heavy volley firing most distinctly, as if from artillery—but we have since learned that there was no artillery firing at that time. By Gen. Nelson's orders, the aides were to note the exact time of important events in action; and I noted the time when these volleys were heard. It was 5:20 A.M. by my watch.

I then went to Gen. Nelson's tent and wakened him. Gen. Buell was there. Immediately, all the headquarters officers were in front of the tents, in their underclothes and stocking feet, with their hands to their ears to make sure.

Gen. Nelson turned to me and asked if my horse was ready. I said "Yes, Sir, at the post." He then said: "Go to the different brigade commanders and order them to get breakfast—strike tents—pack wagons and park them, with a regimental wagon guard—have three days' cooked rations in their haversacks and sixty rounds of ball cartridges—and the heads of columns on the road by seven o'clock."—all of which was done. At seven o'clock the General and staff passed along the troops, and I saw the heads of columns on the road. We went down the river, to Gen. Smith's headquarters, the General went in and conferred with Gen. Smith. Grant's steamboat, the "Tigress," was no longer at the landing when we got there; and my impression is that Grant had already gone up the river. I have always so understood. This, be it marked, was at seven o'clock in the morning.

We could find no way of getting up the river by land, without making a long march to the rear to get on to the ridge where there was a road leading to the river opposite Pittsburg Landing. The staff was scouting everywhere to find someone who might know a path nearer the river.

MRS. W. H. CHERRY
RESIDENT OF SAVANNAH, TENNESSEE

Mrs. Cherry's family home in Savannah had been commandeered as General Grant's headquarters. Writing in Nashville 30 years after the Battle of Shiloh, Cherry sought to dispel postwar rumors that the Federal commander had been intoxicated when the fighting broke out.

You will please accept my assurance . . . that on the date mentioned I believe Gen. Grant was thoroughly sober. He was at my breakfast-table when he heard the report from a cannon. Holding, untasted, a cup of coffee, he paused in conversation to listen a moment at the report of another cannon. He hastily arose, saying to his staff officers, "Gentlemen, the ball is in motion; let's be off." His flagship (as he called his special steamboat) was lying at the wharf, and in fifteen minutes he, staff officers, orderlies, clerks, and horses had embarked.

During the weeks of his occupancy of my house he always demeaned himself as a gentleman; was kind, courteous, genial, and considerate, and never appeared in my presence in a state of intoxication. He was uniformly kind to citizens, irrespective of politics, and whenever the brutality to citizens, so frequently indulged in by the soldiers, was made known to him, he at once sent orders for the release of the captives or restoration of the property appropriated.

The photograph at right, taken in October 1861—one of Ulysses Grant's earliest wartime portraits—shows the recently appointed brigadier general sporting a dress uniform and a long, square-cut beard. This image of Grant is unusual: Later in the war he was known for the simplicity of his dress, and he generally wore his beard cropped close.

"General Cleburne came to us again and said, 'Boys, don't be discouraged; that is not the first charge that was ever repulsed; fix bayonets and give them steel.'"

BRIGADIER GENERAL PATRICK R. CLEBURNE
Brigade Commander, Army of the Mississippi

A native of County Cork, Ireland, and a veteran of the British army, Patrick Cleburne was a charismatic and fiery leader who inspired the admiration and devotion of his troops. Shiloh was his brigade's first battle, and more than a third of his 2,750 men would fall in the two days of fighting.

His line was lying down behind the rising ground on which his tents were pitched, and opposite my right he had made a brestwork of logs and bales of hay. Everywhere his musketry and artillery at short range swept the open spaces between the tents in his front with an iron storm that threatened certain destruction to every living thing that would dare to cross them. An almost impassable morass, jutting out from the foot of the height on which the enemy's tents stood impeded the advance of my center, and finally caused a wide opening in my line. The Fifth Tennessee and the regiments on its left kept to the left of this swamp, and the Sixth Mississippi and Twenty-third Tennessee advanced on its right. My own horse bogged down in it and threw me, and it was with great difficulty I got out. My brigade was soon on the verge of the encampments and the battle began in earnest. Trigg's battery, posted on some high ground in the woods in my rear, opened over the heads of my men, but so thick were the leaves, he could only see in one direction, while the enemy were playing on him from several. . . .

The Sixth Mississippi and Twenty-third Tennessee charged through the encampments on the enemy. The line was necessarily broken by the standing tents. Under the terrible fire much confusion followed, and a quick and bloody repulse was the consequence.

PRIVATE JAMES A. WHEELER
23D TENNESSEE INFANTRY, CLEBURNE'S BRIGADE

Initially repulsed in their attack on Buckland's Federal brigade, Cleburne's men rallied around their commander and renewed the assault. More Confederate units came forward to bolster the advance, and five hours after the fight had begun, the Yankee lines near Shiloh Church were swept northward in disarray.

Just in our front was a ridge, a peach orchard, and the Federal encampment. General Cleburne told us to prepare for a charge. Soon it was ordered and we moved forward at double-quick, passed through the encampment, down the slope on the north side of the ridge near to a branch. Here a line of infantry rose up and poured such a destructive volley into our ranks that we recoiled and fell back to the first ravine. Here we rallied, and General Cleburne came to us again and said, "Boys, don't be discouraged; that is not the first charge that was ever repulsed; fix bayonets and give them steel." Then he ordered, "Forward! Charge!" We leaped forward with a deafening cheer and drove the infantry out of the ravine, but firing from the battery and a line of infantry was so heavy just in rear of the battery that we again fell back, with great loss, but soon reformed, and were ready for the third charge, when a Louisiana brigade was brought up to our support. Another charge was ordered and we moved forward over the dead and wounded, this time to reach the goal that had cost the lives of many of our best men. But the struggle was not yet over for the battery, as the boys in blue fired some of the guns when we were within ten feet of their muzzles. Here we had a hand-to-hand contest over the guns, but we were triumphant, and this fine battery of twelve guns was ours.

Captain Pleasant G. Swor (left) commanded a company in the 5th Tennessee of Brigadier General Alexander P. Stewart's brigade. Initially held in reserve, Stewart's troops were brought forward to bolster the attack on the Union camps.

PRIVATE SAMUEL H. EELS
HOSPITAL STEWARD, 12TH MICHIGAN INFANTRY, PEABODY'S BRIGADE

After a desperate stand against overwhelming odds, Peabody's brigade fell back through their camps with heavy loss. There was no time to evacuate casualties, and the wounded and their medical attendants were soon in Rebel hands. As Eels noted, they continued to assist the wounded of both sides. Promoted to assistant surgeon of his regiment, Eels died of tuberculosis in January 1864.

The wounded came in pretty fast and soon filled up the hospital and then they were laid down on the ground outside. We were all hard at work and only just begun at that when the rout began. Everybody else was running off as fast as possible, but the surgeons resolved that they would not leave their wounded and I was not going to go either, when my services were most required. Most of the hospital attendants ran away but some remained and we continued our work of attending to the wounded though the bullets began to come unpleasantly near. One passed through the tent and within three inches of my head as I was dressing a wounded man, smashing a bottle of ammonia liniment that stood on a box beside me and sending the fluid right into my face and eyes. Very soon the rebels came pouring in on all sides. We of course made no resistance, and they did not fire upon us though some leveled their guns at us and we rather expected to be shot than otherwise. I know I expected every moment to get hit, for the balls were flying all around although I do not think they were meant for the hospital or any of us around there. The ground outside was covered with the wounded all around and the yellow flag was over the tent. I did not know but what I should get frightened in the first battle, but I believe I didn't. I was too busy, and if I had been ever so much scared I don't think I could have run off and left our wounded crying for help. It was a pitiful sight I can tell you, I hope never to see the like again. Such groans and cries for help and especially for *"Water! Water!"* all the time. We could not attend to them half as fast as they needed though we worked as hard as we could. Soon after the first appearance of the rebels, Gen. Hindman of Arkansas rode up and placed a guard over us and assured us we would not be molested though we must consider ourselves prisoners. Two rebel Surgeons came up too and established their hospital right by ours and made liberal use of our medicines and hospital stores. There we worked all day upon the rebel wounded as well as our own, for there were a great number of them brought there.

"I shall never forget my feelings when I saw the first man killed."

PRIVATE RICHARD L. PUGH
WASHINGTON ARTILLERY OF NEW ORLEANS, ANDERSON'S BRIGADE

The owner of a Louisiana sugar plantation at age 25, Dick Pugh joined the elite Washington Artillery with his brother, brother-in-law, and a cousin. Although Shiloh was his battery's first test on the battlefield, the six guns were instrumental in forcing the Yankees from successive defensive positions, firing nearly 800 shells and taking heavy losses in gunners and horses.

It was a beautiful place, a magnificent encampment, behind which, and protected by dense undergrowth, they managed to sustain the charge of three or four regiments And here we suffered terribly, for although, when we first opened fire, several men had been slightly wounded by the bursting of shells, here for the first time we were placed face to face with them, and for the first time found out the danger of sharpshooters, who were not more than two hundred yards off behind trees, aiming deliberately at us. The balls hissed around our heads and struck at our feet, striking men and horses.

I shall never forget my feelings when I saw the first man killed. He was within thirty feet of me, and held the position of No 4 (in other words, the one who fires the piece) on the piece next to my piece, and just as he was about to fire the gun, a ball struck in front of the ear, and he fell backwards expiring without a groan. . . . I received two bullets through the legs of my pants.

Gunners of the 5th Company, Washington Artillery of New Orleans, pose near their tent in the spring of 1861. Their commander, Lieutenant William M. Owen, wrote that "the finest material in the state of Louisiana" filled the regiment's ranks.

PRIVATE R. S. SPROUX
40TH ILLINOIS INFANTRY, McDOWELL'S BRIGADE

General Sherman praised the troops of the 40th Illinois and their commander, Colonel Stephen Hicks, for the determined manner in which they waged a fighting retreat from the embattled encampments, despite the fact that they were nearly out of ammunition. Of 216 casualties in the regiment, 71 men were killed or mortally wounded.

Up to that hour the enemy seemed to crush our lines just as fast as he could find them. When Gen. Sherman rode up to our Colonel, with his wounded hand in a sling, accompanied by only one Aid, and said, "Colonel, can't you take your regiment and check the enemy until I can form my division?" Hicks's reply was: "I think I can." Then Sherman galloped away, and Hicks called attention, and says: "Come on, my Suckers!" They all went, but they didn't all return. We passed by the 13th Wis. and almost to the enemy's line, but the shower of bullets became so terrible that it was beyond endurance, though we stayed long enough to accomplish the desired result, when we fell back a short distance, halted, about-faced, lay down, and held our position until we received orders from the General to take our places upon the line which he had established, and which never was broken by the enemy, though he charged repeatedly that day. We abandoned the line only when it became necessary for us to advance and attack the enemy on his own ground.

The battle flag of Major Franklin Clack's Louisiana Guards Response Battalion of Anderson's brigade bears witness to hard service. Clack had two horses shot from under him while trying to rally his men.

CORPORAL LEMUEL A. SCARBROUGH

13TH TENNESSEE INFANTRY, RUSSELL'S BRIGADE

Pushing through demoralized units unable to breach the Federal line at Shiloh Church, Colonel R. M. Russell's brigade—part of Bragg's corps—eventually cleared the enemy from their front. During the fighting Corporal Scarbrough was shot in the right foot, a wound that put him out of action for nearly five months.

While lying at the lowest part of a ravine supporting a Louisiana Regiment the 11th I think—who were engaging the enemy, spent balls dropped about us. But we were not long to remain simply onlookers at the carnage being enacted in front of us. The enemy threw a few charges of grape shot and musketry among the Louisianians, who becoming panic stricken broke ranks and turning fled in confusion, many of them throwing down their guns in order to expedite their speed to the rear, charging over our Regiment, who were ordered to present bayonets and stop their retreat. But our efforts to stop them were vain, they brushing our guns aside and thru our ranks.

Immediately we were ordered to advance. We charged up the incline thru an old field and among the enemys tents from which they had retreated to an eminence in our front.

Through shot and shell and grape our Regiment rushed in perfect order and keeping in line, not wavering. The first to fall in our Company was Bert Moore who was struck by a grape shot on the shoulder. It chanced to be a glancing ball—but came with such force as to crush him to the ground. I shall never forget the anguish depicted on his countenance, as hearing the ball strike him only a few feet from me.

In this hand-colored tintype, Private Thomas Holman of Company C, 13th Tennessee, wears a trimmed battle shirt typical of early-war Confederate uniforms. Wounded on April 6, Holman was among the regiment's 137 casualties.

"'Who were them hell-cats that went into battle dressed in their graveclothes?'"

from Texas across the country by way of Alexandria, not thinking army blue a healthy color for my men to wear in battle, I sent an agent with a requisition on the quartermaster at New Orleans for Confederate uniforms. When we received and opened the packages at Corinth, we found they were made of wool as white as that on the back of a Kentucky bluegrass sheep. It was a case of Hobson's choice, and some Yankee prisoners inquired: "Who were them hell-cats that went into battle dressed in their graveclothes?"...

No enemy being visible in the thick timber in front, our line moved forward under orders to swing round about a quarter circle to the left. As there was pretty thick undergrowth, any experienced soldier can guess the result of this brilliant evolution by raw troops. My regiment, being on the right, would have to describe a longer curve than either of the others. Things worked well enough for a few yards, but soon intervals were lost, the line broken into as many sections as there were regiments, and some lost sight of each other in the brush, and the general either lost us or we lost him—at least, it is a positive fact that I did not see him or another regiment of the brigade until we returned to Corinth. We felt like orphans when we found ourselves alone in the woods. We moved somewhat in a northwest course it seemed, but the Lord only knew where. After advancing a mile or two a staff officer discovered us, and ordered us to halt until further orders.

COLONEL JOHN C. MOORE

2D TEXAS INFANTRY,
J. K. JACKSON'S BRIGADE

West Point educated and a veteran of Indian fighting in Florida and on the frontier, Moore had left the Regular Army and was a professor at Shelby College in Kentucky when the Civil War began. He organized and commanded the 2d Texas, and won promotion to general for his bravery at Shiloh.

After carrying the enemy's position with a rush early in the day and close on their heels, we were unexpectedly ordered to halt and await further orders. This seemed to be due to our advancing in front of the line on our right occupied by Chalmer's brigade, which was stopped by a heavy force in front. As they seemed pretty hard pressed, I took the responsibility of detaching three or four companies from my right and sending them to reenforce Chalmers. When the enemy saw the Texas boys coming at double-quick and yelling like Comanches, "dressed in their graveclothes," as a Yankee prisoner expressed it, they were not long in retiring to the rear. In explanation of the term "graveclothes" let me say that the regiment reached Corinth just before the battle dressed in "army blue" captured at Texas military posts and issued to the men while at Galveston. When ordered

COLONEL JOSEPH WHEELER

19TH ALABAMA INFANTRY,
J. K. JACKSON'S BRIGADE

With the left flank of the beleaguered Federal forces bent back at nearly right angles to their former position, division commander Hurlbut ordered a counterattack that halted the advance of Chalmers' Confederate brigade. The units of J. K. Jackson's brigade soon regained the momentum, and the Rebel assault pushed on.

Paris P. Casey, a private in the Cherokee Rangers, Company I of the 19th Alabama, sent this ambrotype home to his family not long before the battle. Records indicate that Casey, who served in the ranks of J. K. Jackson's brigade, did not survive the war, although the circumstances of his death are unknown.

Hearing a heavy fire to my left and front, I moved rapidly in that direction, encountering in a burning wood a large force, which retreated after a sharp engagement. About 3 o'clock I came upon two Mississippi regiments warmly engaging a long and dense line of battle.

The Federals largely outnumbered and outflanked the Mississippians, and were forcing them back, while the Mississippians were fighting at close range, most gallantly and doggedly holding every foot of ground for as long as possible, the men seeming to turn and fire upon the advancing enemy at nearly every step.

The color-bearers of the two regiments were very near the advancing line, and General Chalmers himself was gallantly riding among the troops. I was impressed that this was a persistent effort on the part of the enemy to penetrate our line, and I determined to resist and prevent it at all hazards. I advanced my entire brigade, fully 1,600 strong, in one handsome, regular line. General Chalmers and his battle-worn troops passed to my rear, and I took up the fight with all possible determination.

"We saw the 71st Ohio making for the rear, on the run; its great colonel (250 lbs. avoirdupois) in the lead."

CORPORAL ROBERT OLIVER

55TH ILLINOIS INFANTRY, STUART'S BRIGADE

Irish-born farmer Robert Oliver was left wounded on the field when his unit collapsed in the face of Chalmers' attack. He later recounted how a comrade came to his rescue. Oliver was promoted through the ranks to captain; in March 1865 he was again severely wounded, at the Battle of Bentonville, North Carolina.

All at once in front of me, by a big elm tree, stood Parker B. Bagley, orderly-sergeant of Company B, of our regiment. He exclaimed, "Crooker, are you hurt too?" and I fell down by the tree, and faintly asked for water. He had a full canteen, and placed it to my lips. It seemed as though new life was given. He then told me he had been to the rear to help his nephew, and was on his way back to the regiment. I told him it was gone, and to go further that way meant capture. Meanwhile the bullets from distant firing were singing through the air high overhead, and the steady crackling of musketry, deepened by the boom of innumerable cannon, made the diapason of battle complete. Presently a bullet hit the tree just overhead, indicating the necessity of moving. Getting upon hands and knees, I tried to stand up, but could not. With wounds stiffened and limbs swollen, I subsided with a groan at the foot of the tree. Bagley came to my side and put his arms around me, and I clambered up at his right side, clinging to his strong manly form for support. Thus slowly and painfully we dragged our way for a few rods. He reached his left hand in front of his body

to take me by the arm, and the movement pulled up his blouse sleeve and disclosed a bandage around that arm. I exclaimed, "Good God! Bagley, are you hit? Then leave me." His reply is remembered well, they were the last words of a hero; they were uttered with the last breath of a man who lost his life helping me save mine; they are burned into my memory by the one great tragedy of a life-time. These words were: "That does not amount to anything; lean on me just as heavily as you have a mind to; I feel just as well as I ever did." Instantly rang out clear and distinct from the edge of the ravine, a rifle shot. A burning sensation passed along my back, and we fell together—two quivering, bleeding human beings.

LIEUTENANT ELIJAH C. LAWRENCE

55TH ILLINOIS INFANTRY, STUART'S BRIGADE

While many raw Federal units fought hard and stood their ground, several of Stuart's regiments panicked and broke for the rear. A Chicago merchant, Lawrence—seen here in a postwar photograph—was among the wounded. The portly colonel he refers to was Rodney Mason, former adjutant general of Ohio.

Perhaps our movement to the rear was accelerated by the booming of the cannon, which just then opened fire with shell upon our camp. Our retreat down that hill, for some distance, was a little more rapid, naturally, than the ascent. Soon showers of bullets were singing their merry songs in the tree-tops at such a reassuring distance above us that our men turned and began to fire back at the solid line then moving down the hill, firing volley after volley over our heads. Our skirmishers kept up a running fire, with all the rapidity possible with muzzle-loading muskets, falling back in line of, and firing from behind large trees, taking deliberate aim, and doing visible execution. This was kept up all the way back through the woods, until we reached the open field of our drill ground and camp, across which we ran without stopping to look back or fire, and rejoined our regiment, with the loss of only one man. As we entered the woods back of our camp, we saw the 71st Ohio making for the rear, on the run; its great colonel (250 lbs. avoirdupois) in the lead, with his horse at full gallop.

The field officers of the 55th Illinois—Major William Sanger, Colonel David Stuart, and Lieutenant Colonel Oscar Malmborg (from left)—posed for a studio photographer soon after their unit was organized. At Shiloh Sanger served on General Sherman's staff, Stuart was placed in charge of the brigade, and command of the 55th fell to the Swedish-born Malmborg.

SERGEANT HAROLD M. WHITE
11TH IOWA INFANTRY, HARE'S BRIGADE

When ordered by General McClernand to march to the sound of the guns and shore up Sherman's faltering division, the troops of Colonel Abraham Hare's brigade moved resolutely forward, as Sergeant White recalled. But soon after the four regiments took position, Hare's line was broken, and White and his mates were driven back by the sledgehammer blows of the charging Southern brigades.

About a quarter of a mile beyond our camp, we found the road and woods literally swarming with soldiers of Prentiss's Division, who were retreating from the outposts. As we were passing them, going on "double quick" to meet the enemy, some of our boys asked them why they were running away? They replied: "Don't go out there—they will *give you hell!* We are all cut to pieces." Our reply was, "Out there we are going, and if the rebels have any *hell,* we intend to go through it!" and on we went, not stopping. A short distance further on, we met a Government wagon, in which were some rebel prisoners. . . . As we passed them they commenced cursing our Regiment, calling us "damned Yankees," and swearing that they would give us enough of "Dixie's land" before that day's work was over. I never felt more like shooting a rebel.

Hornet's Nest

Notwithstanding their stunning success, by late morning the advancing Confederate forces had become nearly as disorganized as the retreating Federals. Many Rebel soldiers stopped to pillage the captured Yankee camps, stuffing empty haversacks with their enemy's abandoned rations and hunting for souvenirs. Because Johnston rode forward with the assault, overall direction of the attack fell to Beauregard, who had established his headquarters in Sherman's old camp near Shiloh Church. Beauregard was committing troops piecemeal, ordering commanders to lead their troops to the sound of the heaviest firing. The inevitable result was a chaotic intermingling of regiments and brigades, scattered across a five-mile front in rugged terrain and in many cases separated from their respective divisions. The Confederate high command had clearly lost control of the battle.

Though reeling from the shock of the surprise attack, many Federal units rallied around their officers and regimental colors and fell into line alongside General Prentiss' survivors and the as yet unbloodied brigades of Hurlbut's and W. H. L. Wallace's divisions. By 10:30 a.m. nearly 5,000 Union soldiers and a half-dozen artillery batteries were in position along the sunken road, with its fringe of tangled thickets and scattering of timber that provided the Yankees a natural stronghold from which to breast the Rebel tide. In order to get to Pittsburg Landing the Confederates would first have to cross a bullet-swept open field and seize the Yankee position—soon to be dubbed the Hornet's Nest.

Johnston inadvertently granted the Federals a crucial hour to establish their new line when he diverted two fresh Confederate brigades advancing toward Prentiss, sending them to the Rebel right flank to ward off a suspected counterattack there. The supposed threat turned out to be one of Sherman's brigades—a mere three regiments commanded by Colonel David Stuart—that had become separated from their division. At 11:00 a.m. one of Brigadier General Benjamin F. Cheatham's brigades charged the Hornet's Nest, but it lacked support and was easily repulsed.

Profiting from the Confederates' lack of tactical coordination, the Union line threw back several more assaults over the next hour. Then, at 12:30 p.m., General Bragg ordered Colonel Randall Lee Gibson to hurl the four regiments of his brigade against the center of Prentiss' line. Three times Gibson's Arkansas and Louisiana troops charged into an onslaught of musketry and canister, only to be hurled back with staggering loss. At one point the Southerners actually got among the guns of Captain Andrew Hickenlooper's Ohio battery before being driven out by the counterattacking 8th Iowa Infantry. By 2:30 p.m. Gibson's brigade had been virtually annihilated, with little to show for its sacrifice.

While the defenders of the Hornet's Nest continued to hold their embattled position, the troops on their right—elements of Sherman's and McClernand's divisions—were coming under heavy pressure from Polk's Confederate division, aided by scattered units of Hardee's and Breckinridge's commands. By midafternoon the Union right was beginning to give way, exposing the western flank of W. H. L. Wallace's division, which began to bend back toward Prentiss.

The Confederates were also gaining ground on the Yankee left, where Stuart's isolated brigade was retreating before the assault of Brigadier General James R. Chalmers' brigade. Meanwhile General Johnston took personal charge of a renewed effort to smash the Hornet's Nest salient. By 2:00 p.m. Brigadier General John McArthur's brigade on the eastern end of the Union line had given way and was falling back on Pittsburg Landing. Shouting "I will lead you!" Johnston spurred his horse, Fire Eater, along the battle line, exhorting his troops to charge with the bayonet.

Two of Breckinridge's brigades, led by Brigadier General John S. Bowen and Colonel Winfield Scott Statham, swept through a 10-acre peach orchard just to the east of the Hornet's Nest. The assault crushed back the left flank of Hurlbut's position, bending the Federal line into the shape of a horseshoe and raking the defenders of the Hornet's Nest with a deadly cross fire. Caught up in the enthusiasm of the moment, Johnston either failed to notice or chose to ignore a wound in the calf of his right leg. At about 2:30 p.m. Johnston's staff officers were shocked to see the general suddenly reel in the saddle. They helped him to the ground, and before they could determine the extent of his injuries, Johnston bled to death. Command of the Confederate forces on the field now fell to General Beauregard, though it was some time before word of Johnston's mortal wounding reached him.

Meanwhile, Breckinridge's troops continued their attack, shoving Hurlbut's division back up the Hamburg-Savannah road and pushing on toward Pittsburg Landing. As the noose continued to tighten around the Hornet's Nest, Brigadier General Daniel Ruggles paved the way for a climactic Confederate assault by massing 62 cannon that unleashed a torrent of iron on the wavering Union defenders. By 5:00 p.m. the Hornet's Nest was virtually surrounded, and the Rebel ranks closed in for the kill.

Many of W. H. L. Wallace's men managed to cut their way out to the north, though Wallace himself was shot from his horse with a fatal wound. At 5:30 p.m. General Prentiss surrendered what was left of his division, and within half an hour the last resistance had collapsed. Some 2,300 Union soldiers were marched to the rear as prisoners, while hundreds more lay dead and wounded in the blood-soaked thickets.

The stand at the Hornet's Nest, though ultimately futile, had bought precious time for the Federal army to regain its equilibrium. Sherman and McClernand had been able to retreat with their units more or less intact, and as stragglers were rounded up and brought forward into line, Grant was able to throw together a formidable new defensive position to confront the Rebel onslaught.

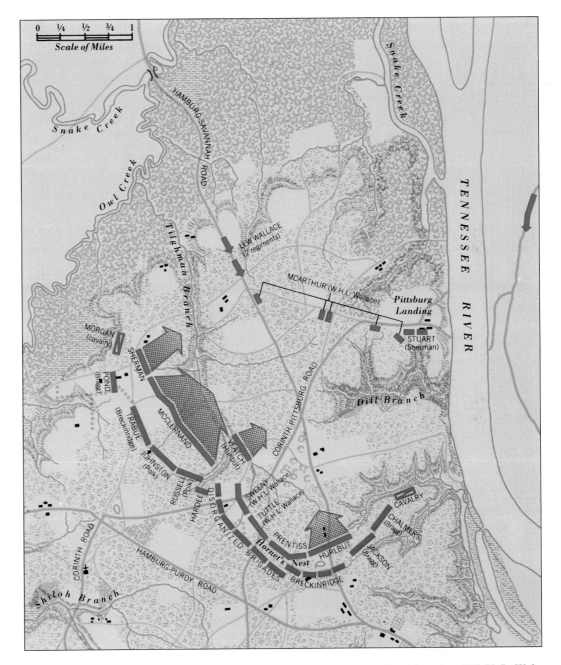

At about 10:30 a.m. on April 6, survivors of General Prentiss' brigade, reinforced by units of W. H. L. Wallace's division, formed a line in a sunken road connecting the Corinth-Pittsburg and Hamburg-Savannah roads. The strong position, dubbed the Hornet's Nest, was the scene of fierce fighting through the day.

"Soon we were on the battle field here and there we saw the bodies of dead men—friends & foes lying together."

Wreathed in smoke, Colonel William T. Shaw's 14th Iowa Infantry fires a volley at the attacking Confederates from the Federal position behind the sunken farm lane that formed the natural defense for the Hornet's Nest. To their right are the four brass 12-pounder James rifles of Captain Emil Munch's 1st Minnesota Light Artillery. The painting, part of a 400-foot-long panorama by Théophile Poilpot, was based upon interviews with veterans of the battle.

CAPTAIN ANDREW HICKENLOOPER
5TH INDEPENDENT BATTERY, OHIO LIGHT ARTILLERY, PRENTISS' DIVISION

Despite the loss of two brass James rifles during the opening Confederate attacks, Captain Hickenlooper remained ready to fight. He posted his remaining four guns on a slight knoll behind the sunken road occupied by Prentiss' division. By filling the gap between Hurlbut's and W. H. L. Wallace's divisions, they formed the "hinge" for the two battle lines that became the Hornet's Nest.

Thus Nature had here providentially supplied that which our commanders had so singularly neglected to provide, a defensive line upon which to rally, with a prominent knoll upon which to place the battery, and a protecting parapet only a few inches in height, but enough to partially protect the infantry, with front covered by an almost impenetrable growth of underbrush. . . .

. . . Soon the shells gave warning, and the skirmish fire grew stronger and deeper. Then came long triple lines of bristling steel, whose stern-faced bearers, protected and yet impeded by the heavy undergrowth, came pressing on, until our cannon's loud acceptance of their challenge and the infantry's crashing volleys caused the assailants to hesitate, break in confusion and hastily retire. . . .

This temporary defeat of the attacking forces had given time for caring for the wounded and for the hasty strengthening of the defensive line; it had also allowed the smoke to clear away, thus affording a better view of the Confederate lines as they again moved forward in a charge of increased impetuosity.

The ear-piercing and peculiar "rebel yell" of the men in gray and the answering cheers of the boys in blue rose and fell with the varying tide of battle; and with the hoarse and scarcely distinguishable orders of the officers, the screaming and bursting of shell, the swishing sound of canister, the roaring of volley-firing, the death screams of the stricken and struggling horses, and the cries and groans of the wounded, formed an indescribable impression, which can never be effaced from memory.

Quickly came the orders sharp and clear: "Shrapnel," "Two seconds," "One second," "Canister." Then, as the enemy made preparations for their final dash, "double canister" was ordered delivered with such rapidity that the separate discharges were blended into one continuous roar.

PRIVATE A. H. MECKLIN

15TH MISSISSIPPI INFANTRY, STATHAM'S BRIGADE

At about noon, the men of Colonel Winfield Scott Statham's brigade, part of General Breckinridge's Reserve Corps, were deployed against the left flank of the Hornet's Nest. Private Mecklin recalled the scene as his regiment pushed through the wreckage of Prentiss' camps toward the Sarah Bell peach orchard and the waiting Yankees. Mecklin, a 28-year-old student, survived Shiloh, his first battle, but was discharged the following month with a chronic illness.

From the formation of our men into line of battle until we entered the battle in good earnest, we went through a series of movements whose object I am unable to explain & where made I cannot now tell. Our brigade under command of Genl Stotham was composed of our Reg with those of Col. Shellier's 22nd Miss, Col Bottles 45th Tenn Col. Cummings & Col. Mitchel's. Sometimes we would advance in column of attack. Then we would march by the right flank. Sometimes our move was to the right & sometimes to the left, but always forward. In front of us we heard a continual roar of musketry far above this, the deep mouthed cannon uttered uproarous thunder. Word was brought us occasionally that our men were successful in every move, that the enemy were driven & that their camps were in our possession. Our men answered these favorable reports by loud cheers. Our movements became more brisk & our officers more excited. It was evident from all these indications that we were near the scene of action & must soon be into it. Our blankets were thrown aside & a guard placed over them. Just at this juncture while making a rapid march at double quick one of our Lieut's was shot through the hand accidentally by his own pistol & just at the same moment almost, our Adjutant—the Lieut's Bro. was stabbed accidentally in the thigh with a bayonet. Resting for some time we went on towards the firing. We passed several wounded men & occasionally squads of wounded Yankees. Soon we were on the battle field here and there we saw the bodies of dead men—friends & foes lying together.

COLONEL RANDALL LEE GIBSON

BRIGADE COMMANDER, ARMY OF THE MISSISSIPPI

Son of a wealthy Louisiana planter, Gibson graduated from Yale University in 1853 and secured a law degree from the University of Louisiana two years later. He was appointed colonel of the 13th Louisiana Infantry in 1861 and led a brigade at Shiloh. Gibson was promoted to brigadier general in 1864.

I was then commanded by Major-General Bragg to attack the enemy in a position to the front and right. The brigade moved forward in fine style, marching through an open field under a heavy fire and half way up an elevation covered with an almost impenetrable thicket, upon which the enemy was posted. On the left a battery opened that raked our flank, while a steady fire of musketry extended along the entire front. Under this combined fire our line was broken and the troops fell back; but they were soon rallied and advanced to the contest. Four times the position was charged and four times the assault proved unavailing. The strong and almost inaccessible position of the enemy—his infantry well covered in ambush and his artillery skillfully posted and efficiently served—was found to be impregnable to infantry alone. We were repulsed.

PRIVATE JOHN G. DEUPREE

1ST MISSISSIPPI CAVALRY, POLK'S CORPS

Private Deupree's company, the Noxubee Cavalry Squadron, was one of a number of independent Mississippi cavalry units consolidated under the command of Colonel Andrew J. Lindsay on April 2, 1862, the day before the Confederates began their march on Pittsburg Landing. Lindsay's regiment spent most of the morning of April 6 screening the left flank of General Cheatham's division.

Being in the rear of Cheatham's division, we were not under direct fire till about 10 o'clock, when the infantry were lying down in front of us, and our cavalry became a target for the artillery and sharp-shooters of the enemy. A Federal battery began to play upon us with a good degree of accuracy. We could hear the heavy missiles whizzing around and above us; and some of them, too, were distinctly visible. One great shot I shall never forget. As it came through the air it was clearly seen. Capt. Foote saw it as it [ricocheted], and spurred his horse out of the way. Lieutenant T. J. Deupree was not so fortunate. The same shot grazed his thigh, cut in two the saber hanging at his side, and passed through his noble stallion, which at once sank lifeless in his tracks. It also killed a second horse in the rear of Lieutenant Deupree, and finally striking a third horse in the shoulder felled him to the ground without disabling him or even breaking the skin. That ball was then spent. My own horse, "Bremer," in the excitement and joy of battle raised his tail on high, and a cannon-ball cut away about half of it, bone and all; and ever afterwards he was known as *"bob-tailed Bremer."* Many solid shot we saw strike the ground, bounding like rubber balls, passing over our heads and making music in their course. Colonel Lindsay at this time counter-marched the regiment and took shelter in a neighboring ravine. Thus, while in supporting distance of the infantry, we were often under fire, unless protected by the nature of the ground, by dense thickets, or by deep ravines.

Col. Campbell 13th La.

This rough sketch shows the position occupied by McClernand's division behind the Corinth-Pittsburg road to the northwest of the Hornet's Nest. As Confederate pressure mounted on the Federal right, General Hurlbut dispatched his brigade commanded by Colonel James C. Veatch to bolster the faltering Federal line.

Ill tempered and authoritarian by nature, General Braxton Bragg, the Confederacy's eighth-ranking general officer, constantly complained of the poor discipline of his troops. When at his order Randall Gibson's small Louisiana brigade failed to break the Hornet's Nest line after four bloody repulses, Bragg unjustly accused Gibson of being an "arrant coward."

Captain Francis Lee Campbell (left) commanded Company B of the 13th Louisiana Infantry and was wounded in the attack on the Hornet's Nest. Recovering from his wound, Campbell fought with his regiment in most of the major engagements of the Army of Tennessee, rising to the rank of colonel.

CAPTAIN WILLIAM W. JACKSON
STAFF, BRIGADIER GENERAL STEPHEN A. HURLBUT

A commissary officer on Brigadier General Stephen A. Hurlbut's staff, Captain Jackson witnessed the repeated assaults ordered by General Bragg against the left wing of the Hornet's Nest. Jackson recalled that the attacks lasted for more than three hours, and he wrote that "in no instance could it be said that there was any relaxation in the endeavor to turn our left flank." Jackson ended the war with a major's brevet for meritorious service.

In columns massed as before, but in double their former numbers, on came the Confederate troops; but they did not on this occasion appear so musical as on the first occasion; and when, as before, they had reached the proper position, the same tactics were used to check their advance, by the delivery of a steady and effective fire of infantry and artillery from four batteries upon their massed columns. The effect was awful. Whole lines went down like grass before the scythe, but were as often replaced by others from the rear, urged on by their officers, until the field was literally covered by the dead and wounded, while shout and cheer went up from our side and doubtless lent its aid in rendering it impossible for their officers to rally their men. Back to the cover of a friendly wood again went the disconcerted masses, to again form under its protection for another attack and another repulse quite as sanguinary as either of its predecessors.

GOVERNOR ISHAM G. HARRIS

STAFF, GENERAL ALBERT S. JOHNSTON

After serving two terms in the U.S. Congress, Isham Harris, a Democrat, was elected governor of Tennessee in 1857. A staunch supporter of secession, Harris was forced to flee the state after the fall of Forts Henry and Donelson, and he volunteered as an aide-de-camp on the staff of General A. S. Johnston.

I was acting as volunteer aid to Genl Johnston on the field. He was upon the right wing where the enemy being strongly posted made an obstinate stand. As you remember, our troops, after a long and desperate struggle wavered for a moment when Genl Johnston rushed in front of the line of battle, rallied the troops ordered and led the charge. The enemy fell back between a fourth & one half mile, when the firing became very heavy on each side. Our advanced position exposed our troops to a raking fire of a battery of the enemy on our left. The last order the Genl gave was to direct me to "order Col Statham of Mississippi to charge that battery." I immediately delivered the order and rode back to the side of the Genl, said to him "Genl your order is delivered and being executed" just at this moment the Genl sank down in his saddle leaning over to the left I instantly put my left arm around him pulling him to me saying "Genl are you wounded?" He said "yes and I fear seriously." Capt Wickham being on his left & I upon his right we held him upon his horse until we guided his horse from the crest of the hill to the ravine, where we lifted him from his horse, laid him upon the ground. I took his head in my lap. He never spoke after answering my question though continued to breathe for 25 or 30 minutes. Immediately after dismounting the Genl Capt Wickham went for the Surgeon. I sent a soldier to bring any staff officers he could find to me.

General A. S. Johnston lies dying on the battlefield at Shiloh in this sketch by an unknown artist. While leading an attack against Federal positions in the peach orchard, Johnston was fatally wounded by a Minié ball that severed an artery in his right leg.

LIEUTENANT GEORGE W. BAYLOR
STAFF, GENERAL ALBERT S. JOHNSTON

Born on the Texas frontier in 1832, George Baylor was a well-known Indian fighter by the time of the Civil War. As a lieutenant in the Regular Army he served in Arizona in 1861 before accepting the post of aide to General Johnston. After Shiloh, Baylor was given command of the 2d Texas and fought in Louisiana. In April 1865 he shot and killed his commanding officer, Major General John A. Wharton, in a duel in Houston, Texas.

After riding some distance and hearing of the General's staff in several places, I saw an officer riding rapidly toward me, and soon recognized Major O'Hara. He had taken me for a surgeon. When we started out in the morning, Dr. David M. Yandall, chief surgeon to General Johnston, said to me: "George, we are going to have some hot work to-day, and that coat of yours is a bad color." I had on an officer's blue coat worn by the Federals, with the insignia of a first lieutenant of cavalry of the Confederates; had borrowed it at the fight at San Augustine Springs, N.M. So we swapped coats, his being gray with black trimmings. Major O'Hara then told me that General Johnston was seriously if not fatally wounded, and his staff were looking for a surgeon. Seeing me in the uniform of one, he had come after me. He said the General was in an awfully hot place, but I said I was going to him, and he replied, "We will go together."

We soon joined as sad a group as ever assembled on a battle field or around a dying bed. General Johnston was such a lovable man that his staff as well as his soldiers worshipped him; and his staff seemed stupefied with grief at the great calamity. He was not seriously wounded—a six-shooter navy ball or buckshot had severed an artery just below the right knee, and he had slowly bled to death. There was a little stream of dark blood that had run along on the ground and formed a little puddle six feet from where he was lying. A simple torque made with a stick and a handkerchief would have stopped the flow of blood until medical aid could have been had. Unfortunately, Dr. Yandall had been ordered by the General to stop and attend to a lot of wounded Confederate and Union soldiers. No doubt his kind heart was moved when he saw the old familiar blue uniform and recalled his brother officers and the scenes they had passed through together.

"General Johnston was such a lovable man that his staff as well as his soldiers worshipped him; and his staff seemed stupefied with grief at the great calamity."

James E. Slaughter resigned from the Regular Army to join the Confederacy in 1861. Commissioned a brigadier general in March 1862, he became assistant inspector general on A. S. Johnston's staff. When Johnston was mortally wounded at Shiloh, Slaughter and his fellow staff officers reported to General Beauregard.

PRIVATE ALBERT A. BARNES
2D IOWA INFANTRY, TUTTLE'S BRIGADE

Moving toward the sound of the fighting, two of General W. H. L. Wallace's brigades, those of Colonels James M. Tuttle and Thomas W. Sweeny, took position along the sunken road to the north of the Hornet's Nest. Private Barnes wrote an article, published in the National Tribune in 1903, describing his regiment's fight on the afternoon of April 6. Barnes was commissioned a lieutenant in December 1863 and was given the office of regimental adjutant.

Looking across the field at long musket range, we could see, during the day, the movements of the Confederate troops to the right and to the left. In the afternoon we could see indistinctly their manuvers in the vicinity of the "Hornet's Nest." They would arrange their ranks and then rush into the thickets on our left. We could hear the awful roar of battle when they assailed the three Iowa regiments, and those of Prentiss beyond. Invariably, they returned, "without form and void."

About 4 p.m. the enemy made a rapid movement to our left. All sounds on our right had passed toward our rear. Wallace's right never did connect with any troops, the nearest command in that direction, Veach's Brigade, having been driven back, exposing Wallace to attack in his rear. In our front all was quiet, the firing being nearly in our rear. Some one passed hurriedly with orders. We were quickly moved over the knoll, and then we could see a great deal. Looking backward from the high ground, and seeing only the 2d and 7th Iowa coming, I remarked to a comrade: "Some one has blundered. Good-by to the 14th Iowa and those other fellows."

With ranks compact, our guns at right shoulder-shift, we followed "Old Yaller"—Tuttle's war horse, going at a double-quick when the ground was favorable. To our right, as far as we could see through the open timber, a great mass of blue was slowly receding, a thin fringe of smoke shooting backward from its rear. Following the blue was a tumultuous host clad in gray and butternut, carrying an assortment of flags, yelling exultantly, but doing little firing. On our left, a greater distance but with more persistent show of defense, a similar scene was being enacted on a smaller scale.

As the Iowans trotted through the gap, the Confederates within short musket range, shouted: "Bull Run!" "Run, you nigger thieves! We'll get you yet." The regiments quickly ran the gantlet, and

reached a point where a line was being formed in front of about 40 cannon. The panic-stricken passed on over the river bluff, while the others stopped and presented a solid, contracted front to the enemy, who surged forward without order or control.

PRIVATE ENOCH COLBY JR.
WILLARD'S BATTERY A, 1ST ILLINOIS LIGHT ARTILLERY, W. H. L. WALLACE'S DIVISION

When the brigade of John McArthur, forming the left flank of the Hornet's Nest, gave way, Battery A was left without infantry support. The Illinois gunners had no choice but to limber up under heavy fire to save their guns. Private Colby came through the battle unhurt and was commissioned a lieutenant in May 1865.

Then Lieut. Wood's voice rang out clear and strong, "Limber to the rear," "Get your guns out of this." Then there was a scramble, No. 1, 3, 4 and 6 guns fell back at once. Not so with 2 and 5. Squad 5 had but three cannoniers and gunner Sherrill left, Dolan and Stiger and Crocker having gone with Flanigan to an ambulance. Four of their horses, including Bailey's Gray Eagle, were badly wounded. The three cannoniers were unable to run up the gun and hook it on. A. C. Hall, alias "Garibaldi," jumped off his horse, and putting his shoulder to the wheel, helped to run it up, the others holding up and pulling on the trail. Just at this time Charley Kimbell came hopping on one leg from squad 2 gun, having been badly wounded in the other, and he was caught and tossed on the foot-board of the limber. "Garrie" remounted his horse, and just as the gun was started, he was hit in the head with a shot and knocked off. I jumped and grabbed the near lead horse by the bit, Foster, the near swing horse, and Colby, the near wheeler, and away we started on a run, the rebels less than a hundred yards from us, making a desperate effort to capture at least the two guns that were delayed in getting away. Poor "Garrie" and Bailey were left behind to the tender mercies of the rebels, as we supposed, but Garrie recovered his senses just as they were about to gather him in, and picking himself up, skipped away and escaped to the landing. At the same time Stiger and Dolan came through the woods hunting for the Battery, and found Bailey sitting against a tree, and each catching him by the arm, escaped safely with him to the landing, thus saving all our wounded from being captured.

At the time the order was given, "Limber to the rear," squad two was in worse shape than squad five. The off wheel horse was the only one remaining. The squad, having disengaged all but him, attempted to haul off the gun, which they could easily have done with his help, but he obstinately refused to move. Matters were growing desperate. The rebels were so close their brass buttons could plainly be seen. Minnie balls were rattling like hail, five of the seven men at the gun were hit within five minutes. Lieut. Wood ordered several men from the other guns to come back and help them, which they did promptly.

Just as they reached the gun a minnie ball struck the horse squarely in the root of the tail, and it effectually performed an instantaneous cure for balking.

With Commissary Chase acting as nigh wheel horse, the gun with its wounded, was rushed back about a quarter of a mile, where the other guns were in battery on a small hill ready to cover our retreat, which they did in good shape, and thus was averted what at one time seemed to be inevitable, the losing of a gun-squad and gun.

CAPTAIN WILLIAM H. HARDER
23D TENNESSEE INFANTRY, CLEBURNE'S BRIGADE

William Harder, a 32-year-old resident of Perry County, Tennessee, raised a 100-man company of his neighbors in 1861 and his mother, Harriet, made their uniforms. Harder's regiment, the 23d Tennessee, was heavily engaged throughout much of the morning of April 6 before being allowed a brief respite. In the late afternoon, the regiment came under harassing fire from the heavy cannon aboard the Federal gunboats Lexington and Tyler.

We fell back out of the gap and were resting along the side of the ridge while our detail went to the rear for cartridges. I was sitting by a white oak tree and on the spur of the root that made a kind of a flat seat along the ground, when the gunboats opened an artillery fire on us. I saw the first shot cut through Col. Smith's of Mississippi line and come in a few inches of me. I told the men to be still as there would be another along close, and had hardly spoken when I saw it cut two of Smith's men down and felt myself flying in the air. It had come through the tree, splintered the spur I sat on and torn it off and sent me whistling about 20 feet.

Still wearing prewar gray militia uniforms, a gun crew of Company A of the Chicago Light Artillery pose with their 12-pounder howitzer in the summer of 1861. Redesignated Battery A, 1st Illinois Light Artillery, the battery of four 6-pounder and two 12-pounder howitzers fought at Shiloh, where the crew suffered 30 casualties.

Private Frederick E. Ransom of the 11th Illinois painted this watercolor of his regiment's line of battle, part of C. Carroll Marsh's brigade, fighting to stem the Confederate attacks on the Federal right flank. Ransom's brother, Colonel Thomas E. G. Ransom, depicted here on horseback, was severely wounded in the fighting.

PRIVATE A. H. MECKLIN
15TH MISSISSIPPI INFANTRY, STATHAM'S BRIGADE

As Colonel Winfield Statham's brigade of Mississippi and Tennessee troops entered the clearing of the Sarah Bell farm, they halted to swap fire at long range with the Federals of Colonel Nelson Williams' brigade, whose line extended through the peach orchard. During the long exchange of musketry, Private Mecklin's rifle became foul with powder residue.

For the first time in my life, I heard the whistle of bullets. We took shelter behind the tents & some wagons & a pile of corn & returned the fire of the enemy with spirit. The bullets whistle around my ears. I was near the front & firing, lay down to load. Soon men were falling on all sides. Two in Co. E—just in front of me, fell dead shot through the brain. On my left in our own Co. . . . were wounded. I fired until my gun got so foul that I could not get my ball down. Taking a short stick that lay near, I drove the ball down. Again the tube became filled up & not being able to get it off, I called to one of Co. E. to throw me the gun of a wounded man by him. I fired this until the tube became filled. Throwing it down I went to the rear & picking up my bro. gun held on until the battle was over. We had fired but a few more rounds, when we were ordered to cease firing and fall back. We did so & formed under cover of the hill were ordered to charge bayonet. . . . We ran forwards as rapidly as we could but being nearly exhausted we were unable to make but a little speed. The minie balls were falling thickly around us.

Private Joseph B. Phillips of the Louisiana Crescent Regiment, part of Colonel Preston Pond's brigade, wore this uniform at Shiloh. Phillips had joined the regiment in March 1862 and survived the battle uninjured, only to die of "unknown causes" at Tupelo, Mississippi, less than a month later.

CHAPLAIN DAVID SULLINS

19TH TENNESSEE INFANTRY, STATHAM'S BRIGADE

David Sullins, a Methodist minister, was elected chaplain of the 19th Tennessee in July 1861. He was appointed quartermaster with the rank of major in January 1862 but resigned in March to resume his duties as chaplain. In his account of Shiloh, printed in Confederate Veteran in 1897, Sullins confused the 1st Louisiana Infantry of Gladden's brigade for the Crescent Regiment. The Federal battery he refers to was Mann's Missouri battery.

From early morning we had driven the Federals from hill top to hill top, till one wing touched the river. Gen. Breckenridge, with whom as quartermaster I pitched my tent for many a day, was commander of the reserve corps, composed of Tennessee, Kentucky, Mississippi and Louisiana troops. He sat upon his horse on the crest of a long ridge, his staff about him and the soldiers flat on the ground just back of the hill top. Col. Frank M. Walker, of the Nineteenth Tennessee Regiment, sat upon his horse at the head of his command, within speaking distance of the General. During the delay caused by the death of Gen. Johnston, the Federals had planted a strong and well supported battery on a hill in our front, which was raining death among us. The Crescent Regiment of New Orleans had been ordered to dislodge it, and the brave fellows charged down the hill through the brush and fallen timber, firing and yelling as they went. They passed the hollow and began the ascent of the opposite hill. The watchful and quick Yankees saw what was coming and, knowing their desperate opportunity, turned every murderous gun upon them. All their hearts were aching, and those large blue eyes of Breckenridge filled with tears as through the rifting smoke he saw the line begin to waver and then to fall back. A fearful moment! Death shrieking in a thousand shells! Somebody must go to the help of those brave men and silence the battery! Breckenridge, turning to his staff, said: "Is there a regiment here that can relieve those men and take the battery?" Col. Walker, modest as a woman and brave as he was modest, spurred his horse forward quickly, and touching his cap, said: "General, I think the Nineteenth Tennessee can!" "Give them the order, Colonel," came the quick reply, and in another moment a thousand East Tennesseans sprang to their feet with a yell and swept down that hill like an unbridled cyclone.

PRIVATE ALEXANDER G. DOWNING

11TH IOWA INFANTRY, HARE'S BRIGADE

As Confederate pressure mounted against the Hornet's Nest, McClernand's division on the Federal right also faced a crisis. Downing, a 21-year-old farmer from Davenport, Iowa, described the furious action. After Shiloh, he participated in the Vicksburg, Atlanta, and Carolina campaigns.

We lay down on the brow of a hill awaiting the approach of the rebels in front. While in this position, Thomas Hains of Company E took off his hat, placed it upon his ramrod, and holding it up, shouted to the boys along the line to see what a close call he had had while out in front, for a minie ball had passed through the creased crown of his hat, making four holes. Before he could get his hat back on his head, a small shell burst over us and mortally wounded him. . . .

My musket became so dirty with the cartridge powder, that in loading it the ramrod stuck fast and I could neither get it up nor down, so I put a cap on, elevated the gun and fired it off. But now I had no ramrod, and throwing down my musket, I picked up a Belgian rifle lying at the side of a dead rebel, unstrapped the cartridge box from his body, and advanced to our company, taking my place with the boys. While in this position I witnessed a wonderful sight—thickly-flying musket balls. I have never seen hail falling thicker than the minie balls were flying in the air above us, though too high to do any harm. Our ammunition soon ran out and the entire regiment was ordered to the rear to replenish our cartridge boxes.

CORPORAL WILBUR F. CRUMMER
45TH ILLINOIS INFANTRY, MARSH'S BRIGADE

By midafternoon the battered brigades of Sherman and McClernand on the Federal right flank came under increased pressure as Rebel forces lapped around their right. Private Crummer's regiment found itself low on cartridges, a predicament shared by many Federal units whose camps, and ammunition reserves, had been overrun by the Confederates.

About 3 o'clock our cartridges began to run low, and we borrowed each of the other until all was gone; we were holding the enemy, but now our guns were silent. What a helpless man a soldier is in a battle with no ammunition. We marched to the rear left in front in search of cartridges, and none too soon either, for a troop of the enemy's cavalry were seen on our right, trying to get in our rear and take us prisoners. We had not gone far when we met a line of fresh troops, of whom we begged cartridges, but the caliber was not the right size for our Enfield rifles and we could not use them, and we started on again hunting for cartridges, the enemy pressing us so hard that the Captain of the rear company went rushing up to the Colonel, exclaiming breathlessly:

"My God, Colonel, they are not fifty yards from my company, and we haven't a shot to defend ourselves."

"Keep cool," said the Colonel, "and don't say anything, the enemy don't know we are out of ammunition, and we will come out all right yet."

We had not gone far when we met a wagon loaded with cartridges. Caliber 58. Did you ever see a hungry lot of men wade into a bang-up dinner?

Will was the first to mount the wagon and rip open one of the boxes in quick order, the men scrambling up into the wagon, and crying out: "Give me some, give me more!" The cartridge boxes and pockets were filled in short order. We then took our position on the right of our brigade, supporting a battery.

Lieutenant Colonel Addison H. Sanders of the 16th Iowa Infantry receives his cap and gauntlets from a valet in this wartime photograph. The inexperienced 16th Iowa, part of Benjamin Prentiss' brigade, was detached to support McClernand's troops on the Federal right and suffered more than 136 casualties attempting to stop the Confederate onslaught. When the 16th's colonel was wounded, Sanders took command and rallied the broken regiment.

LIEUTENANT BASIL W. DUKE

MORGAN'S KENTUCKY CAVALRY,
TRABUE'S BRIGADE

Duke, a Kentucky native, practiced law in St. Louis before joining the cavalry command of his brother-in-law, John Hunt Morgan. At Shiloh, Morgan's cavalry covered the Confederate left flank, but as the Union right crumbled, they were ordered to charge a Federal battery on the Hamburg-Savannah road. Duke was badly wounded in the assault.

The Federal troops at this point were posted upon an eminence, covered with underbrush, and in front of which was a ravine. Eighteen or twenty pieces of artillery, strongly supported, were planted on this hill, and were playing furiously. For perhaps an hour Hardee's efforts to advance were foiled. The position was taken, I believe only after it had been enfiladed. Our squadron approached this point while the advance was thus checked and General Hardee sent an aide to learn "what cavalry that was?" When told it was Morgan's he expressed pleasure and said that he would send it "to take that battery." This was a truly gratifying compliment, but we received it with sobriety; and as we formed for the charge, which we were told would soon be ordered, indulged in no extravagant expressions of joy. I am even inclined to believe that we were not so sanguine of the result as General Hardee seemed to be. The General sat on his horse near Shoup's gallant battery, which was replying, but ineffectually, to the vicious rain of canister and shell which poured from the hill. He seemed indifferent to the hot fire, but very anxious to take those guns.

We had never seen anything like that before. We had occasionally been fired upon by a single piece of artillery, when we had closely approached the enemy's encampments on Green river; and we used to think that hardly fair. Now the blaze and "volleyed thunder" of the guns on that hill seemed to our excited imaginations like the output of a volcano in active operation.

An hour or two previously, a young fellow, belonging to some Confederate battery which had been disabled, had asked permission to serve with us for the rest of the day. He was riding an artillery horse and had picked up a rifle and a cartridge box on the field, so I put him in the ranks. While we were expecting the order to charge, my eye happened to fall on this youngster, and it occurred to me that I might get from him valuable information germane to the business on hand. I therefore took him aside, and remarked: "You say you have served in the artillery for a year, and you ought to know a good deal about it. Now, General Hardee is going to order us to charge that Yankee battery yonder, and I want you to post me about the way to charge a battery."

"Why, good Lord, Lieutenant!" he exclaimed with much emphasis. "I wouldn't do it, if I was you. Why your blamed little cavalry won't be deuce high agin' them guns."

I became angry, because I was not feeling hopeful or comfortable, and his prediction "mingled strangely with my fears."

"Haven't I told you," I said, "that General Hardee will order us to take those guns? Now, don't express any opinion, but answer my question, 'What's the best way to charge a battery?'"

He looked me squarely in the eye for a few seconds, and then said very earnestly: "Lieutenant, to tell you the God's truth, thar' ain't no good way to charge a battery."

In a wild stampede, survivors of Dressler's battery, 2d Illinois Light Artillery, vainly attempt to save their guns from Bushrod Johnson's Confederate brigade.

MAJOR FRANCIS A. SHOUP
CHIEF OF ARTILLERY, HARDEE'S CORPS

An Indiana native and West Point graduate, Shoup served briefly with the Regular Artillery before resigning his commission in 1860 to open a law practice in St. Augustine, Florida. At the Battle of Shiloh he helped Brigadier General Daniel Ruggles mass 62 cannon into a grand battery to bombard the Hornet's Nest.

About this time Gen. Beauregard ordered me to attend to removing the captured artillery, which lay scattered in every direction, to the rear. I put a number of parties at work, using stragglers chiefly. They did remove a large number of pieces, which we finally secured; but I have always thought if we had finished up the work that day we could have removed them at our leisure. I went to the front as soon as I could, and struck the point from which the enemy's line bent back toward the landing. There was a little old field just to the right of this point. I saw the opportunity for some more flank fire, and set to work to gather the fragments of our batteries, scattered about in all directions, and held them under cover of a skirt of woods on the further side of this little field until all were ready. I suppose there were over twenty pieces, but hardly a whole battery together. The order was that when the piece on the left advanced and fired all were to come into action. The fire opened beautifully, but almost immediately the blue coats on the heights over against us began to break to the rear, and we soon saw white flags. It was here that Prentiss surrendered his command.

With his arm resting on the muzzle of a 12-pounder howitzer, Captain Arthur M. Rutledge poses with the officers of his Battery A, 1st Tennessee Light Artillery. Rutledge's guns, attached to Statham's brigade of Breckinridge's corps, were part of the massed battery organized by Ruggles to blast the Yankees out of the Hornet's Nest.

LIEUTENANT CHARLES P. SEARLE
8TH IOWA INFANTRY, SWEENY'S BRIGADE

Searle, a clerk from Davenport, Iowa, was captured when his regiment, part of a brigade holding the right flank of the Hornet's Nest, was encircled by the Confederates. Searle was paroled at Richmond in October 1862 and served with the rank of captain until his discharge for disability in January 1865.

Retreating on the double quick, with leaden and iron hail flying thick around us, a soldier a pace in front of me fell, and I was so close that I fell over him. At the same time a spent ball struck my left arm and another went through my canteen. My arm tingled with pain, and the little water left in my canteen was warm and running over me as I fell to the ground. I thought it was my life blood. In fact, I was sure I was killed, but spying a "Reb" close by, coming with all speed, for they had us on the run, I made one grand, desperate effort to gain my feet, and much to my surprise, succeeded without trouble. I assure you I was a pretty lively corpse, for I left old "Butternut" far in the rear, and did not even say "Good day."

The poor fellow that I stumbled over was not so fortunate. He had received his final discharge.

A short distance further on, who would I see but General Prentiss holding aloft the white flag. The day's work was done. Those able to travel received an urgent invitation to go South on a pleasure trip, at the expense of the Southern Confederacy. It appeared that they would not take "no" for an answer, and our experience in that "neck of the woods" had already convinced us that it was a very unhealthy place. This, together with other circumstances over which we had no control, influenced three thousand of us to accept the urgent invitation of the "chivalry" and take a trip into the sunny South. However, we were like the Irishman, "compelled to volunteer."

I had expected to be killed, but it had not occurred to me that we were to be prisoners of war. When I got back where the congregation were assembling, I found that we were safe, and being strongly guarded and surrounded by those whom we had never seen before, but who were solicitous for our safety.

Those of our boys who had taken in the situation were busy wrapping their guns around trees, or putting them in such a condition that they could not be used against them or their comrades, which was done, or course, against the earnest protest of the Rebels. But, driven to desperation, the work went on, and many a poor boy who, during the ten hours of rain of leaden hail, had escaped unharmed, was shot down in this last effort for his country. . . .

My time had come to receive personal attention. A big, burly Rebel captain stepped up to me and said, "You D——d Yankee, give me your sword!" Oh, how I did want to give it to him point first. But discretion prevailed, and I gave it to him hilt first, which probably saved the burial squad two interments.

First Sergeant John P. Wright was killed when his regiment, Colonel John A. Logan's 32d Illinois Infantry, tried to stop the Confederates as they advanced to envelop the left of the Hornet's Nest.

" 'It is useless to fight longer, I must stop this slaughter.' "

CAPTAIN
JOHN H. STIBBS
12TH IOWA INFANTRY,
TUTTLE'S BRIGADE

Stibbs was commissioned a captain in December 1861. Captured at Shiloh, he was exchanged in December 1862 and rose to the rank of colonel. He received a brigadier general's brevet at the war's end and sat on the court-marshal that condemned Henry Wirz, commander of the Andersonville, Georgia, prisoner of war camp.

ol. Lynch of the 58th Illinois attempted to organize enough men to force an opening to the rear, calling on the men to fall in line and saying he would lead them but before anything material was accomplished the Colonel's horse was shot, falling on him and injuring his leg and for the time being totally disabling him. I know of no other attempt being made to force our way further to the rear. We simply stood there and fought until finally Gen. Prentiss, as I heard him describe repeatedly, said, "It is useless to fight longer, I must stop this slaughter," and he stepped forward on to a stump and waved his handkerchief in token of surrender.

Just before the firing ceased one of my boys called to me and said that Lieut. Ferguson had been wounded

and I went to where he lay and he lifted his shirt and showed me a horrible wound in his abdomen, which I saw at a glance would prove fatal. A few moments after our surrender was completed I called Ferguson's cousin, Private N. G. Price, and we went to where Gen. Polk and his staff were grouped a short distance from us. Just in front of me was Capt. S. R. Edgington, who after saluting Gen. Polk said, "Gen. Polk, I am Capt. Edgington of Company 'A', 12th Iowa Infantry, I am the senior Captain and in command of the regiment, I wish to surrender my command, and to ask for my men all the consideration due to brave men captured in battle," and thereupon he tendered his sword blade foremost. Gen. Polk said, "Reverse that sword and hand it to my Adjutant." Edgington did so and then Gen. Polk said to the Adjutant, "Now return that," and turning to Edgington, said, "On your honor as a soldier and a gentlemen," "On my honor as a soldier and a gentleman," repeated Edgington and received the sword, placed it in the scabbard and retired. Then I got the General's eye, saluted, gave my name and pointing to Ferguson, said, "General, the officer lying there is my 1st Lieut., he is every inch a gentleman and a soldier and is my best friend; he is mortally wounded; Private Price here is his cousin and I want to ask if you will permit Price to remain to care for him. "Most certainly," said the General, "Corporal Price, you remain with your cousin and if any one attempts to interfere with you tell them you are there by the order of Gen. Polk."

Kneeling to escape the smoke from burning brush in their front, the men of Colonel Hugh B. Reed's 44th Indiana, part of Lauman's brigade, fire at advancing Confederates. The engraving, printed in the May 7, 1862, edition of Leslie's Illustrated was based on a sketch by artist Henri Lovie.

PRIVATE ALVAN Q. BACON
14TH ILLINOIS INFANTRY, VEATCH'S BRIGADE

Private Bacon, a member of the color guard of Colonel Cyrus Hall's 14th Illinois, was captured when the Confederates drove his regiment from its position on the Corinth road, where it had made up part of the Federal right flank. Sent to a prison in Macon, Georgia, Bacon escaped to the coast, traveling the last 60 miles in a stolen canoe before being picked up by a Federal gunboat.

The white flag was raised, and two thousand and two hundred men laid down their arms; but not in disgrace as was reported by the press and by General Grant, but as men who had nobly contested every inch of ground during the day—only giving up when it was more than useless to continue the fight. . . .

It was a difficult matter to stop the firing after the flag was raised; some were unaware of it, while others had become reckless and would sooner die than become prisoners. One little incident that occurred may not be uninteresting: A Lieutenant-Colonel in the Rebel service came riding over the ridge from the flag of truce; the boys had not seen the flag; he spoke to them, saying: "My God! Men, lay down your arms; you will all be killed." One of our men leveled his gun at him and fired. He fell from his horse a dead man. It looked hard, for he was working for our benefit; but such are the results of war, and such our soldiers have to become familiar with. . . .

But we will now return to our prisoners. They were searched for side-arms, and the rebels took the opportunity to supply themselves with jack-knives, pocket-forks and various other articles, too numerous to mention.

PRIVATE JOHN G. DEUPREE
1ST MISSISSIPPI CAVALRY, POLK'S CORPS

Shortly after Prentiss surrendered, General Polk ordered Colonel Lindsay to take his 1st Mississippi Cavalry and "go toward the river to cut off the enemy's retreat." As his troopers pushed through the undergrowth they spotted Battery B, 1st Michigan Artillery, withdrawing their guns. The Mississippians captured the battery's four 10-pounder Parrott rifles and one brass 6-pounder.

We rode in a sweeping gallop till we came to the place where General Prentiss had just surrendered, when Colonel Lindsay reported to General Polk for orders. It was now after 5 o'clock, and Col. Lindsay was directed to take command of all the cavalry on this part of the field, to go up the river, and to cut off the enemy's retreat. In obedience to this order, Col. Lindsay attempted to collect other cavalry, meantime directing Lieutenant-Colonel Miller to take command of the First Mississippi. The ever impetuous and daring Colonel Miller at once put himself at the head of the regiment and shouted: "Charge boys, charge! Colonel Lindsay says, Charge!" Then we rushed at full speed for more than a quarter of a mile, yelling like devils incarnate. A Federal battery was observed about three hundred yards ahead, with horses attached, evidently intent on making its escape. But on discovering us the artillerymen turned, unlimbered, and made preparations to open fire upon us. But we came on them so rapidly, they could neither fire nor escape. Every man, every horse, and every gun was captured. By this time Col. Lindsay, who failed to find other cavalry, had ridden to the front of our column. Giving orders to Col. Miller to send this captured Michigan battery, with its six brass Napoleons and all its caissons under escort to General Polk, and seeing another battery just across a deep ravine, he put himself at the head of Foote's company, the Noxubee Cavalry, and rushed forward to seize it. We at once captured one of the caissons, but coming upon the battery we found ourselves in the immediate presence of Federal infantry drawn up in line, evidently belonging to Nelson's division of Buell's army, who were just taking position on the field. They fired at us; but, from excitement, they fired so wildly and so high in the air, that we all escaped unharmed into the ravine and there rejoined the regiment.

Though slightly wounded, Color Sergeant John R. Kirkman carried the 14th Illinois' silk regimental flag (left) and the regiment's national colors to safety when the Federal line collapsed.

Final Line

Following the capture of the Hornet's Nest, an hour of daylight remained for the Confederates to follow up their costly success. But heavy casualties, the intermingling of units from dozens of different brigades, and the death of General Johnston made a coordinated advance impossible. Having battled for 12 straight hours, hundreds of exhausted Rebels simply stopped where they were and began cooking their evening meal, while others wandered off to loot the captured Yankee camps. Far in the rear of his disorganized forces, General Beauregard was out of touch with the situation at the front, and the job of carrying on the fight fell to his subordinates, most of whom had no clear idea of what was expected of them.

While Southern officers attempted to sort out the confusion, Grant continued to strengthen his new line of defense. On the right of the line, he posted the remnants of Sherman's and McClernand's divisions along the Hamburg-Savannah road to screen the long-awaited approach of Lew Wallace's troops down that route. Exasperated by Wallace's dilatory advance from Crump's Landing, Grant was relieved to learn that the 6,000 fresh soldiers were finally nearing the scene of battle.

The lead elements of Buell's Army of the Ohio were also arriving on the field. Buell himself had come ashore at Pittsburg Landing early in the afternoon, and by 5:30 p.m. Colonel Jacob Ammen's brigade had been ferried across the Tennessee. Ammen was accompanied by his division commander— huge, hot-tempered Brigadier General

William "Bull" Nelson—who ordered his troops to force their way at bayonet point through the throng of fugitives that obstructed his route of march to the bluffs overlooking the landing. With the remainder of Nelson's division beginning to cross the river, Ammen's brigade filed into line and prepared to meet whatever the enemy would throw against them.

Braxton Bragg, the dour and irascible commander of Beauregard's Second Corps, was one of the few Southern leaders who recognized the importance of pressing the attack before night fell. Seeing that the Yankees were strengthening their defenses opposite the Confederate right, at 6:00 p.m. Bragg instructed two of his brigade commanders to form their ranks for an assault. "Sweep everything forward," the general ordered. "Drive the enemy into the river."

Obeying Bragg's command, Brigadier Generals James R. Chalmers and John K. Jackson led their troops toward the far left of the Federal line. Both brigades had seen heavy fighting earlier in the day, and although Chalmers' soldiers had replenished their cartridge boxes from captured ordnance supplies, Jackson's men were almost out of ammunition and would have to rely on the bayonet alone.

A stream known as Dill's Branch flowed through a steep and brush-filled ravine directly in front of the Yankee line, and this natural moat slowed and disorganized the advancing Southern brigades. Suspecting that the Confederates might attempt to cut him off from the river, Grant had deployed more than 60 artillery pieces along a half-mile front

opposite the Rebel right flank, including a battery of siege guns. These five huge cannon, originally intended to be used against the defenses of Corinth, hurled their heavy-caliber shells into the oncoming ranks, while on the Tennessee the gunboats *Tyler* and *Lexington* added their salvos to the barrage. The roar and shriek of 53-pound naval shells —exploding overhead and blasting entire trees to splinters—had a demoralizing effect on the Confederate attackers, and when the Yankee infantry opened fire, the Rebel brigades recoiled.

At 6:30 p.m., with the sun going down, General Beauregard decided to call off the assault. He would rest his exhausted troops and resume the offensive on the following morning, April 7. In the meantime Beauregard dispatched news to the Confederate government in Richmond announcing "a complete victory." But as events would soon show, victory was far from won.

All through the hours of darkness, as a chill rain added to the suffering of the wounded and the misery of the men hunkered down in line of battle, the Federal reinforcements continued to arrive. Lew Wallace had finally made his appearance and deployed his fresh division on the Union right, extending the Federal line to the banks of Owl Creek. By midnight four brigades of the Army of the Ohio had disembarked at Pittsburg Landing and taken a position above the Dill's Branch ravine. With more troops arriving by the hour, General Buell hoped to have three divisions on hand by daybreak.

Buell was scornful of the fighting abilities

of Grant's soldiers and considered himself independent of Grant's authority. Without consulting his fellow army commander, Buell told his officers to prepare to launch a dawn counterattack.

But Grant was equally determined to seize the initiative from the Confederates, remarking to one of his staff officers, "I propose to attack at daylight, and whip them."

Having captured the Hornet's Nest, the Confederates pushed northward, becoming increasingly disorganized. Aware that the chance for victory might be slipping away, several Confederate commanders ordered one last push toward Pittsburg Landing. While Hardee and Polk continued to press the Federal right, General Braxton Bragg sent the brigades of James Chalmers and John K. Jackson across Dill's Branch toward the landing. As the Confederates attacked, they were halted by well-directed fire from Federal artillery massed near the river. Even so, by late evening General Beauregard considered the victory to be his and ordered his scattered commands to cease fighting for the night.

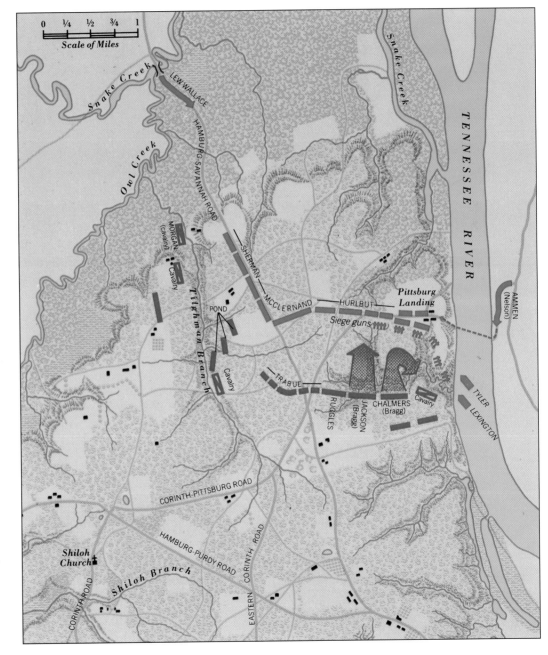

BRIGADIER GENERAL JAMES R. CHALMERS

Brigade Commander, Army of the Mississippi

Chalmers' brigade, along with that of John K. Jackson, attacked toward the river in the late afternoon of April 6, only to be halted by a cross fire from the formidable line of Federal batteries posted near the landing and the gunboats in the river.

In a photograph taken shortly after the battle, Federal soldiers stand near the 24-pounder siege guns of Captain Relly Madison's Battery B, 2d Illinois Light Artillery. Intended to besiege Corinth and strengthen Grant's final line of defense, the guns were dragged into line facing south along the road to Pittsburg Landing.

It was then about 4 o'clock in the evening, and after distributing ammunition, we received orders from General Bragg to drive the enemy into the river. My brigade, together with that of Brigadier-General Jackson, filed to the right and formed facing the river and endeavored to press forward to the water's edge, but in attempting to mount the last ridge we were met by a fire from a whole line of batteries protected by infantry and assisted by shells from the gunboats. Our men struggled vainly to ascend the hill, which was very steep, making charge after charge without success, but continued to fight until night closed hostilities on both sides.

LIEUTENANT COLONEL DAVID C. KELLEY
FORREST'S REGIMENT OF CAVALRY, STATHAM'S BRIGADE

As a young man, David Kelley, a Tennessean, spent several years in China as a missionary for the Methodist Episcopal Church. In 1861 he resigned his calling and raised a company of cavalry that would be assigned to Forrest's regiment. As the last Confederate attacks of the day at Shiloh faltered, Forrest's command rode toward the Federal left flank in an attempt to cut behind the Yankee lines.

I had been ordered after our charge and capture of Gen. Prentiss's command to conduct the prisoners to the rear. Col. Forrest, not inclined to the duty of guarding prisoners, had taken a squadron of our regiment and moved toward the right of our line. Returning from the duty assigned me, riding in the direction of the firing, we came in sight of a long line of Confederate infantry forming at the base of a not very elevated ridge. Leaving a group of officers sitting their horses just in rear of this line, a staff officer galloped to the head of our column, saluted, and said: "Gen. Bragg's compliments, and requests to know what cavalry this is?" The reply was given, "Forrest's Regiment," when the officer added: "Gen. Bragg requests that you place your command in position to attack the battery on the hill in flank when he moves to the attack in front.". . . I rode to the top to get full knowledge of the ground over which the charge would have to be made. While making my observations, two guns from the battery moved rapidly to the rear; the others were deserted, and there was not left on the field a single Federal gun in action. The gunboats were firing, but the balls were passing high over our heads through the tree tops; the banks of the river did not allow their depression.

Returning to my command I conveyed to one of Gen. Bragg's staff the results of my observations, adding: "The whole Federal army in sight is in utter disorder, and will surrender in five minutes after your line of infantry appears on the top of the ridge." He replied: "Gen. Bragg will be on the top of the ridge in five minutes." Not more than five minutes had passed when the whole line of infantry extending to my right farther than the eye could reach threw down their arms and lay at ease on the ground. When I sought the meaning of this sudden change, an officer of Gen. Bragg's staff said to me: "Gen. Bragg has just received an order from Gen. Beauregard to move his command from under the fire of the gunboats and bivouac for the night," adding, "Gen. Bragg is foaming at the mouth like a mad tiger."

Born in Genoa, Italy, Abraham Vacarro immigrated to the United States in 1851 and settled in Memphis, Tennessee. He enlisted in Forrest's cavalry regiment in 1862 and within a month saw his first action at the Battle of Shiloh. Vacarro was later detailed to duty in Richmond and served until the end of the war.

LIEUTENANT HORACE N. FISHER

STAFF, BRIGADIER GENERAL WILLIAM NELSON

As night fell on April 6, Federal transport steamers began ferrying General Buell's Army of the Ohio across the Tennessee River to Pittsburg Landing. As the soldiers disembarked they found chaos along the riverbank. Lieutenant Fisher recalled the reaction of his commander, General William "Bull" Nelson, to the mass of fugitives who crowded the Federal rear areas.

The face of the bluff—something over one hundred feet high—was black with runaways, packed so thickly that the first comers had been gradually shoved down until they were knee-deep in the river and some swimming trying to regain a foothold. How many there were in this mass of runaways no man can say; Buell's estimate is 5,000 early in the day, increasing to 15,000 towards evening, the wreck of a hard-pressed army verging upon a collapse. As we approached in the boat, the Captain rang the bell to stop. Gen. Nelson asked him why he did not go on. The Captain replied "I am afraid of running over some of these men." Gen. Nelson's remarks were very energetic and un-complimentary to them. The boat went on.

The moment our boat touched the shore, the first company jumped ashore and cleared the landing at the point of the bayonet; the gang-planks were run out and the second company landed and enlarged the cleared space; then the horses were led ashore to crash through the crowd higher up. Nelson mounted his big black horse "Ned" (17 hands high), himself a giant in full uniform—over six feet high, weighing 300 pounds. "Two aides on each side of me, other mounted officers in second line," "Gentlemen, draw your sabres and trample these —— into the mud! Charge!" And thus we charged cutting through the mob of runaways who tumbled over each other in abject terror.

Our three companies of infantry, well-closed up, followed in the wake of the horsemen, all of us in dead earnest and hesitating at nothing. Then Nelson, turning in his saddle gave the order: "Shout 'Buell'" and he beat time with his sabre as we rushed up the road from the landing.

Leslie's Illustrated artist Henri Lovie sketched this view of the flotilla of riverboats that transported General Don Carlos Buell's forces to relieve General Grant's hard-pressed army. By daybreak the boats had delivered more than 7,500 fresh soldiers to bolster the Federal lines near Pittsburg Landing.

"'Gentlemen, draw your sabres and trample these —— into the mud! Charge!' And thus we charged cutting through the mob of runaways who tumbled over each other in abject terror."

ASSISTANT SURGEON CHARLES B. TOMPKINS
17TH ILLINOIS INFANTRY, RAITH'S BRIGADE

A graduate of Rush Medical College, in Rushville, Illinois, Tompkins was commissioned an assistant surgeon in the 17th Illinois in May 1861. Driven out of camp by the Confederate attack, he worked in the field hospitals behind the lines. He described the experience in a letter to his wife, Mary, written the day after the battle.

I had ordered all of our things packed up, packed my own trunk & sent the team on towards the river before I left the camp & after I first went to the Reg't in the morning I went back to the camp & remained there until our (U.S.) men had fallen back & the shot were coming into our camp so fast that it was impossible to remain & live (there was 109 bulletholes in my tent) I remained on the field for four hours & our men were driven back evry time & the wounded could not be taken care of there & finally I went to the river & found several of our wounded in a building on the top of the hill & I stopped there & was busy until night dressing wounds & as fast as I could fix them up I sent our boys aboard a boat & Wilson was there to receive them with plenty of help to bathe their wounds & get them something to eat. Towards evening I went on the boat & was there until 9 oclock.

LIEUTENANT HENRY O. DWIGHT
20TH OHIO INFANTRY, WHITTLESEY'S BRIGADE

Shortly after 7:00 p.m. on April 6, Brigadier General Lew Wallace's brigades belatedly began to arrive on the battlefield after their seven-hour march from Crump's Landing, a distance of only 14 miles. Lieutenant Dwight recalled the unpleasant experience of taking a position at night in the face of the enemy. After the war Dwight followed his father's calling and gained prominence as a missionary in Turkey and an expert in Turkish affairs.

We were put into line in the camp of the 81st Ohio Regiment, which was among those driven out of their tents in the battle. The enemy was so near that we could have no lights or fires. Hungry and tired, we prowled about the tents seeking something to eat or a place to rest, until we found dead men in the tents, and then we concluded not to prowl in the dark any more. . . .

I here began to taste the sweets of my new position as an officer. My baggage, blanket and overcoat I had left behind, and our cook was not on hand with the food. Then it began to rain, and poured steadily all night. It was an awful night. To lie on the ground was an impossibility, for the water was flowing in torrents. There were no logs or stones on which to sit, and all that weary night I stood or walked about in the pitiless rain, soaked through and through. In front of us were wounded men lying on the ground and crying for help, but none dared to try to help them for every movement and every sound brought volleys of musketry from the enemy.

LIEUTENANT COLONEL MANNING F. FORCE
20TH OHIO INFANTRY, WHITTLESEY'S BRIGADE

As colonel of the 20th Ohio, Force saw action at Fort Donelson and Shiloh. He later fought at Vicksburg and was severely wounded in the Battle of Atlanta on July 22, 1864. He ended the war as a brevet major general and in 1892 was awarded the Medal of Honor for his conduct at Atlanta.

The men were kept lying down. Col. Whittlesey was mounted, and at our left, and I (all regimental horses having, by order, been left with a guard at the crest where we were first directly fired on) had to walk the length of the battalion several times to receive orders. I heard an occasional pop, and an occasional ball whistle by, but gave no heed, till the men lying down said, "Colonel, there's a sharpshooter firing at you; I see his head every time just beyond that peach-tree." I looked and saw the man aim and fire. This time I was standing still; the ball grazed my leg, and struck one of Company D in the head. It glanced, however, and was not a serious wound. I sent out a party of skirmishers around the field, and in a few minutes they returned with a young man in butternut, his fine Enfield Green pattern loaded and capped. They had killed another and scattered more, who had been deliberately firing at Col. Whittlesey, the Major, and me, sometimes waiting for a line shot.

ACTING COMMISSARY JAMES H. WILEY
22D ALABAMA INFANTRY, GLADDEN'S BRIGADE

As the exhausted Confederate forces halted their attacks, they found themselves in the midst of abandoned Federal camps. In a letter to his wife, Josie, James Wiley recounted the vast store of loot, ranging from food to camp equipment, that he encountered in the well-supplied Yankee camps.

The enemy fled and our forces took possession of their camp. Here was a perfect curiosity shop. Every thing in the eating and wearing line, in fact every tent told of high and extravagant living. While the Confederate troops are lying on the bare ground with one or two blankets and eating fat pork and pickled beets. They have their mattresses and feathered beds blankets, quilts, and comforts and every thing that ones appetite could crave to eat and with stoves to cook on in their tents. All this fell into our hands as we could not move them the greater part of them were destroyed. There were 5 or 6 camps like this. The first 5 or 6 miles from the river were the gun boats lay one every mile or sometimes nearer. We drove them thro' all of their camps on to their gun boats. This was on Sunday, but on Monday they got there almost ruined camps back again.

SERGEANT MAJOR AMBROSE BIERCE
9TH INDIANA INFANTRY, HAZEN'S BRIGADE

Ambrose Bierce enlisted in the 9th Indiana at the age of 18 and rose to the rank of lieutenant as a topographical engineer on the staff of Colonel William B. Hazen. After the war he moved to California and embarked on a career in journalism that would make him one of America's most popular writers.

The night was now black-dark; as is usual after a battle, it had begun to rain. Still we moved; we were being put into position by somebody. Inch by inch we crept along, treading on one another's heels by way of keeping together. Commands were passed along the line in whispers; more commonly none were given. When the men had pressed so closely together that they could advance no farther they stood stock-still, sheltering the locks of their rifles with their ponchos. In this position many fell asleep. When those in front suddenly stepped away those in the rear, roused by the tramping, hastened after with such zeal that the line was soon choked again. Evidently the head of the division was being piloted at a snail's pace by some one who did not feel sure of his ground. Very often we struck our feet against the dead; more frequently against those who still had spirit enough to resent it with a moan. These were lifted carefully to one side and abandoned. Some had sense enough to ask in their weak way for water. Absurd! Their clothes were soaked, their hair dank; their white faces, dimly discernible, were clammy and cold. Besides, none of us had any water.

> "Very often we struck our feet against the dead; more frequently against those who still had spirit enough to resent it with a moan."

Henri Lovie sketched the scene behind Grant's final line near Pittsburg Landing at about 6:00 p.m. on April 6. In the foreground a Federal column pushes its way through a tangle of ambulances and battery horses while infantry and the siege guns of Madison's battery fire at the oncoming Rebels.

ANN DICKEY WALLACE
WIFE OF BRIGADIER GENERAL WILLIAM H. L. WALLACE

On April 4 Ann Wallace, shown at left with her daughter, Isabel, enlisted the aid of the chaplain of the 20th Illinois to travel to Pittsburg Landing on the steamer Minnehaha to pay a surprise visit to her husband. Arriving on the morning of April 6, she found that the battle was under way. Late that afternoon she was given the news that her husband had fallen.

Looking still more depressed, he came near me and a little behind me and said, "This is an awful battle." I replied, "Yes, but these fresh troops will yet win the day." He said, "You have a great many relations on this field, you cannot hope to see them all come in safe." I answered, "They all came safely through Donelson, and to-day my husband is in command of a division and is comparatively safe." He repeated from behind my shoulder, "It is an awful battle." ... I turned to console him and raising my eyes to the face of Hartley, who sat in front of me, and whose countenance reflected horror as he gazed full in the face of Elder Button, the dread truth fell on my heart like a thunderbolt, like the cold hand of steel.

Words needed not to tell it; 'twas before me! I was stunned, chilled, almost paralyzed. Suffering came hours afterwards. ...

On Monday morning about ten o'clock, as I was sitting beside a wounded man just brought in, Cyrus came to me with the word that Will had been brought in (after the rebels were put to flight) and Oh! joy, he was breathing. I flew to the adjoining boat, where he was. There on a narrow mattress on the floor in the middle of the cabin he lay mortally wounded. His face was flushed, but he was breathing naturally, so like himself, save for that fearful wound in his temple. A ball had passed through his head in a manner that made it marvelous that he could still live. But the greatest joy was yet to come—Will recognized my voice at once and clasped my hand. I was thrilled and exclaimed, "He knows me; he knows me!"

MAJOR FRANCIS A. SHOUP
CHIEF OF ARTILLERY, HARDEE'S CORPS

Sick with a respiratory infection and out of contact with his command, Beauregard dispatched orders that the Confederate forces were to break off the action for the day. Then he sent a telegram to Richmond reporting "a complete victory." Writing after the war, staff officer Shoup viewed the cease-fire as a major mistake and described the confusion in the Confederate command as darkness set in.

Beauregard was sick, and in truth he seemed not to know the condition of affairs. He was back at Shiloh Church. At least Col. Sam Lockett, of the Engineers, told me that he was there with him, and heard the order given which closed the action on the first day. He repeated the very words, which were about as follows: "Order the firing to cease. The victory is sufficiently complete. There is no need to expose the men to the fire from the gunboats." However, Beauregard knew that Buell was at hand, and that no time was to be lost in preventing a junction with Grant. There was really nothing to be feared from the gunboats, for, as I am informed, the bluff is so high their fire would have had very little effect. It was a fearful blunder, and the way in which it was executed made it worse. I took the miscellaneous batteries back to what I thought a safe distance and prepared to camp for the night, but I found the infantry whirling past me to the rear, and I had to move farther back till I got some infantry camps in front of me. Nobody knew where anybody else was. I waited a long time expecting an orderly or staff officer to give information as to where headquarters were, and calling the Generals together for consultation. At last, tired to death though I was, I mounted my horse and started out to find somebody's quarters. I rode up and down in every direction, but the only General I found was Pat Cleburne. He was sitting on a stump drinking coffee out of a bucket, and was as utterly in the dark as I was. He knew where nobody was, had a few of his own men with him, and didn't know who was next to him. I gave it up and went back to my camp. The fact is, there was no conference of any sort that night.

DOUGLAS PUTNAM JR.
STAFF, MAJOR GENERAL ULYSSES S. GRANT

A member of the Ohio State Paymaster's Department, Douglas Putnam was sent to Savannah to oversee payment of the Ohio troops. When the firing started at Pittsburg Landing, Putnam asked to accompany General Grant as a volunteer aide. After the Battle of Shiloh he sought service as a line officer and became the 92d Ohio Infantry's lieutenant colonel. Severely wounded at Missionary Ridge, Putnam was given a medical discharge in 1864.

"The reply came quick and short: *'Retreat? No!* I propose to attack at daylight, and whip them.' "

A group of officers was gathered around General Grant about dusk, at a smoldering fire of hay just on top of the grade—the rain was falling, atmosphere murky, and ground covered with mud and water. Colonel McPherson rode up, and Grant said: "Well, Mac; how is it?" He gave him a report of the condition as it seemed to him, which was, in short, that at least one-third of his army was *"hors du combat,"* and the rest much disheartened. To this the general made no reply, and McPherson continued: "Well, General Grant; under this condition of affairs, what do you propose to do sir? Shall I make preparations for retreat?" The reply came quick and short: *"Retreat? No! I propose to attack at daylight, and whip them."*

Grant's headquarters steamer, *Tigress,* lies moored between two government transports at Pittsburg Landing in a photograph taken shortly after the battle. Grant arrived from Savannah aboard the Tigress to take command at Shiloh on the morning of April 6. Just visible on the opposite bank are the gunboats Tyler and Lexington.

Federal Resurgence

General Beauregard's Confederate army was in no condition to resume the offensive on April 7. "Our force was disorganized, demoralized, and exhausted," corps commander Braxton Bragg recalled. Despite the fact that many regiments were nearly out of ammunition, and some entirely so, Bragg observed angrily that officers had failed to provide for their troops: "Although millions of cartridges were around them, not one officer in ten supplied his men, relying on the enemy's retreat." To the rear, however, Beauregard was more sanguine. Unaware that Lew Wallace's division and half of Buell's Army of the Ohio had arrived on the field, Beauregard was confident that all he had to do was hold his ground while Grant retreated across the Tennessee. To Beauregard it seemed highly unlikely that the Federals would attempt to counterattack, and he chose to rest his men rather than have them dig in overnight. But with some 45,000 troops on the field—more than twice what the Rebels had on hand—Grant was determined to strike back and regain the ground that had been lost the previous day.

The lead elements of Buell's army advanced at sunrise, and Nelson's division quickly routed the startled Southern pickets to their front. At 7:00 a.m. Brigadier General Thomas L. Crittenden's division extended Nelson's line to the west, followed an hour later by Brigadier General Lovell Rousseau's brigade of McCook's division. By 8:00 a.m. Buell had 15,000 soldiers in position across a mile-wide front, ready to launch a full-scale assault.

Shocked at the sudden appearance of the Yankee formations deploying in his front,

General Hardee dispatched several brigades at 10:00 a.m. to blunt the vanguard of Nelson's division as it advanced near the peach orchard where so much heavy fighting had taken place the day before. At first the Federals wavered, but Colonel William B. Hazen's brigade shored up the line and pushed on to take part of a Rebel battery. In a desperate effort to maintain the Confederate right flank, brigades led by General Chalmers and Colonels Preston Smith and George Maney again lashed out at Nelson's division. The counterattack gained ground in heavy fighting but was brought to a halt by point-blank canister fire from Captain William Terrill's battery of the 5th U.S. Artillery.

While Nelson was fighting to the east, Crittenden's and McCook's troops—advancing in the Federal center—were slowed by heavy underbrush and faced with stout resistance from a line Bragg had patched together with scattered Confederate units. But on the western edge of the battlefield, Lew Wallace's 6,000-man division had been steadily gaining ground since going on the offensive at 6:30 a.m. Wallace was supported by some 7,000 troops formed from the battered remnants of Sherman's and McClernand's divisions, anxious to recapture the camps that had been overrun the previous day. Spirited counterattacks by Daniel Ruggles and Sterling Wood slowed but could not halt the Federal onslaught, and by 11:00 a.m. the Union advance was nearing the intersection of the Corinth and Purdy roads, a half-mile north of Shiloh Church.

Believing there was an opportunity to split

the Federal line at the junction of Wallace's and Buell's forces, Braxton Bragg ordered Patrick Cleburne to launch an attack with his brigade. With only 800 fighting men left, Cleburne questioned the wisdom of such a move, but Bragg was adamant and the attack proceeded. Caught in a lethal cross fire, Cleburne's brigade collapsed before the advance of Sherman's and McClernand's men. Benjamin Cheatham led his brigade to Cleburne's support and fiercely assailed the pursuing Federals. Their nerves frayed from the battle on April 6, numbers of Sherman's and McClernand's troops broke for the rear. But when Rousseau's brigade swung down on Cheatham's flank, the Rebels gave way. With the line restored, the Union juggernaut lumbered on toward Shiloh Church.

At 2:30 p.m. Beauregard issued orders for a general withdrawal toward the defenses of Corinth, and over the next hour he committed his last reserves in an attempt to stem the tide of blue-clad soldiers. Realizing too late that Buell's Army of the Ohio had joined Grant on the field, Beauregard took personal charge of the last-ditch defense, riding among his demoralized troops and exhorting them to a final effort. For a time the remnants of Ruggles' division and Wood's brigade held near Shiloh Church, but soon they too were streaming from the field in retreat. In obedience to orders the Southern soldiers set fire to the tents and equipment in the captured Yankee camps before trudging down the muddy road to Corinth.

With more than two hours of daylight remaining, the Federals might well have pressed on with little effective resistance from their beaten foe. But both Grant and Buell were content to have driven the enemy from the field, while regaining all the ground that had been lost the day before. The Union armies had lost more than 13,000 men—11,000 of them in Grant's Army of the Tennessee. And with a quarter of his original force killed, wounded, or missing, Grant considered his troops "too much fatigued to pursue."

The Confederate loss was equally horrific—some 10,700 men—but the blow to Southern morale cut much deeper. Having come so close to victory, to abandon the bloody field where so many comrades lay was enough to shake even the stoutest resolve and raise grave doubts as to the future of the Southern Confederacy in the war's western theater.

Throughout the night of April 6, the Confederates made no attempt to regroup, but Grant continued to feed the fresh brigades of Buell's army into his line in preparation for a morning advance. Pressing forward at dawn, Grant's 45,000 men easily repulsed the 20,000 Confederates who were still able to resist. Despite launching desperate local counterattacks, the Confederates were steadily pushed back toward Shiloh Church. Shortly after 2:30 p.m., Beauregard ordered a withdrawal to Corinth, forming his rear guard near the church.

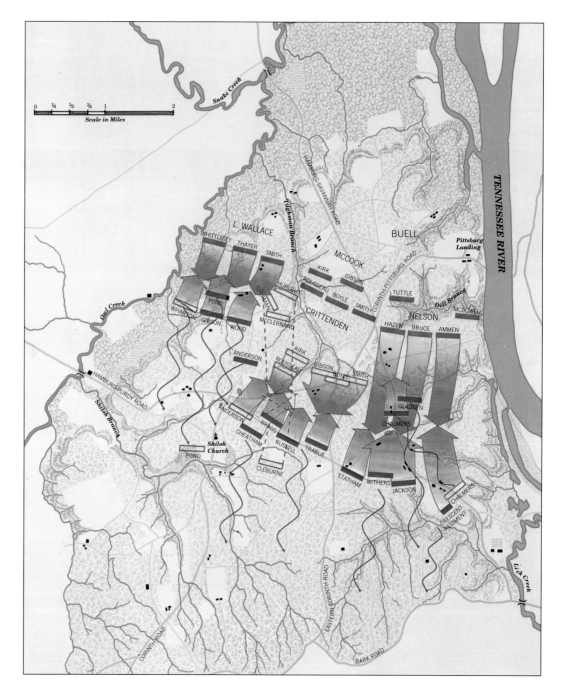

"The Rebels ... would retreat a short distance and then rally and fight like devils. There is no use to talk about their being cowardly, for they will fight and fight well."

SERGEANT MICHAEL S. BRIGHT
77TH PENNSYLVANIA INFANTRY, KIRK'S BRIGADE

Colonel Edward N. Kirk's brigade debarked from their transports at first light on April 7. They, along with the other fresh brigades of Brigadier General Alexander M. McCook's division, formed a line of battle that linked up with Lew Wallace's division on the Federal right. Sergeant Bright tersely described the morning's actions in a letter to his uncle, Emanuel Stotler.

We were landed at the Pittsburgh Landing, ten miles above Savannah. This was Monday morning, the second day of the fight.

We marched off the boat, took breakfast, if breakfast we may call it, and then we piled up our blankets, for we had left knapsacks, overcoats, everything but blankets in the wagon. We filled our haversacks and our canteens, and started out to fight. We had only gone a short distance when the bullets could be heard whizzing over our heads. The next thing, we formed line of battle and marched forward, passing over the dead. Nearly every few yards a body was stretched out.

For some time the battle raged furiously, and I tell you now I commenced to think we were going to get thrashed. But the scale turned at last, and the Rebels commenced to give ground. They would retreat a short distance and then rally and fight like devils. There is no use to talk about their being cowardly, for they will fight and fight well.

The 77th Pennsylvania Infantry's silk color was presented to the regiment by Governor Andrew G. Curtin in Allegheny City, Pennsylvania, on October 7, 1861. The 77th was the only unit from Pennsylvania to see action at Shiloh; its flag was "literally riddled" by the explosion of a Rebel shell.

PRIVATE HENRY M. STANLEY
6TH ARKANSAS INFANTRY, HINDMAN'S BRIGADE

At dawn on April 7, Stanley was sent forward as a skirmisher for Cleburne's depleted brigade and was quickly captured by the advancing Federals. Sent to Camp Douglas, Illinois, he endured two months as a prisoner of war before volunteering for the U.S. artillery to gain freedom. Discharged for physical disability, Stanley returned to England. He came back to the United States in 1863 and enlisted in the U.S. Navy for the remainder of the Civil War.

At daylight, I fell in with my Company, but there were only about fifty of the Dixies present. Almost immediately after, symptoms of the coming battle were manifest. Regiments were hurried into line, but, even to my inexperienced eyes, the troops were in ill-condition for repeating the efforts of Sunday. However, in brief time, in consequence of our pickets being driven in on us, we were moved forward in skirmishing order. With my musket on the trail I found myself in active motion, more active than otherwise I would have been, perhaps, because Captain Smith had said, "Now, Mr. Stanley, if you please, step briskly forward!" This singling-out of me wounded my *amour-propre,* and sent me forward like a rocket. In a short time, we met our opponents in the same formation as ourselves, and advancing most resolutely. We threw ourselves behind such trees as were near us, fired, loaded, and darted forward to another shelter. Presently, I found myself in an open, grassy space, with no convenient tree or stump near; but, seeing a shallow hollow some twenty paces ahead, I made a dash for it, and plied my musket with haste. I became so absorbed with some blue figures in front of me, that I did not pay sufficient heed to my companion greys; the open space was too dangerous, perhaps, for their advance; for, had they emerged, I should have known they were pressing forward. Seeing my blues in about the same proportion, I assumed that the greys were keeping their position, and never once thought of retreat. However, as, despite our firing, the blues were coming uncomfortably near, I rose from my hollow; but, to my speechless amazement, I found myself a solitary grey, in a line of blue skirmishers! My companions had retreated! The next I heard was, "Down with that gun, Secesh, or I'll drill a hole through you! Drop it, quick!"

Private John Dimitry of the Louisiana Crescent Regiment wore this shell jacket at Shiloh. On April 7, as he was tending his wounded captain, he was shot through the hip. He was evacuated to a hospital in Corinth and then to New Orleans. When that city fell to Federal forces in late April, Dimitry made his way to Richmond and was discharged shortly afterward for medical disability.

PRIVATE M. E. BOYSELL

58TH OHIO INFANTRY, THAYER'S BRIGADE

Private Boysell's regiment attacked along with the rest of General Lew Wallace's division on the far right of the Federal line. Using the marshy ground of Owl Creek to protect his right flank, Wallace ordered his line of battle to wheel left to turn the Confederate left flank. As they advanced, Private Boysell found that the disorganized Rebels were not quite beaten.

Someone recently mentioned the wonderful resources of old Tennessee—its iron, stone, marble, timber, etc. I have seen some valuable timber in my time, but a fine young oak at Shiloh, during that terrific two-days' struggle, April 6 and 7, 1862, was the most valuable piece I ever saw.

I was seized with that "tired feeling" and jumped behind this tree, when a sudden and terrible crash came of musketry, grape, and canister. It was here I fell—that is, I fell into line to assist in resisting a fearful onslaught of Cleburne's Division. The tree was hit by a cannon-ball or shell about 10 feet from the ground. "What fools!" I thought. "If you wanted to kill me, why didn't you aim lower, and you would have done the work."

The woods were full of smoke and flame for a time, and when the smoke of battle cleared away the ground was strewn with the dead on both sides. There were not trees enough for all. With many the cruel war was over, and they would never draw rations again.

The rebels were retreating in good order, while we were trying to wipe them off the earth. A retreating army is often like the "business end" of a crippled wasp. The rebels turned suddenly on our advancing columns and the assault was terrific.

This bugle was shot from the hands of Private Frederick Barnhart of Company B, 15th Indiana Infantry,
during the action on April 7. After the battle, Barnhart recovered the battered horn as a memento.

PRIVATE CONRAD WISE CHAPMAN

3D KENTUCKY (C.S.) INFANTRY, TRABUE'S BRIGADE

Born in Alexandria, Virginia, Chapman moved to Rome in 1850 with his father, artist John Gadsby Chapman. He returned to the United States when the war broke out and, unable to reach Virginia from New York, he made his way to Bowling Green, Kentucky, and enlisted in the 3d Kentucky Infantry. After recuperating from the severe head wound he received at Shiloh, Chapman fought with his regiment at Vicksburg before transferring to a unit from his native Virginia.

I could feel that my wound had been made by a musket ball, but whether the intruder was in their or not [I] of course could not be sure, although I supposed it must have made its exit otherwise I would not have my thoughts about me. I began to feel more and more faint, and should have dropped over, but for one of the ambulance corps of the third who recognized me and took me to an ambulance and thence to the Drs Tent. When old Dr Thompson looked into my wound for a moment, his usual gruff joking tone changed, and he told me in a soft kind voice, which scared me, that it looked bad, and that I would have to get out and he would see what he could do for me, but that it was no use to do anything then, but as I could not get on, I had better lay quietly in his tent, and if the Yankees came up I would be taken care of all the same, I got out and the ambulance went back for more wounded—The Dr gallopped off to meet another ambulance coming up and I remained with my wound still bleeding at tremendous rate by a tree—Reports came in that our troops were still holding the position but it was not certain how long they would be able to—A little wiery unhurt man was near me and offered to help me along so with a stick to lean on and his shoulder I managed to get on, one fellow I passed through me his hand-kerchief another his hat and thus with my wound doubly covered I did not feel the cool breeze playing with it and my hear—My little friend had a supply of Yankey candy he had got which he gave me to eat, and I could not help smiling at his kindness and forethought for the journey, which promised to be a slow one for me at least. We stopped by a running brook and an old negroe lent me his tin cup to bathe my wound—and drink—[F]urther on we were abruptly stopped by a cavalry man, who dashed up at such a rate that he knocked off my hat, but as soon as he did it apologized, and turned to my companion to know if he was hurt. Otherwise he had orders that none should pass. The little fellow whined out I am looking out after my poor friend and thus passed through the line of guards to prevent just his tribe of stragglers from getting away. However he got me this far, and if he had not done intirely his duty through the day I felt thankful to him for what he had done for me. I stopped to rest a few moments afterwards and he stepped aside and never returned.

The 1st Ohio and a battalion of the 15th U.S. Regulars overrun two guns of Captain Robert Cobb's Kentucky battery in the area used as a review field for the Federal camps. William R. McComas, who sketched the action for Leslie's Illustrated, depicted Federal soldiers manning the captured guns. In fact, the artillery pieces had been rendered useless when the Confederate gunners spiked their vents.

"The two opposing lines were deliberately standing and pouring into each other a perfect hailstorm of bullets, while men were dropping like slaughtered beeves on both sides."

CORPORAL JOHN G. LAW
154TH (SENIOR) TENNESSEE INFANTRY, JOHNSON'S BRIGADE

As Federal pressure mounted, the Confederates attempted a series of local coun-terattacks to try to halt the enemy advance. Corporal Law, separated from his command like hundreds of his comrades, fell in with Cleburne's brigade, which had been ordered by General Bragg to make a lone charge against the Yankees.

I fell in with the first organized body that came in sight, which proved to be a part of Bowen's division, advancing in line of battle to the support of a battery that seemed to be hard pressed, and was pouring a stream of fire into the enemy at short range. Recognizing my old friend, Cad. Polk, of Columbia, Tenn., who was the Adjutant of an Arkansas regiment, I at once fell into line with his regiment. As we crossed a little ravine and ascended the slope of the hill, the battery retired under a heavy fire of musketry through our ranks and went into position on the opposite side of the ravine. We were ordered to lie down while the battery opened fire over our heads. At the same time a heavy volley of musketry was poured into our line by the enemy, who were plainly visible a few hundred yards in our front. The boys in gray then rose to their feet and delivered their fire with such deadly effect that the advance of the enemy was checked, the blue line staggered under the fire, reeled, broke, and rolled back in confusion, like a wave that breaks upon the rock-bound shore and spends its fury in vain. Then, resuming my search for my own regiment, and attracted by heavy firing on the left, I started in that direction, and passed over a part of the woods from which we had just driven the enemy. The ground was dotted with the blue uniforms of the dead and wounded, while canteens and haversacks were scattered here and there in great abundance. Having no water in my plain tin canteen, I picked up a splendid one, well covered and full of water, and threw it hastily over my shoulder. Some Yankee had kindly left it for my accommodation. Soon after coming into possession of this valuable property my heart was touched by a piteous cry for water. I stopped, and kneeling by the side of a Federal soldier, who was badly wounded, placed the canteen to his lips, expressed sympathy for him in his terrible suffering, and then, hurrying on, was soon in another line of battle hotly engaged with the enemy, who were plainly visible in heavy force through the open woods. There was no charging, but the two opposing lines were deliberately standing and pouring into each other a perfect hailstorm of bullets, while men were dropping like slaughtered beeves on both sides. A gallant officer was riding along the Confederate lines giving orders and inspiring the men by his valorous deeds, and heroic courage in the face of death. It was Colonel Richmond, of General Polk's staff. My nerves grew steadier, and advancing to the front, I found myself all at once fighting in the ranks of the old One Hundred and Fifty-fourth Tennessee regiment. There was no time to look for my company, so raising my gun, I took deliberate aim and fired. It was my only shot, for as I was in the act of loading a ball came crashing through my canteen, and as the water poured out and soaked through to my skin, I imagined that the blood was gushing from a mortal wound, and, without waiting to see what damage my body had sustained, started off to the surgeon.

PRIVATE J. N. JONES
39TH INDIANA INFANTRY, GIBSON'S BRIGADE

As the victorious Federals pushed on, they found the Confederates exhausted and disorganized, but still defiant and aggressive. In an article he wrote for the National Tribune in 1907, Private Jones recalled an incident that occurred as his regiment fought near Shiloh Church.

After the order to cease firing we came to an order arms, and had been standing thus perhaps ten minutes when a rebel officer riding a dark bay horse at a brisk canter made his appearance to the left of the house and about opposite the foot of the 39th. He would have struck the head of the regiment had he kept on, but when opposite the colors and within 150 yards of them he raised his hat and swung it over his head as much as to say "defiance to you;" then turned his horse and rode over in a diagonal direction to the right of the house. The regiment stood watching him, like myself wondering what he meant; but when he raised his hat and turned his course, every man who had a load in his gun fired at him, and from the noise of the volley most of the boys evidently had loads. He neither fell from his saddle nor quickened his speed, but rode back to cover unscathed.

The silk national flag of the 14th Wisconsin Infantry, part of General Prentiss' division, was made by Gilbert Hubbard & Co. of Chicago and presented to the regiment on December 20, 1861. On April 7 the flag was being carried when the regiment captured and spiked two guns of Cobb's Kentucky battery.

In this sketch by Henri Lovie, a Federal battle line moves forward against the Rebels near Shiloh Church around 3:00 p.m. in one of the last actions on the field. Despite the artist's notations, General Grant was not personally in charge of this attack.

CAPTAIN WILLIAM H. HARDER

23D TENNESSEE INFANTRY, CLEBURNE'S BRIGADE

Shortly before noon General Patrick Cleburne's brigade, reduced by the fighting of the day before from 2,700 to about 800 men, launched an unsupported attack on the Union center at the order of General Bragg. Wounded in the fight, Harder was captured and sent to a Federal hospital at Mound City, Illinois. Exchanged in July, he rejoined his company and served to the war's end.

For about thirty minutes the firing was a continuous blaze. My men knelt down and delivered a steady fire, and in that time many of them sent out one hundred cartridges to the man.

The federals answered it with a heavy fire but delivered too high. Our loss was great and theirs much greater as they had more men in line. A minie at length went cutting through my neck and shoulder entering on the right and bearing down on backward to the left, and leveling me to the earth.

When I became conscious I was bleeding in a round full stream from the right of my neck and could feel the hot blood running down my left side under the clothes. I immediately emptied my Navy and then turned over on my left side, when another minie stuck in the right groin and turned me on my back. I had a Silver mounted Derringer in my right pants pocket. . . . The Silver mounting doubled around the minie and prevented it from penetrating my flesh, but it bruised me dreadfully.

When my men that were still not wounded, and also the wounded that could get back all left me, thinking I was dead. Save Corp. Jett Patton, he was wounded and staid with me.

The firing almost ceased for a few minutes and then the federal advanced and made me and Patton prisoners. As the federals came over me a drunken man plunged his bayonet at my breast, and would have finished me but for his Lieutenant, who shoved him forward as he made his plunge. His bayonet went up to the hilt in the ground, between my breast and right arm, and bent off at right angles with his gun about the same moment of time I saw a federal drive his bayonet at the breast of Sergt Wagoner and I thought at the time he was killed but it did not hurt him. The lieutenant placed a guard over me and went forward after taking my Sword and Navy.

A Federal soldier stripped this D-guard fighting knife and belt from the body of a Louisiana Confederate after the Battle of Shiloh. The massive knives, popular among early-war Confederates, were often made by local blacksmiths and cutlers.

PRIVATE W. E. YEATMAN
2D TENNESSEE INFANTRY, CLEBURNE'S BRIGADE

Yeatman joined the 2d Tennessee in April 1861 in Nashville, shortly before the regiment was ordered to Virginia. He saw his first action at Manassas in July and spent the war's first winter encamped in northern Virginia. In February Yeatman and his comrades reenlisted and received a furlough home to Tennessee where, after 60 days, they were reassigned to Cleburne's brigade in time to fight at Shiloh.

"As the federals came over me a drunken man plunged his bayonet at my breast."

This was late in the afternoon of the 7th and it seemed to me that we had been holding that place for "three mortal hours"—repulsing every attack, getting out of ammunition again and again, and as often resupplied, and holding on. We did not want to quit, but we did feel that we ought to have had more support. When Breckenridge did come in we imagined that we were preparing for a final charge that we felt was to end in a perfect victory. Instead our order was to march at once to the rear, while Breckenridge held the ground we had fought for the whole afternoon. That night was one of horrors. The shrieks of the wounded as they were hauled past us in rough ambulances and even rougher wagons, will live in my memory while memory lasts. The storm of the night before was bad, but this, with its battle accompaniments, drivers swearing at balky teams, shrieks from the jolted, dying wounded, was as near a perfectly horrible scene as words can describe. On the weary night march, commands scattered. One would lay down in a fence corner and be followed at once by a dozen; a mile farther this would be repeated, and so on until a regiment at halting time would be as if deployed as skirmishers for miles.

Lieutenant Samuel T. Foreman (below, right), adjutant of the 4th Kentucky (C.S.) Infantry of Trabue's brigade, was killed during the desperate fighting north of the Purdy road and Shiloh Church. His brother, Colonel James Foreman (below, left), of the 15th Kentucky (U.S.), was serving in Buell's Army of the Ohio but was on detached service at Huntsville, Alabama, at the time of the battle.

Dismal Retreat to Corinth

As General Beauregard's exhausted Confederate troops stumbled back toward Corinth on April 8, the day after the battle, Nathan Bedford Forrest and 350 of his cavalrymen rode as a rear guard. Right on Forrest's tail came four Federal infantry brigades commanded by Sherman, who intended to make sure that the enemy had in fact cleared out.

Forrest, spoiling for a fight, soon spotted Sherman's skirmishers threading their way through a belt of downed trees—the place became known as Fallen Timbers—and immediately decided to attack. Yelling "Charge! Charge!" he led his troopers forward, bugles blaring and sabers slashing, straight for the spot where Sherman and his aides were observing the action. "We ingloriously fled pell mell through the mud," Sherman recalled, adding that "if Forrest had not already emptied his pistols as he passed the skirmish line, my career would have ended right there."

But Forrest himself careened on too far, outdistancing his men and riding straight into the Federal main line. Finally realizing that he was alone, he whirled his horse and tried to cut his way out. Then, though wounded by a Federal bullet, he reached down, snatched up a Union soldier by the collar, and flung

him onto his horse's rump. With a human shield guarding him from further fire, Forrest galloped away, throwing the frightened soldier to the ground when out of range.

The fierce little skirmish at Fallen Timbers proved to be the only notable fight on April 8. General Grant, although he was eager to follow and destroy the Confederate army, feared that neither his exhausted men nor General Buell's troops were up to the demanding task. As Grant wrote, he "had not the heart to order the men who had fought desperately for two days, lying in the mud and rain whenever not fighting," and "did not feel disposed to positively order Buell, or any part of his command, to pursue."

Though unharried by the Federals, the Confederate retreat to Corinth was still a gruesome ordeal, especially for the wounded, who were often piled two deep in crude wagons that lurched and plunged and slithered along the muddy, rutted road. It was all made worse when about nightfall another violent storm hit with driving sleet and hailstones, some of which were, a Confederate officer recalled, "as large as partridge eggs."

Finally Beauregard's half-frozen, bone-weary survivors straggled into Corinth—

which itself became a scene of horror as more than 5,000 wounded men were laid out on floors and porches and sidewalks, and surgeons worked around the clock cutting off bullet-shattered limbs. At most 30,000 men remained ready for duty, and 10,000 of those would soon be ill with typhoid and dysentery when Corinth's water supply turned foul.

Grant's and Buell's armies, 70,000 strong, could well have smashed into Corinth after a few days' rest and destroyed Beauregard's crippled force. But Grant, failing to move immediately, had thrown away his chance. By April 11 General Halleck had arrived from St. Louis on a gunboat to take personal command in the field.

Halleck's first move was to rudely shove Grant, whom he still distrusted, into a powerless subordinate position so humiliating that Grant almost resigned from the army on the spot. Halleck then spent three weeks reorganizing his force, dividing it into what amounted to three corps under Generals Buell, Thomas, and Pope. Now leading a huge army of at least 110,000 men, Halleck nevertheless exhibited caution in the extreme, taking almost a month to move the 20 miles from Pittsburg Landing to the outskirts of Corinth. After each short forward move the troops were ordered to lay networks of corduroyed roads. At every stop they dug elaborate entrenchments—just in case, as Halleck constantly imagined, the Confederates counterattacked.

Halleck's extraordinary caution was hardly necessary. Beauregard had in fact received some reinforcements—about 12,000 men led by Major Generals Sterling Price and Earl Van Dorn. But the battered Confederates, at most 55,000 strong, were in no condition to hold off Halleck's juggernaut.

Beauregard's only option was to get his army out of Corinth before it was smashed to bits. To mask the retreat he contrived an ingenious deception. On his orders, dozens of railroad trains were shunted into Corinth, each one greeted with rousing cheers as though they were bringing in a constant stream of reinforcements. The trains clattering into Corinth were in fact empties while those going out were loaded with equipment and supplies Beauregard was trying to save.

The ploy was good enough to fool Halleck, who remained convinced his army was in mortal danger. Finally on May 30, when Buell's and Pope's advance units were poised at last to smash into Corinth, a large explosion rocked the town, plainly indicating that the Confederates were destroying some last bits of ammunition. Rushing in, the Federals found no enemy soldiers, virtually no equipment, and hardly a morsel of food. Corinth had been stripped—except for mocking signs reading, "These premises to let; inquire of G. T. Beauregard," painted here and there by departing Confederates.

Proclaiming his retreat "equivalent to a brilliant victory," Beauregard hustled his army 50 miles south to the area of Tupelo, Mississippi. Once there he was abruptly fired from command by President Jefferson Davis, who was furious that Corinth had been lost without a fight and alarmed that a huge Federal army was ready to rampage throughout the Deep South almost unopposed.

But Davis need not have worried so much. Halleck, satisfied with taking Corinth, was not about to rampage anywhere. Sending General Pope on a brief and halfhearted pursuit of the Confederates, Halleck busied himself sending telegrams to Washington trumpeting his great victory in the battle that never was.

Then, in one of the Civil War's most bizarre moves, he split up his own powerful army, sending Buell off to the northeast on what proved a futile campaign to take Chattanooga, sending Grant to Memphis, and leaving Pope to sit protecting Corinth. In doing so, Halleck all but negated the victory at Shiloh and frittered away a chance, as Grant later wrote, to prosecute a "great campaign for the suppression of the rebellion" that might well have ended the war.

SHILOH CASUALTIES

FEDERAL

Killed	1,754
Wounded	8,408
Missing	2,885
Total	13,047

CONFEDERATE

Killed	1,723
Wounded	8,012
Missing	959
Total	10,694

LIEUTENANT WILLIAM C. THOMPSON
6TH MISSISSIPPI INFANTRY, CLEBURNE'S BRIGADE

Lieutenant Thompson joined Company B of the 6th Mississippi—known as the Simpson Fencibles—in July 1861. After the Battle of Shiloh he served with his regiment in most of the battles fought by the Army of Tennessee, until his capture in December 1864 at the Battle of Franklin. Exchanged in March 1865, Thompson was on a medical furlough when the war ended.

The heart-rending scene at the hospital is one I would like to forget. Piles of dead soldiers were all around, and lying in rows were others who were dying. Doctors and their assistants were moving among the wounded, examining and aiding those who were not beyond help. The screams from the operating table resounded through the woods, for the surgeons were taking off arms and legs of a succession of men carried to them. Teams drawing ambulances were being urged to hasten, hauling the wounded from the field and back to a safer place. Other wagons were collecting and bringing in more wounded. They were being unloaded like so many butchered hogs, and the wagon beds were streaming blood. Once unloaded, the wagons were off to the front again, to collect more unfortunates. Many were dead when unloaded, others died soon afterwards.

CORPORAL WILBUR F. CRUMMER
45TH ILLINOIS INFANTRY, MARSH'S BRIGADE

Thousands of dead from both armies lay scattered across the battlefield under the warm April sun. Since the bodies had begun to decay, immediate burial was essential. Corporal Crummer's company, along with companies detailed from other regiments, was assigned the grisly task of interring the dead in 50-foot trenches. Since the Federals held the field, most Confederate dead went unidentified.

A few Sibley tents, torn and riddled by shot and shell, were all we had left. I lost my shirts, blankets, letters from home, my testament (mother's gift) and a picture of the "girl I left behind me." I was more indignant over the loss of my girl's picture than I was over the other articles.

On Tuesday I was detailed with others to bury the dead lying within our camp and a distance of two hundred yards in advance. I had charge of digging the grave, if a trench over sixty feet long and four feet deep, can be called a grave.

The weather was hot, and most of the dead had been killed early Sunday morning, and dissolution had already commenced. The soldiers gathered the bodies up and placed them in wagons, hauling them near to the trench, and piling them up like cord wood.

Steamboats chartered by the U.S. Sanitary Commission lie moored alongside vessels assigned to the medical department at Pittsburg Landing soon after the battle. The Sanitary Commission, a civilian volunteer organization, provided sorely needed medical supplies, nurses, and physicians to the overworked army field hospitals.

We were furnished with plenty of whiskey, and the boys believed that it would have been impossible to have performed the job without it.

When the grave was ready, we placed the bodies therein, two deep; the father, brother, husband, and lover, all to lie till Gabriel's trumpet shall sound. All the monument reared to those brave men was a board, nailed to a tree at the head of the trench, upon which I cut with my pocket knife, the words: "125 rebels."

We buried our Union boys in a separate trench, and on another board were these words: "35 Union." Many of our men had been taken away and buried separately by their comrades. It was night when we finished the task, some of the squad, "half seas over" with liquor, but they could not be blamed, for it was a hard job. The next day we burned the dead horses and mules.

Colonel Julius Raith of Illinois lay wounded on the field for two days before receiving medical care. Surgeons aboard the steamer Hannibal amputated his right leg, but he died from shock and loss of blood on April 11.

PRIVATE SAMUEL H. EELS
HOSPITAL STEWARD, 12TH MICHIGAN INFANTRY, PEABODY'S BRIGADE

After his field hospital was overrun and captured by Confederates on April 6, Private Eels and the wounded were evacuated to a hospital five miles behind the battlefield. In addition to tending the wounded from his own side, Eels assisted with more than 300 injured Confederates. In a letter written on April 13, Eels described the Confederate retreat and his own release from captivity.

They got pretty well beaten on Monday. We could see and hear them all Monday night retreating over the road to Corinth Miss. which passed close by where we were. The road was jammed full of them that night, and they left quantities of stores & provisions along the way most of which they had taken from our camps. As they retreated our forces advanced. We fully expected to be sent on further South. Those of our wounded who were able to travel were sent on but the surgeons & I and some of our hospital attendants were left with those who could not be transported without ambulances which they did not have. Then one of the surgeons of our side made an arrangement with the Surgeons of the other side by which it was agreed that the wounded should be left where they were until they could be carried away & then they should go each to their own party without hindrance from the troops on either side & their Surgeons & attendants should go with them. We were at the time in their power but our pickets were coming pretty near and the prospect was that they would not be captured by our forces they could get away. So we came back last night and now are in our old camp again.

On April 7 Private William S. Lovejoy of the 41st Ohio traded his canteen to a wounded soldier of the 8th Louisiana Infantry for this "CS"-marked drum canteen.

"Along in the night this man on the cot talked very low and weak, and after awhile said he knew he was going to die and bid us good-bye."

LIEUTENANT JOHN T. BELL
2D IOWA INFANTRY, TUTTLE'S BRIGADE

As the victorious Federals regained their camps, many soldiers witnessed pathetic scenes that they remembered for the rest of their days. In his book, Tramps and Triumphs of the Second Iowa Infantry, *Bell described an encounter with a wounded Rebel soldier in an abandoned tent. Bell never found out if the soldier survived.*

During the battle of Sunday the woods were fired and when we regained our outer camps, Monday, found at one point a pile of corn, containing several hundred bushels, gathered with the husks on. Many wounded soldiers crawled to this pile of corn, seeking more comfortable conditions, and when the fire swept through the woods and over the corn, they could not get away and were burned to death. At another place Monday afternoon I found a bright young boy (confederate) lying badly wounded on a cot in a tent. Facing him, on another cot alongside his own, sat a dead rebel with wide-staring eyes, and underneath the cot occupied by the boy was the body of a union soldier. By dropping his left hand the boy could touch this body, and by moving his right hand a trifle he could touch the other. He said: "I was badly wounded yesterday, but managed to get into this abandoned tent and climbed up on this cot. Soon after this man on the other cot crawled in, and just before dark this soldier lying under my cot. They were both hurt worse than I was, but we talked to each other as much as we could for encouragement. Then along in the night this man on the cot talked very low and weak, and after awhile said he knew he was going to die and bid us good-bye. I didn't hear anything after that from the man lying under my cot, and it was awful still from that till morning. When daylight came I found that they were both dead, and I have laid here all day hoping someone would come and help me."

SOPHIA MCCLELLAND
ADMINISTRATOR, U.S. SANITARY COMMISSION

Within days of the battle, Kentucky authorities dispatched a well-equipped steamboat to evacuate wounded Kentuckians from Pittsburg Landing. McClelland, armed with a pass from Secretary of War Edwin M. Stanton, accompanied the Sanitary Commission party and was allowed to travel over the battlefield, where many of the Rebel wounded had not yet been recovered.

I found one man shot through the breast, lying in a little thicket, groaning in great pain.

"Water," he moaned. "For God's sake, give me water!"

I placed my water-flask to his mouth, and as I knelt beside him I noticed that he wore the gray, and belonged to some Georgia regiment. He almost emptied the flask before he took it from his lips, and as he looked up at me gratefully the tears rolled down his cheeks, and he stretched his hands feebly out toward the flask, which I was about to replace in my belt.

"It's pretty good, isn't it?" I asked, when he had taken another draught.

"Good!" he repeated, between gasps. "I should say it was. I've been cryin' for it for six hours, an' I never thought I'd be cryin' for water—anyhow, not to *drink!* But this blamed war has upset things so that there ain't no tellin' what a man will do."

Soldiers kindle a fire to burn the carcasses of some of the thousands of dead horses—the wreckage of cavalry units and artillery teams—that littered the Shiloh battlefield. The engraving was printed in Leslie's Illustrated *on May 17, 1862.*

PRIVATE JOHN E. MAGEE
STANFORD'S MISSISSIPPI BATTERY, A. P. STEWART'S BRIGADE

John Magee, a native of Ohio who had settled in Mississippi, enlisted on November 1, 1861. After Shiloh he was promoted to corporal and fought at Murfreesboro and Chickamauga. Magee was reported to have deserted in May 1864, but he may have been captured by the Federals and paroled. He left his diary with a comrade in the spring of 1864 and never returned to retrieve it.

Things were now in a bad condition, our men repulsed at all points, and badly demoralized, and the enemy with very heavy reinforcements driving us. In the evening it set in to rain, and the battle once more ceased at dark. Thousands of stragglers were seen in every direction, which were turned back, and our army formed a line of battle under Breckinridge to protect our retreat. Batteries wagons and men were moving all night for Corinth. We went 2 mile to the rear and staid all night to collect our men and be ready. It rained all night, and troops suffered very much especially the wounded. Our loss to day was 3 killed 12 wounded and 2 captured prisoners—also 68 horses 4 canon equipments and all. . . .

Tuesday April 8th 1862. A very wet morning—mud knee deep, and still raining. Troops still moving to the rear, we started with our 2 canon and wagons at 1—travelled very slow. Heard no firing in our rear—we had an awful time getting to Corinth—had to lift the wagons out of the mud several times. We however got into our old camp at dark, all very tired and worn out, most of us sick.

Conrad Wise Chapman of the 3d Kentucky painted this scene of the men of his regiment recuperating after the Battle of Shiloh in their camp near Corinth, Mississippi.

GLOSSARY

abatis—A defensive barrier of fallen trees with branches pointed toward the enemy.

barbette—A platform from which artillery can be fired over a parapet.

Belgians—Belgian-made muskets, usually flintlocks, refitted with rifling, or grooves cut in the barrel, and modified to take a percussion cap.

brevet—An honorary rank given for exceptional bravery or merit in time of war. It granted none of the authority or pay of the official rank.

butternut—The color, variously described as yellowish brown, tan, or brownish gray, of the common homespun Confederate uniform for those who could not afford to acquire cloth of the official gray. It became a general Northern term for a Confederate soldier.

caisson—A cart with large chests for carrying artillery ammunition; connected to a horse-drawn limber when moved.

Claybank horse—A horse of a yellowish color.

Columbiad—A large cast-metal, smoothbore cannon adopted for all U.S. seacoast defenses in 1860. The largest, a 15-inch Columbiad, threw a 320-pound shell more than a mile. The tube alone weighed almost 25 tons.

Dimick rifle—Any of a number of models of hunting or sport rifles made by or for the famed gunsmith Horace E. Dimick, of St. Louis.

double-quick—A trotting pace.

embrasure—An opening in a fort wall through which a cannon was fired.

Enfield rifle—The Enfield rifle musket was adopted by the British in 1853, and the North and South imported nearly a million to augment their own production. Firing a .577-caliber projectile similar to the Minié ball, it was fairly accurate at 1,100 yards.

enfilade—Gunfire that rakes an enemy line lengthwise, or the position allowing such firing.

epaulement—A rough, earthen defensive parapet usually intended to protect a position's flank.

flintlock—A firearm with a piece of flint attached to the hammer. When the trigger is pulled, the flint strikes a piece of steel, creating a spark that ignites powder through a vent and fires the weapon.

furlough—A leave of absence from duty granted to a soldier.

garrison—A military post, especially a permanent one. Also, the act of manning such a post and the soldiers who serve there.

grapeshot—Iron balls (usually nine) bound together and fired from a cannon. Resembling a cluster of grapes, the balls broke apart and scattered on impact. Although references to grape or grapeshot are numerous in the literature, some experts claim that it was not used on Civil War battlefields.

hardtack—A durable cracker, or biscuit, made of plain flour and water and normally about three inches square and a half-inch thick.

hors de combat—French for "out of combat," meaning dead or disabled.

howitzer—A short-barreled artillery piece that fired its projectile in a relatively high trajectory.

James gun—Named for its inventor, Charles T. James, this cannon had unique rifling to fire a James shell also of his design.

mess—A group of soldiers who prepare and eat meals together, or to eat such a meal; the place where such a meal is prepared and eaten.

Minié ball—The standard bullet-shaped projectile fired from the rifled muskets of the time. Designed by French army officers Henri-Gustave Delvigne and Claude-Étienne Minié, the bullet's hollow base expanded, forcing its sides into the grooves, or rifling, of

the musket's barrel. This caused the bullet to spiral in flight, giving it greater range and accuracy. Appears as minie, minnie, and minni.

Navy revolver—One of the most popular handguns of the Civil War. Manufactured by the Colt company, it was a .36-caliber, cap-and-ball, single-action revolver accepting either loose or cartridge powder.

Parrott guns—Muzzleloading, rifled artillery pieces of various calibers made of cast iron, with a unique wrought-iron reinforcing band around the breech. Patented in 1861 by Union officer Robert Parker Parrott.

revetment—Support or bracing to hold in place the sides of earthen fortifications, trenches, and gun emplacements. Could be made of cloth, wooden pickets and posts, sandbags, wire mesh, or other material. A fortification so bolstered was said to be revetted.

rifler—A tool for cleaning the rifling in a cannon or shoulder arm.

secesh—A slang term for secessionist.

Sibley tent—A tent resembling the tipi of the Plains Indians; named for its inventor, Confederate general Henry Hopkins Sibley. Conical, erected on a tripod, with a smoke hole at the top, the tent could easily accommodate 12 men and their equipment.

skirmisher—A soldier sent in advance of the main body of troops to scout out and probe the enemy's position. Also, one who participated in a skirmish, a small fight usually incidental to the main action.

smoothbore—Any firearm or cannon with a smooth, or unrifled, barrel.

solid shot—A solid artillery projectile, oblong for rifled pieces and spherical for smoothbores.

stack arms—To set aside weapons, usually three or more in a pyramid, interlocking at the end of the barrel with the butts on the ground.

trail arms—To grasp a musket at about midpoint and carry it at one's side, roughly parallel to the ground.

turnspit—Formerly a small mongrel dog used on a treadmill to turn a spit. An unqualified and incapable person.

Veteran Volunteers—Men or units in the Federal service who reenlisted after serving one term of duty. The Veteran Volunteer Act of early 1864 offered a month's furlough, free transportation home, and a bounty of $400.

Zouaves—Regiments, both Union and Confederate, that modeled themselves after the original Zouaves of French colonial Algeria. Known for spectacular uniforms featuring bright colors—usually reds and blues—baggy trousers, gaiters, short and open jackets, and a turban or fez, they specialized in precision drill and loading and firing muskets from the prone position.

ACKNOWLEDGMENTS

The editors wish to thank the following for their valuable assistance in the preparation of this volume: Stacey Allen, Shiloh National Military Park, Shiloh, Tenn.; Rick Baumgartner, Blue Acorn Press, Huntington, W.Va.; David D. Bowlby, Illinois State Military Museum, Springfield; Charles B. Greifenstein, The College of Physicians of Philadelphia, Philadelphia; Randy W. Hackenburg, U.S. Army Military History Institute, Carlisle Barracks, Pa.; Betty Lou Heintz, Henry County Historical Society, New Castle, Ind.; Steve Hill, Westwood, Mass.; Corinne P. Hudgins, The Museum of the Confederacy, Richmond; Mary Ison and Staff, Reference Library, Prints and Photography Department, Library of Congress, Washington, D.C.; Jimmie Jobe, Fort Donelson National Battlefield, Dover, Tenn.; Lawrence T. Jones III, Confederate Calendar Works, Austin, Tex.; Norwood Kerr, Alabama Department of Archives & History, Montgomery; Diane Kessler, Pennsylvania Capitol Preservation Committee, Harrisburg; Mary Michaels, Illinois State Historical Society, Springfield; Teresa Roane, Valentine Museum, Richmond; Bobby Roberts, Little Rock, Ark.; Donna Marie Schmink, Indiana Battle Flags Commission, Indianapolis; Anne Sindelar, The Western Reserve Historical Society, Cleveland; Fae Sothham, The State Historical Society of Missouri, Columbia; Larry Strayer, Blue Acorn Press, Huntington, W.Va.; John White, University of North Carolina, Chapel Hill; Michael J. Winey, U.S. Army Military History Institute, Carlisle Barracks, Pa.; Lynnette Wolfe, Wisconsin Veterans Museum, Madison; Katherine Wyatt, Nebraska State Historical Society, Lincoln.

PICTURE CREDITS

ington, D.C., photographed by Larry Sherer; Frank and Marie-Thérèse Wood Print Collections, Alexandria, Va.—Chicago Historical Society; USAMHI, copied by A. Pierce Bounds. 54: MASS-MOLLUS/USAMHI, copied by A. Pierce Bounds; Indiana Civil War Battle Flags Commission, Indiana War Memorial, Indianapolis. 55: Bob Coch Collection, copied by Dale Nielson; MASS-MOLLUS/USAMHI, copied by A. Pierce Bounds. 56: Nebraska State Historical Society, Lincoln. 57: Print Collection, Miriam and Ira D. Wallach Division of Art, Prints and Photographs, The New York Public Library, Astor, Lenox and Tilden Foundations. 58: Kentucky Historical Society, Frankfort; Museum of the Confederacy, Richmond, photographed by Larry Sherer. 59: Courtesy collection of Bill Turner, from *The Confederate General*, Vol. 2, edited by William C. Davis, © 1991 National Historical Society, copied by Philip Brandt George. 60: Courtesy Charlie Salter. 61: David Wynn Vaughan. 62: Cook Collection, Valentine Museum, Richmond, Neg. No. 3055; Tennessee State Museum Collection, Nashville, photographed by June Dorman, Artifact No. 73.17. 63: Eleanor S. Brockenbrough Library, Museum of the Confederacy, Richmond. 64: Alabama Department of Archives and History, Montgomery. 65: Library of Congress, Manuscript Division—courtesy Ronn Palm. 66: The Richard K. Tibbals Collection, USAMHI. 67: Courtesy Herb Peck Jr., Nashville; courtesy David R. O'Reilly, from *Fighting for Time*, Vol. 4 of *The Image of War, 1861-1865*, © 1983, The National Historical Society, Doubleday & Co., Garden City, N.Y. 68: Print Collection, Miriam and Ira D. Wallach Division of Art, Prints and Photographs, The New York Public Library, Astor, Lenox and Tilden Foundations. 71: Map by R. R. Donnelley & Sons Co., Cartographic Services. 72: Courtesy Marvin Chandler, from *Mrs. Hill's Journal: Civil War Reminiscences*, by Sarah Jane Full Hill, © 1980 by R. R. Donnelley & Sons Co., copied by Philip Brandt George. 73: State Historical Society of Wisconsin, Madison. 74: Frank and Marie-Thérèse Wood Print Collections, Alexandria, Va. 76: Henry County Historical Society, New Castle, Ind. 77: Tennessee State Library and Archives, Nashville; from *"Respects to All": Letters of Two Pennsylvania Boys in the War of the Rebellion*, edited by Aida Craig Truxall, © 1962 University of Pittsburgh Press, copied by Philip Brandt George. 78, 79: Library of Congress; Pennsylvania Capitol Preservation Committee, Harrisburg. 80: MASS-MOLLUS/USAMHI, copied by A. Pierce Bounds. 81: Western Reserve Historical Society, Cleveland. 82: Tennessee State Museum Collection, Nashville, Neg. No. 82.142.2, photography by June Dorman. 83: Frances H. Rainey. 84: MASS-MOLLUS/USAMHI, copied by Rob-

ert Walch. 86, 87: MASS-MOLLUS/USAMHI, copied by Robert Walch; courtesy State Historical Society of Iowa, Iowa City, from *The Battle of Shiloh*, by Joseph W. Rich, © 1911, copied by Philip Brandt George—courtesy the Illinois State Historical Library, Springfield. 89: National Archives, Record Group 94, copied by Philip Brandt George. 90: Courtesy Anna Lindsey Jones, from *"For My Country": The Richardson Letters, 1861-1865*, compiled and edited by Gordon C. Jones, Broadfoot Publishing Co., Wendell, N.C., 1984, copied by Philip Brandt George. 92: From *Battles and Leaders of the Civil War*, Vol. 1, © 1887 The Century Co., New York, copied by Philip Brandt George. 95: Map by Walter W. Roberts, overlay by Time-Life Books. 96: MASS-MOLLUS/USAMHI, copied by A. Pierce Bounds. 97: Jessie Ball duPont Library, University of the South, Sewanee, Tenn.; National Archives, Record Group 109, copied by Philip Brandt George. 98: Library of Congress; MASS-MOLLUS/USAMHI, copied by A. Pierce Bounds. 99: Frank & Marie-Thérèse Wood Print Collections, Alexandria, Va.; MASS-MOLLUS/USAMHI, copied by A. Pierce Bounds. 100: Old State House, Little Rock, Ark. 101: From *The Autobiography of Sir Henry Morton Stanley*, edited by his wife, Dorothy Stanley, Houghton Mifflin Co., New York, 1909, copied by Philip Brandt George. 102: MASS-MOLLUS/USAMHI, copied by A. Pierce Bounds; National Archives, Record Group 94, copied by Philip Brandt George. 103: Blue Acorn Press, Huntington, W.Va.; MASS-MOLLUS/USAMHI, photographed by James Enos. 104: From *The Story of a Common Soldier of Army Life in the Civil War, 1861-1865*, by Leander Stillwell, © 1920, published by Franklin Hudson Publishing Co., copied by Philip Brandt George. 107: Library of Congress. 108: Library of Congress, Neg. No. LC-USZ62-12995; courtesy Herb Peck Jr., Nashville. 110: MASS-MOLLUS/USAMHI, copied by A. Pierce Bounds. 111: Confederate Memorial Hall, New Orleans, photographed by Larry Sherer—David Wynn Vaughan. 112: Alabama Department of Archives and History, Montgomery, copied by A. Pierce Bounds; MASS-MOLLUS/USAMHI, copied by A. Pierce Bounds. 113: Courtesy collection of Bill Turner, frame courtesy Harris Andrews. 114: Ray Zielin Collection, copied by Richard A. Baumgartner; MASS-MOLLUS/USAMHI, copied by A. Pierce Bounds. 115: MASS-MOLLUS/USAMHI, copied by A. Pierce Bounds. 117: Map by Walter W. Roberts. 118, 119: H. H. Bennett Studio Foundation, Inc., Wisconsin Dells, Wis. 120: Herb Peck Jr., Nashville; courtesy collection of Bill Turner. 121: Courtesy Byron J. Ihle; National Archives, Record Group 94, copied by Philip Brandt George. 122: Courtesy Tennessee State Library and Archives, copied by Karina McDaniel

—Kentucky Historical Society, Frankfort. 123: Alabama Department of Archives and History, Montgomery. 125: Courtesy the Illinois State Historical Library, Springfield. 126: Courtesy the Illinois State Historical Library, Springfield—Confederate Memorial Hall, New Orleans, photographed by Larry Sherer. 127: From *Downing's Civil War Diary*, by Sergeant Alexander G. Downing, The Historical Department of Iowa, Des Moines, 1916. 128: MASS-MOLLUS/USAMHI, copied by A. Pierce Bounds. 129: MASS-MOLLUS/USAMHI, copied by A. Pierce Bounds; Frank and Marie-Thérèse Wood Print Collections, Alexandria, Va. 130: Alabama Department of Archives and History, Montgomery—Tennessee Historical Society, Nashville. 131: Courtesy the Illinois State Historical Library, Springfield. 132: Mark Warren—Library of Congress. 133: Illinois State Military Museum, Springfield. 135: Map by Walter W. Roberts. 136: Library of Congress—Goulet-Buncomb Collection, Southern Historical Collection, University of North Carolina, Chapel Hill. 137: Courtesy Charlie Salter. 138: Print Collection, Miriam and Ira D. Wallach Division of Art, Prints and Photographs, The New York Public Library, Astor, Lenox and Tilden Foundations. 139: Illinois State Historical Library, Springfield, copied by Richard A. Baumgartner. 140: MASS-MOLLUS/USAMHI, copied by A. Pierce Bounds—courtesy Daniel W. Strauss, Elkhart, Ind. 141: Miriam and Ira D. Wallach Division of Art, Prints and Photographs, The New York Public Library, Astor, Lenox and Tilden Foundations. 142: Courtesy the Illinois State Historical Library, Springfield. 143: MASS-MOLLUS/USAMHI, copied by A. Pierce Bounds. 145: Map by Walter W. Roberts, overlay by Time-Life Books. 146: Pennsylvania Capitol Preservation Committee, Harrisburg. 147: Museum of the Confederacy, Richmond, photographed by Larry Sherer. 148: Print Collection, Miriam and Ira D. Wallach Division of Art, Prints and Photographs, The New York Public Library, Astor, Lenox and Tilden Foundations. 149: Fort St. Joseph Museum, Niles, Mich. 151: Flag in collection of Wisconsin Veterans Museum, Madison—Print Collection, Miriam and Ira D. Wallach Division of Art, Prints and Photographs, The New York Public Library, Astor, Lenox and Tilden Foundations. 152: Museum of the Confederacy, Richmond, photographed by Larry Sherer. 153: Courtesy Lee Joyner, photography by George S. Whiteley IV. 156: MASS-MOLLUS/USAMHI, copied by A. Pierce Bounds. 157: Courtesy the Illinois State Historical Library, Springfield; courtesy Russ Pritchard, photographed by Larry Sherer. 158: Frank and Marie-Thérèse Wood Print Collections, Alexandria, Va. 159: Leo J. Oaks, Grants Pass, Oreg.

BIBLIOGRAPHY

BOOKS

Allardice, Bruce S. *More Generals in Gray.* Baton Rouge: Louisiana State University Press, 1995.

Amann, William Frayne, ed. *Personnel of the Civil War, Volume 1: The Confederate Armies.* New York: Thomas Yoseloff, 1961.

Arms and Equipment of the Confederacy (Echoes of Glory series). Alexandria, Va.: Time-Life Books, 1991.

Arms and Equipment of the Union (Echoes of Glory series). Alexandria, Va.: Time-Life Books, 1991.

Bacon, Alvan Q. *Adventures of a Pioneer Boy while a Prisoner of War.* Private printing, [186-].

Barker, Lorenzo A. *Birge's Western Sharpshooters in the Civil War, 1861–1865.* Huntington, W.Va.: Blue Acorn Press, 1994 (reprint of 1905 edition).

Beatty, John. *The Citizen-Soldier, or, Memoirs of a Volunteer.* Cincinnati: Wilstach, Baldwin, 1879.

Bell, John T. *Tramps and Triumphs of the Second Iowa Infantry, Briefly Sketched.* Des Moines: Valley Bank & Trust, 1961 (reprint of 1886 edition).

Bergeron, Arthur W., Jr., ed. *Reminiscences of Uncle Silas: A History of the Eighteenth Louisiana Infantry Regiment.* Baton Rouge, La.: Le Comité des Archives de la Louisiane, 1981.

Bierce, Ambrose. *Ambrose Bierce's Civil War.* Ed. by William McCann. Chicago: Henry Regnery, 1956.

Boatner, Mark Mayo, III. *The Civil War Dictionary.* New York: David McKay, 1959.

Brinton, John H. *Personal Memoirs of John H. Brinton: Major and Surgeon U.S.V., 1861–1865.* New York: Neale, 1914.

Carroll, John M. *List of Field Officers, Regiments & Battalions in the Confederate States Army, 1861–1865.* Mattituck, N.Y.: J. M. Carroll, 1983.

Churchill, James O. "Wounded at Fort Donelson." In *War Papers and Personal Reminiscences, 1861–1865: Read before the Commandery of the State of Missouri, Military Order of the Loyal Legion of the United States.* Vol. 1. Wilmington, N.C.: Broadfoot, 1992.

The Confederate General. 5 vols. Ed. by William C. Davis. Harrisburg, Pa.: National Historical Society, 1991.

Crummer, Wilbur F. *With Grant at Fort Donelson, Shiloh and Vicksburg.* Oak Park, Ill.: E. C. Crummer, 1915.

Crute, Joseph H., Jr. *Confederate Staff Officers, 1861–1865.* Powhatan, Va.: Derwent Books, 1982.

Downing, Alexander G. *Downing's Civil War Diary.* Ed. by Olynthus B. Clark. Des Moines: Historical Department of Iowa, 1916.

Duke, Basil W. *A History of Morgan's Cavalry.* Ed. by Cecil Fletcher Holland. Bloomington: Indiana University Press, 1960.

Dyer, Frederick H., comp. *A Compendium of the War of the Rebellion.* Vol. 2. Dayton: Press of Morningside Bookshop, 1979 (reprint of 1908 edition).

Esposito, Vincent J., ed. *The West Point Atlas of American Wars, 1689–1900.* Vol. 1. New York: Frederick A. Praeger, Publishers, 1959.

Fisher, Horace Cecil. *The Personal Experiences of Colonel Horace Newton Fisher in the Civil War.* Boston: Thomas Todd, 1960.

The Guns of '62. Vol. 2 of *The Image of War, 1861–1865.* Garden City, N.Y.: Doubleday, 1982.

Heitman, Francis B. *Historical Register and Dictionary of the United States Army.* Vol. 1. Urbana: University of Illinois Press, 1965.

Henry, Robert Selph. *"First with the Most": Forrest.* Indianapolis: Bobbs-Merrill, 1944.

Hickenlooper, Andrew. "The Battle of Shiloh." In *Sketches of War History, 1861–1865: Papers Prepared for the Commandery of the State of Ohio, Military Order of the Loyal Legion of the United States.* Vol. 5. Wilmington, N.C.: Broadfoot, 1992.

Hicks, Henry G. "Fort Donelson." In *Glimpses of the Nation's Struggle: Papers Read before the Minnesota Commandery of the Military Order of the Loyal Legion of the United States, 1892–1897.* Vol. 2. Wilmington, N.C.: Broadfoot, 1993.

Hill, Sarah Jane Full. *Mrs. Hill's Journal.* Ed. by Mark M. Krug. Chicago: R. R. Donnelley & Sons, 1980.

Horn, Stanley F., comp. and ed. *Tennessee's War, 1861–1865: Described by Participants.* Nashville: Tennessee Civil War Centennial Commission, 1965.

Huffstodt, Jim. *The Story of General W. H. L. Wallace, General T. E. G. Ransom, and Their "Old Eleventh" Illinois Infantry in the American Civil War (1861–1865).* Bowie, Md.: Heritage Books, 1991.

Illustrated Atlas of the Civil War (Echoes of Glory series). Alexandria, Va.: Time-Life Books, 1991.

Johnson, Robert Underwood, and Clarence Clough Buel, eds. *Battles and Leaders of the Civil War.* 4 vols. New York: Century Co., 1887.

Johnston, William Preston. *The Life of Gen. Albert Sidney Johnston.* New York: D. Appleton, 1878.

Kimbell, Charles B. *History of Battery "A," First Illinois Light Artillery.* Chicago: Franz Gindele, 1885.

Law, J. C. "Diary of Rev. J. G. Law." In *Southern Historical Society Papers.* Vol. 11. Wilmington, N.C.: Broadfoot, 1990 (reprint of 1883 edition).

Lawrence, Elijah C. "Stuart's Brigade at Shiloh." In *Civil War Papers Read before the Commandery of the State of Massachusetts Military Order of the Loyal Legion of the United States.* Vol. 2. Wilmington, N.C.: Broadfoot, 1993.

McDonough, James Lee. *Shiloh: In Hell Before Night.*

Knoxville: University of Tennessee Press, 1977.

Moats, Virgil H. *Shiloh to Vicksburg: Dear Eliza.* Pebble Beach, Calif.: Hedgehog Press, 1984.

Moneyhon, Carl. *Portraits of Conflict: A Photographic History of Louisiana in the Civil War.* Fayetteville: University of Arkansas Press, 1990.

Nevin, David, and the Editors of Time-Life Books. *The Road to Shiloh: Early Battles in the West* (The Civil War series). Alexandria, Va.: Time-Life Books, 1983.

Official Army Register of the Volunteer Force of the United States Army: For the Years 1861, '62, '63, '64, '65. Vols. 3, 5, 6, 7. Gaithersburg, Md.: Olde Soldier Books, 1987 (reprint of 1865 edition).

Purdue, Howell, and Elizabeth Purdue. *Pat Cleburne: Confederate General.* Hillsboro, Tex.: Hill Jr. College Press, 1973.

Putnam, Douglas, Jr. "Reminiscences of the Battle of Shiloh." In *Sketches of War History, 1861–1865: Papers Prepared for the Ohio Commandery of the Military Order of the Loyal Legion of the United States.* Vol. 3. Wilmington, N.C.: Broadfoot, 1991.

The Rebellion Record: A Diary of American Events. Vol. 4. Ed. by Frank Moore. New York: D. Van Nostrand, 1864.

Rich, Joseph W. *The Battle of Shiloh.* Iowa City: State Historical Society of Iowa, 1911.

Richardson, George S. *"For My Country": The Richardson Letters, 1861–1865.* Comp. and ed. by Gordon C. Jones. Wendell, N.C.: Broadfoot, 1984.

Roberts, Bobby:

Portraits of Conflict: A Photographic History of Arkansas in the Civil War. Fayetteville: University of Arkansas Press, 1987.

Portraits of Conflict: A Photographic History of Mississippi in the Civil War. Fayetteville: University of Arkansas Press, 1993.

Sauers, Richard A. *Advance the Colors!: Pennsylvania Civil War Battle Flags.* Harrisburg, Pa.: Capitol Preservation Committee, 1987.

Searle, Charles P. "Personal Reminiscences of Shiloh." In *War Sketches and Incidents: As Related by Companions of the Iowa Commandery Military Order of the Loyal Legion of the United States.* Vol. 1. Wilmington, N.C.: Broadfoot, 1994.

Shadows of the Storm. Vol. 1 of *The Image of War, 1861–1865.* Garden City, N.Y.: Doubleday, 1981.

Sherman, William T. *Memoirs of General William T. Sherman.* Bloomington: Indiana University Press, 1957.

Stanley, Henry Morton. *The Autobiography of Sir Henry Morton Stanley.* Ed. by Dorothy Stanley. New York: Greenwood Press, 1969 (reprint of 1909 edition).

Stillwell, Leander. *The Story of a Common Soldier.* [Erie, Kans.]: Franklin Hudson, 1920.

The Story of the Fifty-Fifth Regiment Illinois Volunteer Infantry in the Civil War, 1861-1865. Huntington, W.Va.: Blue Acorn Press, 1993 (reprint of 1887 edition).

Sword, Wiley. *Shiloh: Bloody April.* Dayton: Press of Morningside Bookshop, 1988.

Tennesseans in the Civil War: A Military History of Confederate and Union Units with Available Rosters of Personnel. Part 1. Nashville: Civil War Centennial Commission, 1964.

Truxall, Aida Craig, ed. *"Respects to All": Letters of Two Pennsylvania Boys in the War of the Rebellion.* Pittsburgh: University of Pittsburgh Press, 1962.

Turner, William A. *Even More Confederate Faces.* Orange, Va.: Moss Publications, 1983.

United States War Department:
  The War of the Rebellion: A Compilation of the Official Records of the Union and Confederate Armies. Series 1, Vol. 7. Washington, D.C.: Government Printing Office, 1882.
  The War of the Rebellion: A Compilation of the Official Records of the Union and Confederate Armies. Series 1, Vol. 10, Part 1-Reports. Washington, D.C.: Government Printing Office, 1884.

Walke, Henry. *Naval Scenes and Reminiscences of the Civil War in the United States: On the Southern and Western Waters during the Years 1861, 1862, and 1863.* New York: F. R. Reed, 1877.

Wallace, Isabel. *Life & Letters of General W. H. L. Wallace.* Chicago: R. R. Donnelley & Sons, 1909.

Wallace, Lew. *Lew Wallace: An Autobiography.* Vol. 2. New York: Harper & Brothers, 1906.

Warner, Ezra J.:
  Generals in Blue: Lives of the Union Commanders. Baton Rouge: Louisiana State University Press, 1964.
  Generals in Gray: Lives of the Confederate Commanders. Baton Rouge: Louisiana State University Press, 1959.

Wheeler, Joseph. "The Battle of Shiloh." In *Southern Historical Society Papers.* Vol. 24. Wilmington, N.C.: Broadfoot, 1991 (reprint of 1896 edition).

PERIODICALS

Anderson, Charles W. "After the Fall of Fort Donelson." *Confederate Veteran,* September 1896.

Barnes, Albert A. "The First Day at Shiloh." *National Tribune* (Washington, D.C.), August 27, 1903.

Baylor, George Withe. "With Gen. A. S. Johnston at Shiloh." *Confederate Veteran,* December 1897.

Boysell, M. E. "A Reminiscence of Shiloh." *National Tribune* (Washington, D.C.), February 3, 1898.

Carrico, Samuel T. "A Story of Shiloh." *National Tribune* (Washington, D.C.), May 5, 1900.

Carrington, George D. "A Drummer Boy at Donelson."

National Tribune (Washington, D.C.), August 30, 1900.

Cherry, Mrs. W. H. "Gen. Grant at Shiloh." *Confederate Veteran,* February 1893.

Dunham, Abner. "Civil War Letters of Abner Dunham, 12th Iowa Infantry." Ed. by Mildred Throne. *Iowa Journal of History,* October 1955.

Dwight, Henry O. "The War Album of Henry Dwight, Part 2: First Sight of War." Ed. by Albert Castel. *Civil War Times Illustrated,* April 1980.

Gillis, Simeon. "The First Gun at Shiloh." *National Tribune* (Washington, D.C.), August 15, 1901.

Jackson, William W. "The Battle of Shiloh." *National Tribune* (Washington, D.C.), December 24, 1885.

Jones, J. N. "Battle of Shiloh." *National Tribune* (Washington, D.C.), March 7, 1907.

Jones, James A. "About the Battle of Shiloh." *Confederate Veteran,* December 1899.

Jordan, Thomas. "The Battle of Shiloh." *New Orleans Picayune,* February 20, 1885.

Kelly, David C. "Mistakes Concerning Battle of Shiloh." *Confederate Veteran,* December 1901.

Lathrop, Barnes F. "A Confederate Artilleryman at Shiloh." *Civil War History* (Iowa City), December 1962.

Lee, E. T. "The Battle of Shiloh." *National Tribune* (Washington, D.C.), June 23, 1887.

Lennard, George W. " 'Give Yourself No Trouble about Me': The Shiloh Letters of George W. Lennard." Ed. by Paul Hubbard and Christine Lewis. *Indiana Magazine of History,* March 1980.

Moore, John C. "Shiloh Issues Again." *Confederate Veteran,* July 1902.

Nixon, Liberty Independence. "An Alabamian at Shiloh: The Diary of Liberty Independence Nixon." Ed. by Hugh C. Bailey. *Alabama Review,* April 1958.

"River Campaign: Part 2, Fort Donelson." *Richmond Dispatch,* February 27, 1862.

Ross, Reuben R. "River Batteries at Fort Donelson." *Confederate Veteran,* October 1896.

Shoup, Francis A. "How We Went to Shiloh." *Confederate Veteran,* May 1894.

Spencer, Selden. "Diary Account of Fort Donelson." *Confederate Veteran,* June 1897.

Sproux, R. S. "The 40th Illinois at Shiloh." *National Tribune* (Washington, D.C.), July 12, 1888.

Sullins, David. "Heroic Deed at Shiloh." *Confederate Veteran,* January 1897.

Thompson, William Candace. "From Shiloh to Port Gibson." *Civil War Times Illustrated,* October 1964.

Throne, Mildred, ed. "Letters from Shiloh." *Iowa Journal of History,* July 1954.

Wheeler, James A. "Cleburne's Brigade at Shiloh." *Confederate Veteran,* January 1894.

Wilkes, John S. "First Battle Experience—Fort Donelson." *Confederate Veteran,* November 1906.

OTHER SOURCES

Confederate Calendar. "May 1995." Austin, Tex.: Confederate Calendar Works.

Deupree, John G. Memoir. Shiloh, Tenn.: Shiloh National Military Park.

Eels, Samuel Henry. Letter, April 13, 1862. Samuel Henry Eels Papers. Washington, D.C.: Library of Congress, Manuscript Division.

Force, Manning Ferguson. Letter, April 22, 1862. Robert W. Lee Papers. Washington, D.C.: Library of Congress, Manuscript Division.

Harder, William Henry. Diary, 1861-1865. Nashville: Tennessee State Library and Archives, Manuscripts Section.

Harris, Isham G. Letter, April 6, 1862. RG94, Records of the Adjutant General's Office, Special File. Washington, D.C.: National Archives and Records Administration.

Magee, John Euclid. Diary, 1861-1863. Durham, N.C.: Duke University.

Mecklin, A. H. Diary, 1862. Jackson: Mississippi Department of Archives and History.

Miller, Thomas F. Letter, February 10, 1862. SC 1050a. Springfield: Illinois State Historical Library.

Moffatt, Thomas William, Sr., and Wallace Wilson Moffatt. "A Union Soldier's Civil War." Unpublished manuscript, 1962. Montgomery: Alabama Department of Archives and History.

Rainey, Isaac N. "Experiences of I. N. Rainey in the Confederate Army." Memoirs, February 1925. Nashville: Tennessee State Library and Archives, Civil War Collection.

Scarbrough, Lemuel A. Journal. Shiloh, Tenn.: Shiloh National Military Park.

Shepherd, Benjamin A. Letter, March 17, 1862. Nashville: Tennessee State Archives.

Stibbs, John Howard. Memoirs. Box F 23, Federal Collection. Nashville: Tennessee State Archives, Civil War Collection, Confederate and Federal, 1861-1865.

Tompkins, Charles B. Letter, April 8, 1862. #5311 Durham, N.C.: Duke University, Special Collections Library.

Wilder, William Frank. Memoirs. Washington, D.C.: Library of Congress, Manuscript Division.

Wiley, James H. Letter. Shiloh, Tenn.: Shiloh National Military Park.

Yeatman, W. E. Memoirs. Box 14, Folder 16, Confederate Collection. Nashville: Tennessee State Archives, Civil War Collection, Confederate and Federal, 1861-1865.

INDEX

Numerals in italics indicate an illustration of the subject mentioned.

TIME® Time-Life Books is a
LIFE division of Time Life Inc.
BOOKS

TIME LIFE INC.
PRESIDENT and CEO: George Artandi

TIME-LIFE BOOKS
PRESIDENT: John D. Hall
PUBLISHER/MANAGING EDITOR: Neil Kagan

VOICES OF THE CIVIL WAR

DIRECTOR, NEW PRODUCT DEVELOPMENT:
Curtis Kopf
MARKETING DIRECTOR: Pamela R. Farrell

SHILOH

EDITOR: Henry Woodhead
Deputy Editors: Harris J. Andrews (principal), Kirk Denkler,
Philip Brandt George
Design Director: Ray Ripper
Associate Editor/Research and Writing: Connie Contreras
Senior Copyeditor: Donna D. Carey
Picture Coordinator: Lisa Groseclose
Editorial Assistant: Christine Higgins

Initial Series Design: Studio A

Special Contributors: Dan Kulpinski, Brian C. Pohanka, David
S. Thomson (text); Michael P. Bub, Charles F. Cooney, Steve
Hill, Robert Lee Hodge, Henry Mintz, Carolyn S. Saper, Liz
Soderberg, Anne Whittle (research); Anne Farr, Mary Beth
Oelkers-Keegan (copyedit); Roy Nanovic (index).

Correspondents: Christina Lieberman (New York).

Vice President, Director of Finance: Christopher Hearing
Vice President, Book Production: Marjann Caldwell
Director of Operations: Eileen Bradley
Director of Photography and Research: John Conrad Weiser
Director of Editorial Administration: Barbara Levitt
Production Manager: Marlene Zack
Quality Assurance Manager: James King
Library: Louise D. Forstall

Consultants

Brian C. Pohanka, a Civil War historian and author, spent six
years as a researcher and writer for Time-Life Books' Civil
War series and Echoes of Glory. He is the author of *Distant
Thunder: A Photographic Essay on the American Civil War* and
has written and edited numerous works on American military
history. He has acted as historical consultant for projects
including the feature film *Glory* and television's *Civil War
Journal.* Pohanka participates in Civil War reenactments and
living-history demonstrations with the 5th New York Volunteers, and he is active in Civil War battlefield preservation.

Larry M. Strayer, an editor with Blue Acorn Press, has written
or contributed to more than a dozen titles on the war's western
theater, including *Yankee Tigers* and the award-winning Echoes
of Battle volumes on the Atlanta and Chattanooga campaigns.
Well known in living-history circles, he serves as adviser for
Accuracy Historical Productions. Focusing on the common
soldier, his next publication will photographically chronicle
Ohio's involvement in the Civil War.

Dr. Richard A. Sauers is a historian specializing in the Civil
War. As chief historian for the Pennsylvania Capitol Preservation Committee he directed the research and documentation
of more than 400 Civil War battle flags and wrote *Advance
the Colors!,* the two-volume study of Pennsylvania's Civil
War flags. He is active in Civil War and local historical soci-
eties and is involved in battlefield preservation. He is assistant editor of *Gettysburg* magazine. His published works
include *A Caspian Sea of Ink: The Meade-Sickles Controversy*
and *"The Bloody 85th": A Supplement to the History of the 85th
Pennsylvania.* He has also compiled a critical bibliography
of the Gettysburg campaign.

First printing. Printed in U.S.A.
Published simultaneously in Canada.
School and library distribution by Time-Life Education,
P.O. Box 85026, Richmond, Virginia 23285-5026.

TIME-LIFE is a trademark of Time Warner Inc. U.S.A.

Library of Congress Cataloging-in-Publication Data
Shiloh / by the editors of Time-Life Books.
     p. cm.—(Voices of the Civil War)
     Includes bibliographical references and index.
     ISBN 0-7835-4707-2
     1. Shiloh, Battle of, 1862. I. Time-Life Books. II. Series.
E473.54.S57 1996
973.7′31—dc20   96-33040
                                                        CIP

OTHER PUBLICATIONS

HISTORY
The Civil War
The American Indians
Lost Civilizations
The American Story
Mysteries of the Unknown
Time Frame
Cultural Atlas

SCIENCE/NATURE
Voyage Through the Universe

DO IT YOURSELF
The Time-Life Complete Gardener
Home Repair and Improvement
The Art of Woodworking
Fix It Yourself

TIME-LIFE KIDS
Family Time Bible Stories
Library of First Questions and Answers
A Child's First Library of Learning
I Love Math
Nature Company Discoveries
Understanding Science & Nature

COOKING
Weight Watchers® Smart Choice Recipe Collection
Great Taste~Low Fat
Williams-Sonoma Kitchen Library

For information on and a full description of any of the Time-
Life Books series listed above, please call 1-800-621-7026
or write:

Reader Information
Time-Life Customer Service
P.O. Box C-32068
Richmond, Virginia 23261-2068